lonely planet

CROATIA

Lucie Grace, Anja Mutić, Isabel Putinja

Meet our writers

Lucie Grace

@LucieGraces; @80bathes

Lucie Grace is a travel and culture writer, based between Croatia and Thailand, who has a lifelong passion for wild swimming.

'An old man selling ice cream in Zagreb once told me Croatia is the "country of joy and dreams" and that sums up how I feel about Croatia. It's a wonder – from the natural sights of inland lagoons on Mljet to architectural marvels that range from the Gothic in Šibenik to Modernism on Krk – it's a country that repeatedly makes my jaw drop.'

Anja Mutić

@everthenomad

Born and raised in Zagreb, Anja returned to Croatia after 20 years spent abroad. From her Zagreb base, she now runs Storyline Studio, a creative content agency for tourism, travel and hospitality.

'The inside–outside perspective is such a gift. I see Croatia with the eyes of a local, aware of all its intricacies and shades of grey. Yet the magic of discovery doesn't wear off; I still get blown away by its beauty and potential.'

Isabel Putinja

@isabelswindow

Isabel Putinja is a travel writer, solo walker and slow traveller living in Istria, Croatia.

'My favourite part of researching this guidebook was travelling up and down the coastline-hugging Jadranska Magistrala, Croatia's most scenic road.'

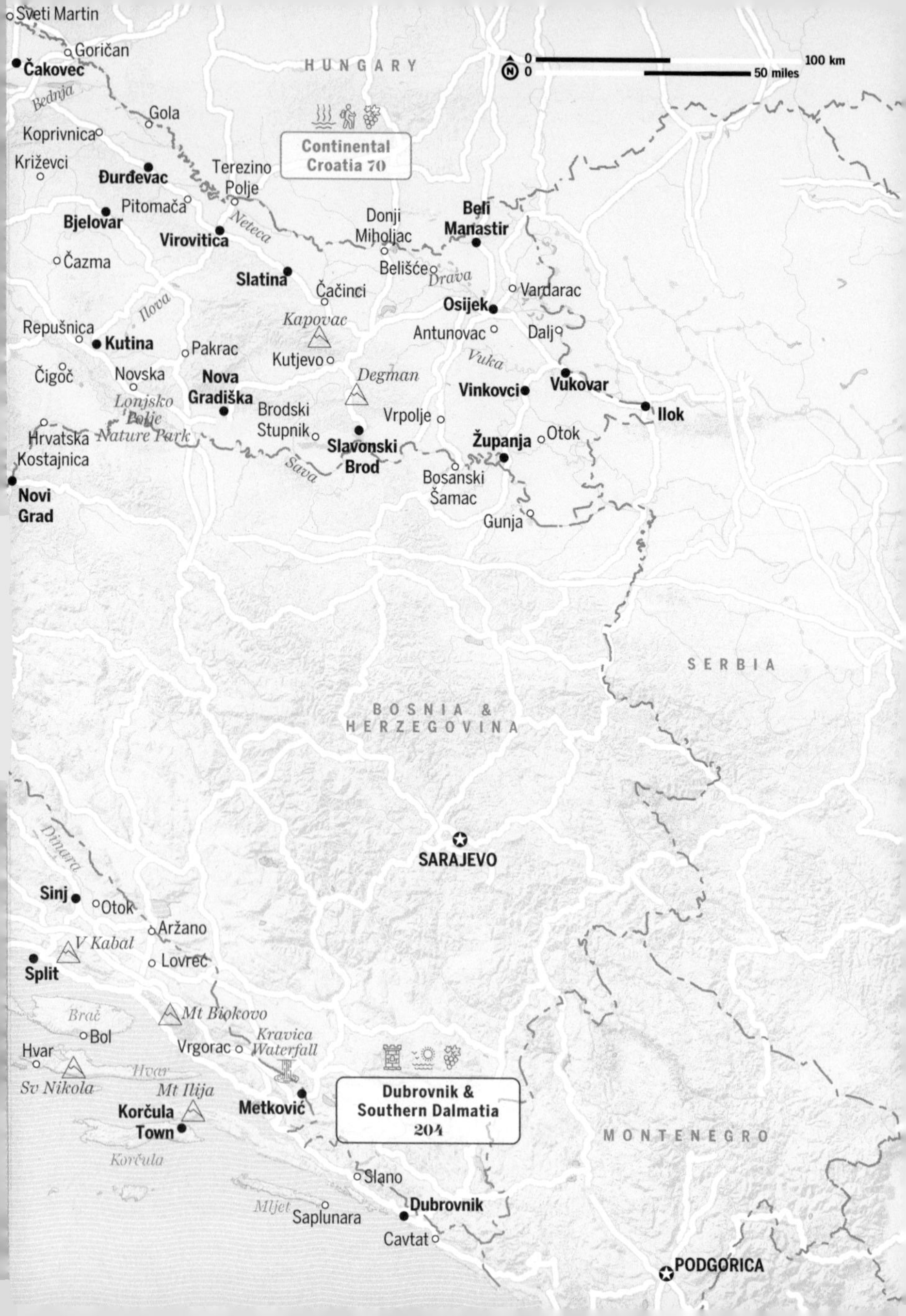

HUNGARY
0
100 km
0
50 miles
Sveti Martin
Goričan
Čakovec
Bednja
Gola
Koprivnica
Križevci
Đurđevac
Terezino Polje
Continental Croatia 70
Pitomača
Bjelovar
Neteca
Virovitica
Beli Manastir
Donji Miholjac
Belišće
Drava
Čazma
Slatina
Čačinci
Vardarac
Osijek
Ilova
Kapovac
Repušnica
Kutina
Pakrac
Antunovac
Dalj
Kutjevo
Vuka
Čigoč
Novska
Nova Gradiška
Degman
Vinkovci
Vukovar
Lonjsko Polje Nature Park
Brodski Stupnik
Vrpolje
Ilok
Hrvatska Kostajnica
Slavonski Brod
Županja
Otok
Sava
Bosanski Šamac
Novi Grad
Gunja
SERBIA
BOSNIA & HERZEGOVINA
Dinara
SARAJEVO
Sinj
Otok
Aržano
V Kabal
Split
Lovreć
Brač
Mt Biokovo
Bol
Kravica Waterfall
Vrgorac
Hvar
Hvar
Sv Nikola
Mt Ilija
Korčula Town
Metković
Dubrovnik & Southern Dalmatia 204
MONTENEGRO
Korčula
Slano
Mljet
Saplunara
Dubrovnik
Cavtat
PODGORICA

Hop between islands to find the perfect beach of your own. Lace up your hiking boots and explore wild, natural beauty spots. Marvel at ancient treasures preserved from thousands of years ago. Seek out edgy art and music in hilltop towns and beachside hot spots. Gaze at cascading waterfalls, raft on rushing rivers and cycle along scenic trails. Sip on world-class vino along off-the-radar wine roads. Savour tasty local bites in secret foodie enclaves and soak in thermal baths.

This is Croatia.

TURN THE PAGE AND START PLANNING YOUR NEXT BEST TRIP →

SLOVENIA
LJUBLJANA
ITALY
Zagreb 40
Oroslavlje
Zaprešić
ZAGREB
Velika Gorica
Crna Mlaka
Obruč
Brest
Mirna
Vrbovsko
Istria 90
Vojak
Rijeka
Viševica
Kvarner 118
Pazin
Poreč
Gračišće
Beli
Crikvenica
Rovinj
Krk Town
Labin
Senj
Žuta Lokva
Selište Drežničko
Marčana
Cres
Pula
Kvarner
Kvarnerić
Bijeli
Lopar
Plitvice Lakes National Park
Premantura
Rab Town
Korenica
Televrina
Cres
Perušić
Ozeblin
Una
Adriatic Sea
Gospić
Donji Lapac
Lošinj
Pag Town
Vaganski vrh
Paklenica National Park
Starigrad-Paklenica
Maslenica
Ist
Veli Rat
Zadar
Knin
Kistanje
Roški Slap
Biograd
Northern Dalmatia 144
Kornat
Murter
Krka National Park
Šibenik
Žirje
Rogoznica
Split & Central Dalmatia 168
ITALY
Vis Town
Vis
Experience Croatia online
Adriatic Sea

Jadranska Magistrala (p198)

Contents

ZORAN PAJIC/SHUTTERSTOCK ©

Mađerkin Breg (p81)

Split's Golden Gate (p179)

ESSAYS

VISUAL GUIDES

ADRIATIC ISLAND HOPPING

Croatia's crystalline waters are speckled with a multitude of islands, and whether you're voyaging by luxury sailboat or travelling by public ferry, exploring them is the ultimate Croatian experience. Some are tiny and unpopulated, while larger islands buzz with bars and restaurants. Landscapes on the islands range from arid and rocky terrain to sandy beaches backed by verdant forests. With 1244 islands to choose from, Croatia has just the perfect island spot for everyone.

Left Pakleni Islands (p197)
Right Tourist boats, Split Harbour (p174)
Below Chartered sailboat (p159)

→ FERRY SERVICES

A fleet of ferries, hydrofoils and tourist boats serve Croatia's islands. Boats run year-round, though strong winter winds sometimes suspend services. Summer has the most departures and the priciest tickets.

ROZHNOVSKAYA TANYA/SHUTTERSTOCK ©

TOURS & FEES

Of Croatia's eight national parks, three are archipelagos: Brijuni, Kornati and Mljet. You can visit Brijuni only on an organised tour, and the other two parks charge admission fees.

RIGHT: MIHA TRAVNIK/SHUTTERSTOCK ©, LEFT: EXTREME-PHOTOGRAPHER/GETTY IMAGES ©

↑ SET SAIL

Chartering your own sailboat with a skipper has become increasingly popular. It's loveliest in spring and autumn when you can have the coves and bays all to yourself.

Best Island-Hopping Experiences

- **Let your hair down on Hvar, party-hearty central, and recoup on the Pakleni Islands.** (p197)
- **Explore the hidden coves and glowing caves of Vis, the most remote of Croatia's main islands.** (p190)
- **Make a loop of lush, posh Lošinj.** (p128)
- **Marvel at the cobalt-hued lakes on long, slender and mesmerising Mljet in the southern Adriatic.** (p223)
- **Sail the dense archipelago of Kornati, with its 140 uninhabited islands.** (p159)

A BEACH **FOR EACH**

From its highly indented coastline to the multitude of islands that line its shores, Croatia has hundreds of beaches to choose from. Whether you like to laze around in standard swimwear, show off the latest designer styles or take your kit off altogether, you'll find your patch under the Croatian sun. Beaches can be sandy, pebbly, shingly or rocky, but what unites them all is the astonishingly clear water.

Left Sveti Jakov Beach (p221)
Right Sea urchin
Below Naturist beach sign, Lokrum Island (p222)

→ PRICKLY URCHINS

Unless you have experience with spotting and avoiding the spiky little sea creatures that inhabit the shallows in large numbers, wear water shoes.

FOTOSR52/SHUTTERSTOCK ©

NO RESERVATIONS

Don't leave your towel or mat on the beach and think you've reserved your spot for the entire day. It's bad manners to take up space unless you're physically present.

RIGHT: ROBYNCHARNLEY/SHUTTERSTOCK ©, LEFT: ROSE LAMOND/SHUTTERSTOCK ©

↑ NUDE RULES

It's fine to go topless on pretty much any Croatian beach. For full-on nudity, look for naturist spots. Istria has many of Croatia's largest and most well-developed naturist resorts and campgrounds.

Best Beach Experiences

- **Feast your eyes on the horn-shaped Zlatni Rat beach on Brač.** (p195)
- **Soak up the sun on the gorgeous Sveti Jakov Beach in Dubrovnik.** (p211)
- **Explore uninhabited Veli Žal's white sands.** (p158)
- **Head out to wild Srebrna on remote Vis Island.** (p197)

NATURE'S BEAUTY **SPOTS**

Croatia's appeal is grounded in nature: its majestic waterfalls, dreamy lakes, dense forests, mighty mountains and dazzling Adriatic coast. Forests cover nearly half the country and are home to many endemic species of flora and fauna. Croatia has more than 400 protected areas, comprising islands, lakes and mountains, making the country a veritable nature wonderland well worth exploring.

↑ NEW NATURE PARK

Designated in 2021, Dinara has been added to Croatia's list of nature parks. It features the highest peak in Croatia, the mighty 1831m-tall Dinara.

LEFT: MLADEN BOZICKOVIC/SHUTTERSTOCK ©, BELOW: SYRINX17/GETTY IMAGES ©

Best Nature Experiences

- **Take a boat trip through the spectacular floodplains of Kopački Rit Nature Park.** (p88)
- **Stroll along the boardwalks of Krka National Park and marvel at its canyons and waterfalls.** (p162)
- **Roam the woodsy Plitvice Lakes National Park with its turquoise ribbon of lakes and falls.** (p164)
- **Hike through the alpine trails and karst canyons of Paklenica National Park.** (p164)
- **Head off the beaten trail and into Gorski Kotar's densely forested Risnjak National Park.** (p83)

← RESPECT NATURE

Don't underestimate the power of the weather, especially in the mountains and deep woods. Wear suitable gear, including hiking shoes. Never go up a mountain in flip-flops.

Above Dinara National Park
Left Hiking, Paklenica National Park (p164)

GRGO JELAVIC/PIXSELL/ALAMY STOCK PHOTO ©

★ **OTHER ARTSY TOWNS**

For an artsy vibe and lots of galleries, plan to visit Trogir (near Split), Stari Grad (on Hvar) and Rovinj (especially during Grisia, an annual art event on the second Sunday in August).

ON THE HUNT **FOR ART & MUSIC**

Croatia isn't all beaches, ancient treasures and stunning nature – it also has a vibrant and happening contemporary culture, from the small, buzzy independent art scene in Zagreb to alternative music in Rijeka. Find art colonies in Istria's medieval hilltop towns of Labin and Grožnjan and dance until the wee hours in the electronic music festival hot spot of Tisno, which draws in crowds from around the globe.

Best Art & Music Experiences

- **Explore the alternative music scene of Rijeka, Croatia's forward-thinking port city with an edgy vibe.** (p132)
- **Catch some theatre, a dance show or a concert during the annual Dubrovnik Summer Festival.** (p216; pictured)
- **Visit contemporary galleries and scope out great street art in Zagreb.** (p44)
- **Hang out with artists and musicians in Istria's dreamy hilltop towns of Grožnjan and Labin.** (p99)
- **Groove in tiny seaside Tisno on Murter Island, which hosts heaps of summertime EDM festivals.** (p161)

Parenzana Trail
On your bike

Hop on two wheels for a cycling adventure along Istria's Parenzana Trail, tracing a historic railway route. Inaugurated in 1903 during the Austro–Hungarian era, the defunct railbed was given a new lease of life as a bike path in 2006.

50 minutes from Pula

▶ p98

Lika
Off-radar adventures

Underrated and offbeat, Lika is perfect if you like a sense of discovery. Go canoeing on the Gacka River, horseback riding with views of the Velebit mountain range or spelunking in Grabovača Cave.

2 hours from Zagreb

▶ p165

GET WILD & ACTIVE

Because so much of the country is covered with pristine natural landscapes, the siren call of the outdoors has a strong pull in Croatia. From mighty, rugged mountains and dense old-growth forests to cascading waterfalls and wild island peaks, Croatia's landscape is an outstanding outdoor playground, with year-round sports and activities to be enjoyed.

Paklenica National Park
Rugged wilderness

Explore the trekkers' paradise of Paklenica National Park, full of karst canyons, dramatic gorges and alpine trails. It's wild and rugged, with high peaks to brave and rough terrain to traverse – a spectacular experience for those with trekking skills.

1 hour from Zadar

▶ p164

Žumberak-Samobor Highlands Nature Park

Woodsy hikes

Roam the wild highlands of this nature park that's strewn with meadows, forests, river canyons, medieval forts, paragliding spots and rock-climbing areas. The trails are well marked and lined with mountain huts and restaurants open for weekend meals.

50 minutes from Zagreb to Samobor

▶ p74

Cetina Canyon

Thrills on the river

Go cliff jumping, rafting or canyon-eering on the rushing Cetina River near Omiš. Throw in breaks for swimming under waterfalls and exploring cave pools. See the river from above on a zip-line adventure across the canyon.

40 minutes from Split to Omiš

▶ p203

Biokovo Nature Park

Mountain adventures

Scale Mt Biokovo and hike the spectacular Biokovo Nature Park, which is crisscrossed by 40 trails. For sweeping views from a unique perspective, take the Tučepi zip line and fly above a forested canyon.

1¼ hours from Split to Makarska

▶ p203

CROATIAN **TIPPLES**

Wine from Croatia might be a novelty to international consumers, but creating and consuming vino has been embedded in this region's lifestyle for more than 25 centuries. Today, the tradition is undergoing a renaissance in the hands of a new generation of winemakers preserving indigenous varietals and revitalising ancestral estates. And there's the popular *rakija* (grappa) too, ranging in flavour from grape and honey to cherry and plum.

↑ HARVEST TIME

Martinje (St Martin's Day) is celebrated in Croatia's wine-producing regions on 11 November. Expect heaps of festivities, lots of feasting and samples of new wines.

Best Wine & Rakija Experiences

- **Take a day trip from Dubrovnik to the Pelješac Peninsula wineries.** (p228)
- **Sample high-quality vintages from the foothills of Motovun.** (p113)
- **Check out the annual Jelsa wine festival on Hvar Island.** (p192)
- **Try the potent local grappa produced on Krk Island.** (p126)
- **Explore the lesser-known wine roads of Slavonia in the east.** (p84)

← TOAST LIKE THE LOCALS

When drinking with Croatians, raise a glass and say *živjeli!* (pronounced *zhee-vye-lee*) while looking straight into your companions' eyes.

Above Grape harvest
Left Wine toast

SECRET SPOTS OF CROATIA

Croatia has seen such a huge increase in visitor numbers, especially during the peak summer season, that it can be tricky to feel a sense of discovery and find secret places with that special something. But luckily, many such places still exist if you know where to look.

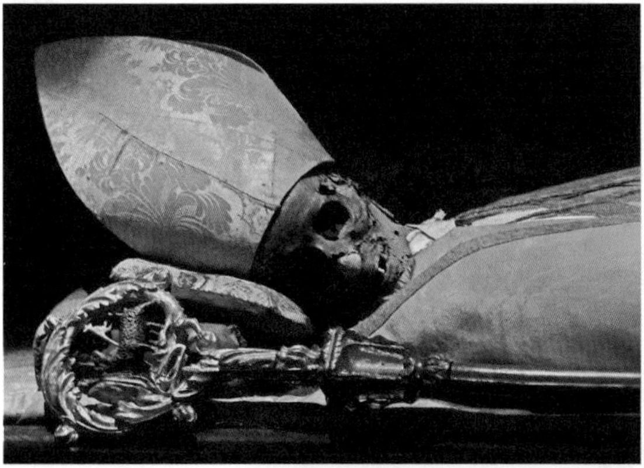

↑ MUMMIES

One of Croatia's most bizarre and creepiest attractions hides in the Istrian town of Vodnjan: four miraculously preserved mummies inside Church of St Blaise's.

Best Secret Experiences

- ▸ **Swim with locals in the Ombla River near Dubrovnik.** (p227)
- ▸ **Check out the food scene on the island of Šipan in the Elaphiti.** (p222)
- ▸ **Discover the scenic island of Šolta on a guided bicycle tour.** (p186)
- ▸ **Spend time in Istria's lovely hilltop town of Oprtalj.** (p99)
- ▸ **Take a dip in the thermal baths of dreamy Međimurje.** (p80)

← RARE TEXTILES

Check out the captivating craft of Konavle embroidery in the off-the-radar villages east of Dubrovnik and at the Konavle County Museum in Čilipi.

Above Mummy, St Blaise's Church, Vodnjan (p215)
Left Konavle embroidery (p213)

ANCIENT TREASURES

Croatia offers a field day for travellers who love stepping back in time. Visit remarkably preserved Roman structures built thousands of years ago that still buzz with life, and admire basilicas, churches and cathedrals that span eras and styles from Byzantine and Gothic to Renaissance and Venetian – and wild architectural mixtures of these.

Left Diocletian Palace (p179)
Right City Walls, Dubrovnik (p234)
Below Historic quarter, Varaždin (p78)

→ TIMING IS KEY

Croatia's A-list old towns (Dubrovnik and the Diocletian's Palace quarter of Split) get jam-packed in summer, so explore them at the crack of dawn before the crowds descend.

UNESCO STAMP

Croatia has 10 UNESCO World Heritage sites, eight of which are ancient sites. (Two are natural landscapes.)

↑ INLAND GEM

Many of Croatia's beautiful old towns are on the coast, but in the country's interior, the baroque beauty of Varaždin's historic quarter shouldn't be missed.

Best Ancient Treasure Experiences

- **Delve into the dazzlingly beautiful old town of Dubrovnik, encircled by 13th-century walls.** (p210)
- **Size up the stunning Korčula Town, a Venetian Renaissance showcase, on the namesake island.** (p216)
- **Stroll around the 4th-century Diocletian's Palace in Split, a Roman delight.** (p178)
- **Gaze at the frescoes inside the Byzantine-era Euphrasian Basilica in Poreč.**(p102)
- **Marvel at the wondrous Gothic-Renaissance beauty of the Cathedral of St James in Šibenik.** (p157)

Summer is a great time to visit continental Croatia because the crowds head to the coast.

Peak season coincides with the best weather. Hvar Island gets the most sun, followed by Split, Korčula Island and Dubrovnik.

↗ Dubrovnik Summer Festival

Taking place since the 1950s, the Dubrovnik Summer Festival features classical music, theatre and dance at venues around the old town.

▶ Dubrovnik

▶ dubrovnik-festival.hr

p216

Dance & Non-Verbal Theatre Festival

The otherwise sleepy Istrian town of Svetvinčenat (San Vincenti) comes alive during this late-July festival showcasing contemporary dance, street theatre, circus and mime acts.

▶ San Vincenti

▶ svetvincenatfestival

p116

JUNE

Average daytime max: 25°C
Days of rainfall (Zagreb): 13

JULY

Croatia in SUMMER

Lovrečeva

Krk's annual festival in mid-August is dedicated to the island's patron saint, St Lawrence, with historical reenactments, folk dances and delicious local food.

▶ Krk

p126

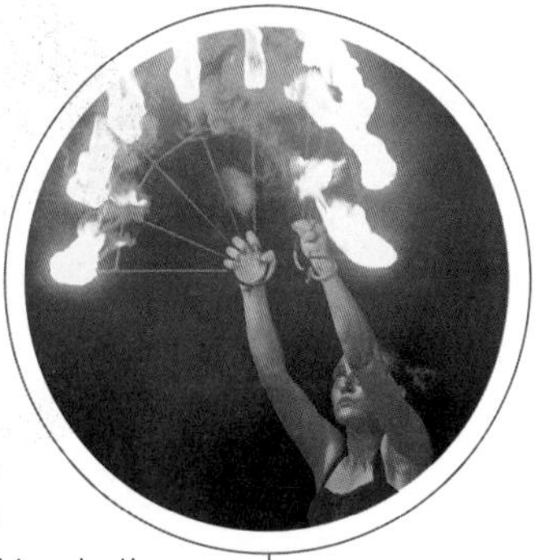

↗ Špancirfest

In late August, this eclectic festival enlivens the streets of Varaždin with world music, acrobats, theatre, traditional crafts and illusionists.

▶ Varaždin

▶ spancirfest.com

p78

Demand for accommodation peaks during July and August. View tours and overnight adventures in advance at lonelyplanet.com.

AUGUST

Average daytime max: 27°C
Days of rainfall (Zagreb): 11

Average daytime max: 26°C
Days of rainfall (Zagreb): 10

Full Moon Festival

During the high-summer full moon, Zadar's quays are lit with torches and candles, and boats lining the quays become floating fish markets.

▶ Zadar

Packing Notes

Bring swimwear, a hat and sunscreen. Summer days are balmy and the sun is strong.

Autumn is a field day for foodies. It's truffle season in Istria. Pick olives along the coast and enjoy the fruits of the grape harvest.

← Festival of Subotina

White truffle season kicks off in Istria with this one-day festival on the second Saturday in September, featuring a giant truffle omelette.

▶ Buzet

The summer rush is over on the coast, but sunshine is still plentiful, the sea is warm and the crowds have largely left.

Many hotels along the coast shut their doors for the season in mid-October, as do many restaurants.

SEPTEMBER

Average daytime max: 22°C
Days of rainfall (Zagreb): 10

OCTOBER

Croatia in AUTUMN

↘ Zagreb Film Festival

Catch film screenings, parties and international film directors competing for the coveted Golden Pram award in November.

▶ Zagreb

▶ zff.hr

↑ Martinje

The Feast of St Martin is celebrated in wine-producing regions on 11 November, with lots of feasting and sampling of new wines. p80

Ferry services wind down their catamaran links and reduce their schedules from October onwards, so check the schedules ahead of time.

NOVEMBER

Average daytime max: 16°C
Days of rainfall (Zagreb): 11

Average daytime max: 9°C
Days of rainfall (Zagreb): 11

Fall foliage in its full splendour is a spectacular sight to catch, especially in Gorski Kotar (p82) and Plitvice Lakes National Park (p164).

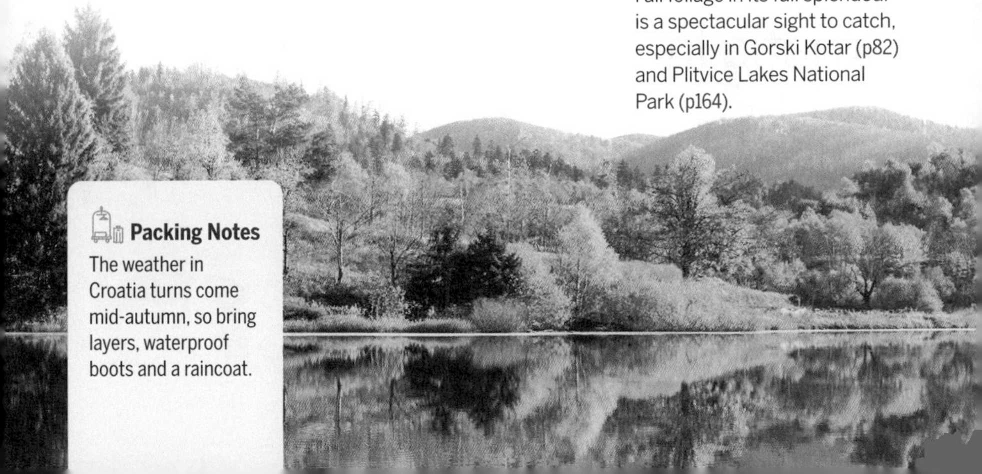

Packing Notes

The weather in Croatia turns come mid-autumn, so bring layers, waterproof boots and a raincoat.

Wintertime brings the wild, bone-chilling wind known as *bura* to the coast, which often shuts down roads and ferry traffic.

↘ Night of the Museums

Dozens of museums and galleries around Croatia throw open their doors to the public for free on the last Friday in January, including the Museum of Contemporary Art (pictured).

↖ Advent in Zagreb

From early December to early January, Zagreb's buzzy Christmas market features activities, street food, mulled wine, craft stores and live music.

▶ Zagreb

▶ adventzagreb.hr

p68

DECEMBER

Average daytime max: 5°C
Days of rainfall (Zagreb): 11

JANUARY

Croatia in WINTER

FROM LEFT: BJANKA KADIC/ALAMY STOCK PHOTO ©, XBRCHX/SHUTTERSTOCK ©, GRGO JELAVIC/PIXSELL/ALAMY LIVE NEWS ©, HAPPY WINDOW/SHUTTERSTOCK © BACKGROUND IMAGE: VIGO-S/SHUTTERSTOCK ©

↘ Feast of St Blaise

On 3 February, the streets of Dubrovnik perk up with folk dancing, concerts and processions, honouring St Blaise, its patron saint.

▶ Dubrovnik p215

↓ Rijeka Carnival

Croatia's most colourful carnival, with pageants, street dances, masked balls, exhibitions and street parades, takes place in February.

▶ Rijeka

▶ visitrijenka.hr/karneval

When the winter ice starts to melt in March, catch the full action of the waterfalls in Plitvice Lakes (p164) and Krka national parks (p162).

FEBRUARY

Average daytime max: 4°C
Days of rainfall (Zagreb): 10

Average daytime max: 7°C
Days of rainfall (Zagreb): 9

Hit the slopes just outside of Zagreb at Sljeme, the main peak of Mt Medvednica, with ski runs and lifts.

Packing Notes

Pack hats, gloves, scarves and other winter accessories for a chilly Croatian trip in winter.

Late spring is a great time to visit the coast. The Adriatic is warm enough for swimming, and prices are lower.

← Holy Week on Hvar

Hvar's 500-year-old, all-night-long Following the Cross procession, starting after Mass on Holy Thursday, is inscribed on UNESCO's Cultural Heritage of Humanity list.

▶ Hvar

During early spring, inland Istria's meadows are dotted with wild asparagus. Do as the locals do and pick some.

The maestral (strong, steady westerly wind) makes for great sailing and rafting. Kayaking is excellent, too, as the rivers swell with water.

MARCH

Average daytime max: 12°C
Days of rainfall (Zagreb): 11

APRIL

Croatia in SPRING

↘ Subversive Festival

Mingle with Europe's activists and revolutionaries at this two-week festival each May that features film screenings and panels by left-leaning movers and shakers.

▶ Zagreb

▶ subversivefestival.com

p68

↓ Sudamja

This weeklong extravaganza peaks with the feast of St Domnius, Split's patron saint, on 7 May. Expect concerts, rowing races, religious rituals and fireworks.

▶ Split

Open Wine Cellar Day

On the last Sunday in May, Istrian winemakers open their cellars for free tastings and grape-fuelled merrymaking.

Average daytime max: 16°C
Days of rainfall (Zagreb): 13

MAY

Average daytime max: 21°C
Days of rainfall (Zagreb): 13

Croatia's bustling pavement cafe culture comes alive again, as terraces get packed with customers after a period of indoor coffee drinking.

Packing Notes

Bring layers for lower temps and rain gear, as it can pour right into May.

ESSENTIAL CROATIA
Trip Builder

TAKE YOUR PICK OF MUST-SEES AND HIDDEN GEMS

The essential Croatian travel itinerary takes in a bit of everything: a stint in the capital of Zagreb followed by the sun-splashed southern cities of Split and Dubrovnik on the Dalmatian coast and an island or two thrown in too.

Trip Notes

Hub towns Zagreb, Split, Dubrovnik

How long Allow 10 days

Getting around Zagreb, Split and Dubrovnik all have airports and frequent flight connections. Long-distance buses and ferries get you to the islands. To travel at your own pace, hire a car.

Tip In peak summer season, the motorway heading south can get jammed, especially on weekends. Travelling midweek in summer is a wise choice.

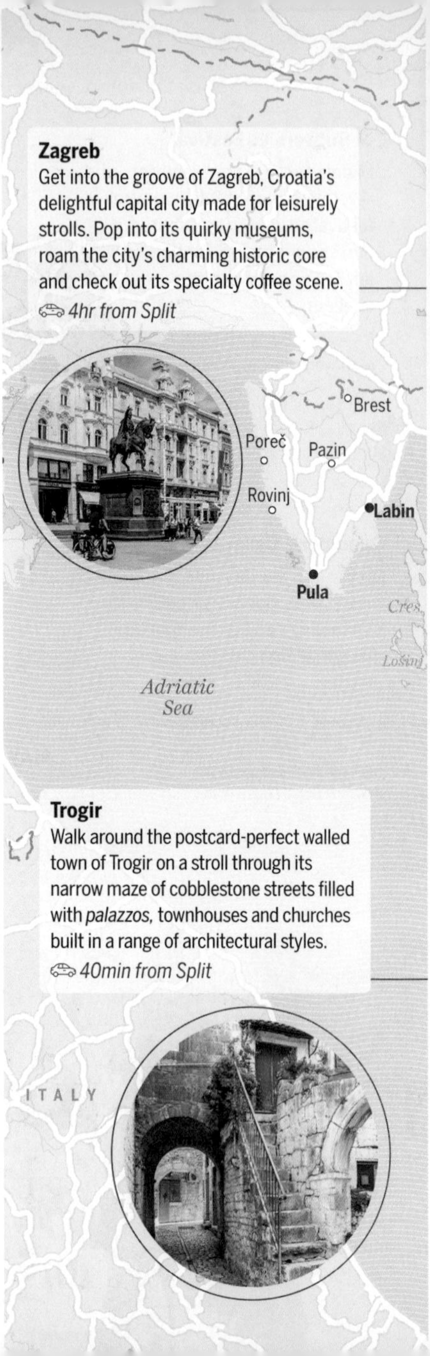

Zagreb
Get into the groove of Zagreb, Croatia's delightful capital city made for leisurely strolls. Pop into its quirky museums, roam the city's charming historic core and check out its specialty coffee scene.
4hr from Split

Trogir
Walk around the postcard-perfect walled town of Trogir on a stroll through its narrow maze of cobblestone streets filled with *palazzos*, townhouses and churches built in a range of architectural styles.
40min from Split

FROM LEFT:TRABANTOS/SHUTTERSTOCK ©, MAZUR TRAVEL/SHUTTERSTOCK ©, ROKAS TENYS/SHUTTERSTOCK ©

Split
Discover Croatia's exuberant second city, the seafront stunner of Split. Poke around Diocletian's Palace, a vibrant ancient quarter perfect for a wander, and dive into Split's great nightlife.
4hr from Zagreb

Brač
Zip over to Brač, an island known for its photogenic beach of Zlatni Rate. Hike up to Vidova Gora, the highest point in the Adriatic islands.
50min from Split

Hvar
Head to the dazzling island of Hvar, which has an intriguing mix of glamour, vibrant nightlife and historic treasures. Explore its pristine beaches, stellar wineries and a string of storybook towns.
1hr from Split

Dubrovnik
Visit the magnificent old town of Dubrovnik, fringed by mighty defensive walls and the sparkling blue Adriatic to witness the beauty of the 'Pearl of the Adriatic' firsthand.
3hr from Split

Korčula
Head to this stunning southern isle with its photo-worthy showcase, Korčula Town, encircled by ancient walls. Leave town to explore the island's beaches, wineries and striking scenery.
& 2hr from Dubrovnik

ISTRIA
Trip Builder

TAKE YOUR PICK OF MUST-SEES AND HIDDEN GEMS

Explore the heart-shaped Istrian peninsula and find its magnificent medley of sights that span coastal 'blue' Istria and 'green' Istria, the hinterland strewn with woods, olive groves and vineyards. Check out the pretty coastal resorts and beaches, hilltop medieval towns, top-rated food and wines, and lovely rural hotels.

Trip Notes

Hub towns Pula, Poreč, Rovinj

How long Allow 1 week

Getting around Pula has an international airport. For the most flexibility, especially if you want to explore the interior at your own pace, hire a car. Roads can be narrow and winding.

Tip Autumn is a wonderful time to visit the Istrian interior. This season brings the olive and wine harvest, and it's amazing for truffle hunting.

Poreč
Zip up the coast to Poreč to gape at its World Heritage–listed Euphrasian Basilica, one of Europe's finest intact examples of Byzantine architecture, with magnificent 6th-century frescoes.
50min from Pula

Rovinj
Stroll the pretty streets of Istria's showpiece resort town. Its steep cobbled roads and piazzas lead to St Euphemia's Church (pictured below), which has a 60m-high tower that dominates the peninsula.
45min from Pula

Pula
Wander the coastal capital of Istria, home to a remarkably well-preserved Roman amphitheatre, locally called the Arena, that overlooks the city's harbour.
3½hr from Zagreb

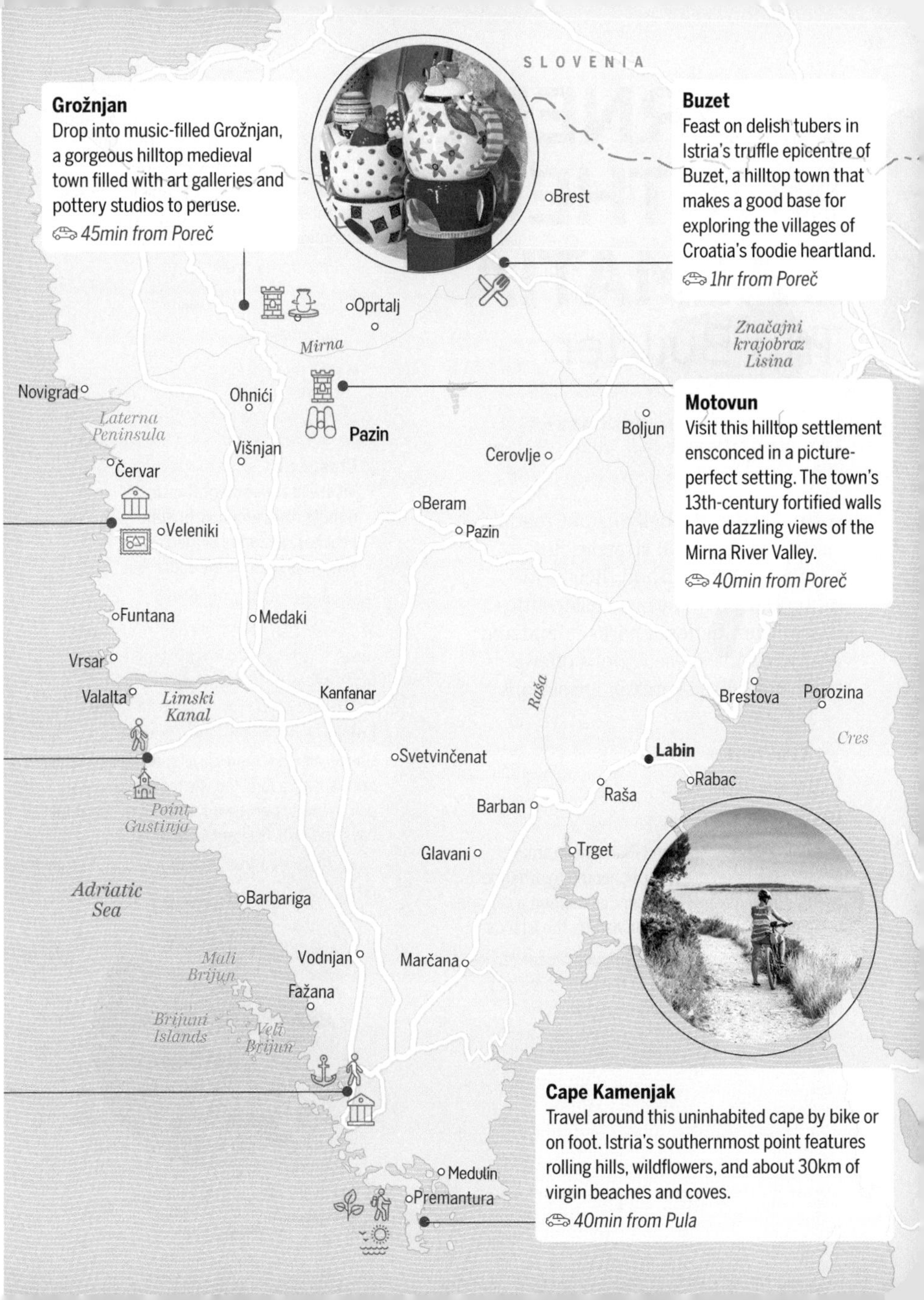

Grožnjan
Drop into music-filled Grožnjan, a gorgeous hilltop medieval town filled with art galleries and pottery studios to peruse.
45min from Poreč

Buzet
Feast on delish tubers in Istria's truffle epicentre of Buzet, a hilltop town that makes a good base for exploring the villages of Croatia's foodie heartland.
1hr from Poreč

Motovun
Visit this hilltop settlement ensconced in a picture-perfect setting. The town's 13th-century fortified walls have dazzling views of the Mirna River Valley.
40min from Poreč

Cape Kamenjak
Travel around this uninhabited cape by bike or on foot. Istria's southernmost point features rolling hills, wildflowers, and about 30km of virgin beaches and coves.
40min from Pula

KVARNER & NORTHERN DALMATIA

Trip Builder

TAKE YOUR PICK OF MUST-SEES AND HIDDEN GEMS

Take in the delights of Croatia's less-trodden coastal stretches in Northern Dalmatia and their wild hinterland. With buzzy seaside cities, magnificent national parks inland and pretty islands, these regions offer a heady and diverse mix of attractions.

Trip Notes

Hub towns Rijeka, Zadar

How long Allow 10 days

Getting around Zadar and Rijeka have small airports, and they are well connected to other parts of Croatia by frequent bus services. Hiring a car and hopping on ferries is best for visiting the islands.

Tip In peak summer season, queues for car ferries can be long, so plan to get to the port at least 1½ hours before the scheduled departure.

Rijeka
Immerse yourself in the laid-back vibe and lively cafe and cultural scene of this thriving port city. Hop over to the elegant seaside resort town of Opatija to admire its belle époque villas.
2hrs from Zagreb

Cres
Visit wild and verdant Cres for remote campgrounds, pristine beaches, a handful of medieval villages and an off-the-radar feel.
& *1½hrs from Rijeka*

Lošinj
Check out Cres' more developed sister island, posh Lošinj, a forested isle that showcases a pair of pretty port towns, a string of beautiful bays and lush, fragrant vegetation.
& *3½hrs from Rijeka*

Krk

Taste Krk's rich grappa liqueur, excellent wines and world-renowned olive oils. Relax on gorgeous beaches on this large and spectacular island that's home to Rijeka's international airport.

1hr from Rijeka

Plitvice Lakes National Park

Spend a day exploring this eye-popping natural wonderland of turquoise lakes linked by a series of waterfalls and cascades.

2hrs from Zadar

Rab

Lounge on the sandy beaches of the Lopar Peninsula and explore postcard-pretty Rab Town, with its ancient stone alleys and the four bell towers that rise above them.

2hrs from Rijeka

Paklenica National Park

Take a hike on the network of alpine trails and canyons through this spectacular national park wilderness. For extra thrills, tackle the park's rock-climbing routes.

50min from Zadar

Zadar

Amble through this vibrant Dalmatian coastal city, which has a medley of Roman ruins, Habsburg architecture and a scenic seafront with the mesmerising *Sea Organ* and *Greeting to the Sun* installations.

3¾hrs from Zagreb

DALMATIA OFF THE RADAR
Trip Builder

TAKE YOUR PICK OF MUST-SEES AND HIDDEN GEMS

Once you've visited the must-dos on Croatia's Dalmatian coast, take in its lesser-known seaside gems in the northern and southern stretches. Vibrant beauty and secret hideaways await in these oft-overlooked towns, islands and natural stunners.

Trip Notes

Hub towns Šibenik, Dubrovnik

How long Allow 10 days

Getting around An extensive bus network connects the major cities in Dalmatia. Hiring a car is best for exploring on your own with more spontaneity.

Tip You can splurge on a private speedboat to the Elaphiti Islands from Dubrovnik or take a group boat trip from the old town harbour, though these get crowded.

FROM LEFT: WIRESTOCK CREATORS/SHUTTERSTOCK ©, RNDMS/SHUTTERSTOCK ©, ANATOLII LYZUN/SHUTTERSTOCK ©

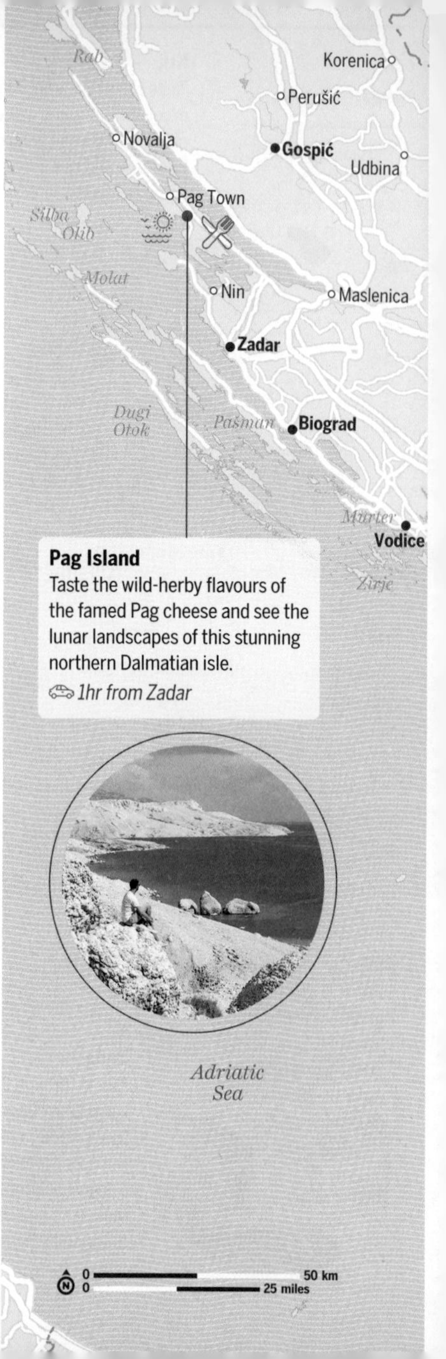

Pag Island
Taste the wild-herby flavours of the famed Pag cheese and see the lunar landscapes of this stunning northern Dalmatian isle.
1hr from Zadar

Krka National Park

Stroll along the boardwalks of this scenic national park. The Krka River rushes through canyons, broadening into emerald lakes and splashing over numerous falls and cascades.

30min from Šibenik

Šibenik

Gape at the sublime Renaissance architecture in this buzzy little Dalmatian city. The UNESCO-listed Cathedral of St James is the centrepiece, and the city also has a clutch of converted Venetian forts.

1hr from Split

Konavle

Discover this verdant border region of green fields hemmed in by mountains and punctuated by cypresses. It hides a gorgeous beach, a remote castle (pictured above) and excellent rural restaurants.

35min from Dubrovnik

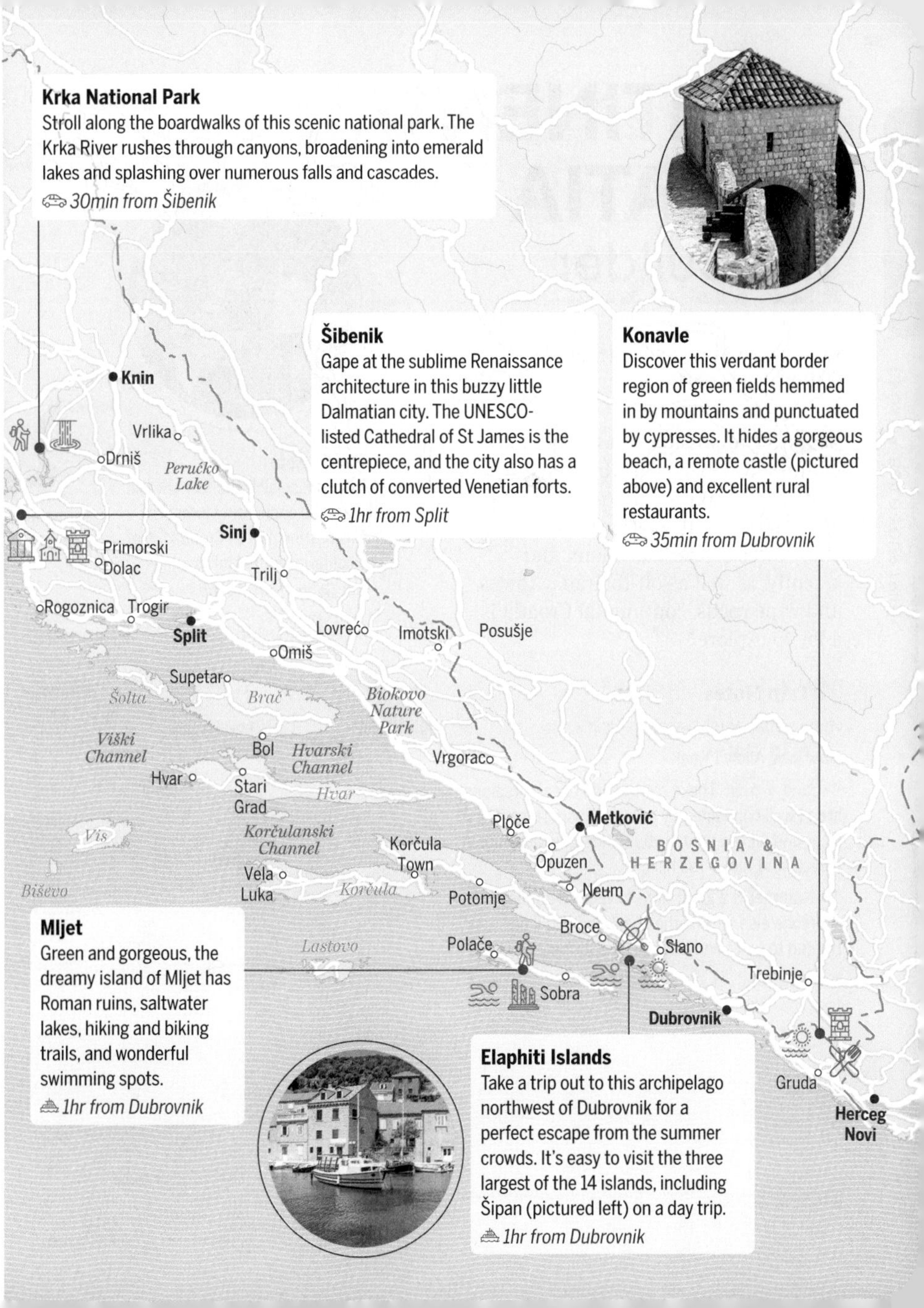

Mljet

Green and gorgeous, the dreamy island of Mljet has Roman ruins, saltwater lakes, hiking and biking trails, and wonderful swimming spots.

1hr from Dubrovnik

Elaphiti Islands

Take a trip out to this archipelago northwest of Dubrovnik for a perfect escape from the summer crowds. It's easy to visit the three largest of the 14 islands, including Šipan (pictured left) on a day trip.

1hr from Dubrovnik

CONTINENTAL CROATIA
Trip Builder

TAKE YOUR PICK OF MUST-SEES AND HIDDEN GEMS

It's impossible not to fall in love with the Croatian coast, but the quiet, understated continent doesn't get the credit it deserves. For travellers who enjoy forests, lakes, farmland and serenity, as well as off-the-radar towns and wine roads, continental Croatia is a joy to explore.

Trip Notes

Hub towns Zagreb, Varaždin, Osijek

How long Allow 1 week

Getting around These continental Croatia regions aren't well connected by public transport, so hire a car and hit the road. If you're adventurous, hire a bicycle and tackle the hills.

Tip Summer is a great time to visit, as almost everyone else storms the coast and you'll be treated to quiet and a sense of discovery.

FROM LEFT: MARIO KRPAN/SHUTTERSTOCK ©, MICHAEL WARWICK/SHUTTERSTOCK ©, SERGE GOUJON/SHUTTERSTOCK ©, STOKKETE/SHUTTERSTOCK ©

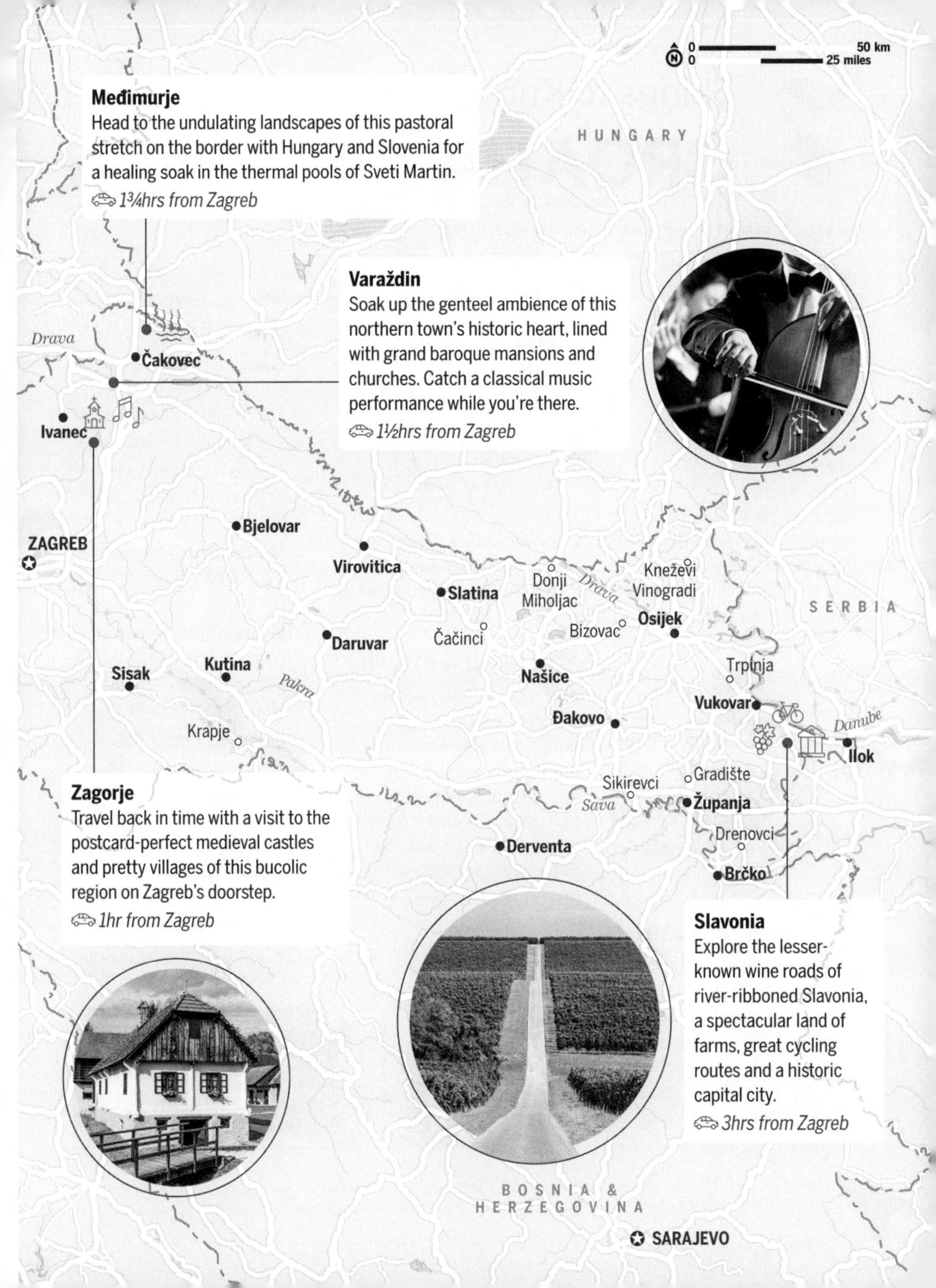

Međimurje

Head to the undulating landscapes of this pastoral stretch on the border with Hungary and Slovenia for a healing soak in the thermal pools of Sveti Martin.

1¾hrs from Zagreb

Varaždin

Soak up the genteel ambience of this northern town's historic heart, lined with grand baroque mansions and churches. Catch a classical music performance while you're there.

1½hrs from Zagreb

Zagorje

Travel back in time with a visit to the postcard-perfect medieval castles and pretty villages of this bucolic region on Zagreb's doorstep.

1hr from Zagreb

Slavonia

Explore the lesser-known wine roads of river-ribboned Slavonia, a spectacular land of farms, great cycling routes and a historic capital city.

3hrs from Zagreb

7 Things to Know about CROATIA

INSIDER TIPS TO HIT THE GROUND RUNNING

1 Going for Coffee

You might think no one in Croatia has a job because the country's cafes are perennially packed during business hours. That's because life – including work – in Croatia happens over coffee *(kava)*, even if you're actually drinking tea. *'Ajmo na kavu'* (let's go for coffee) is an invite you don't want to turn down if you want to get under the skin of Croatian culture.

2 Local Lingo

Bok Use this word to say 'hello' in Croatian, especially in Zagreb and the continental areas.

Da/ne It's important to know how to say a clear yes/no.

Molim Saying 'please' in Croatian can open doors.

Hvala 'Thank you', the magic word, is always greatly appreciated. It's also gender neutral.

Nema na čemu This phrase means 'you're welcome', the response to *hvala*.

Oprostite means 'excuse me', and it's what you'd use to get someone's attention.

▶ See the Language chapter on p252.

3 Summer Rush

If you're travelling around Croatia by road during the July and August peak season, expect stop-and-go traffic jams on motorways. Avoid travelling on weekends, especially Saturdays, and add a few extra hours to your travel time.

4 Getting Around

Though Croatia has a handful of train lines, the bus is the public transport of choice. Buses generally run on time, though they are subject to summer traffic jams.

▶ See the Getting Around section on p242.

5 Beach Shoes

Unless the soles of your feet are used to walking on sharp pebbles and rocks, water shoes are a must for swimming. Water shoes also protect from the prickly sea urchins that are widespread. Believe us, you don't want to step on one and have to pull out their spiky spines lodged in your foot.

6 No Small Talk, but Good Laughs

Small talk, chats about the weather and exchanging pleasantries won't get you far in Croatia. Croatians might appear quite abrupt in their social interactions and often even disinterested and aloof. Part of that is that they stick to their own. Croatia is a cliquey place, with a strong sense of community and tight family relations that occupy much of their social lives and calendar. While Croatians can be friendly to outsiders, they hardly ever invite them in, even to the outer edges of the inner circle.

That said, if you crack a Croatian and break the barrier of strained initial interaction, you'll find they're super warm, welcoming, hospitable, open, loyal and funny. Croatians love to laugh, at themselves and others, and they appreciate a good sense of humour, though you also may have to sit through hours of poorly translated jokes that don't make much sense in English but are still hilarious – to them.

▶ See the Language chapter on p252.

7 Outdoor Gear

While Croatia is known for sun-kissed fun on its beaches, the country also has serious nature and wilderness that you may be tempted to explore. Head out into the wild, but don't underestimate the terrain. Hike in proper shoes and gear, not flip-flops or beachwear.

▶ See the Hiking Safely box on p244.

Read, Listen, Watch & Follow

READ

Chasing a Croatian Girl: A Survivor's Tale
(Cody McClain Brown; 2018) Humorous, contemporary, non-fiction insight into Croatia and its culture.

Zagreb Noir
(various; 2015) A collection of funny crime stories set in Zagreb by contemporary Croatian writers.

Cafe Europa
(Slavenka Drakulić; 1996) Essays on life in Croatia after the collapse of Communism.

Farewell, Cowboy
(Olja Savičević Ivančević; 2010) Captivating debut novel by a Split-based writer; a great holiday read.

LISTEN

Oliver Dragojević
(The Best of Collection; 2015) Croatia's most beloved singer of catchy ballads, this Dalmatian musical icon passed away in 2018.

Let 3
(Two Dogs Fuckin'; 1989) Rock band from Rijeka that represented Croatia at Eurovision 2023 with its provocative song 'Mama ŠČ!'.

Tamarra Obrovac
(Nuvola; 2023) Album by a Croatian ethno-jazz diva who's been on the scene for 25 years.

Dino Dvornik
(Dino Dvornik; 1989) Though he passed away in 2008, the Croatian king of funk is still a beloved music figure.

ALEKSANDAR ZEC/SHUTTERSTOCK ©

Josipa Lisac
(Dnevnik Jedne Ljubavi/Diary of a Love; 1973; picutred above) First solo album by this pop/funk/jazz singer known for her eccentric style.

WATCH

Fine Dead Girls
(Dalibor Matanić; 2002) Gripping Croatian drama set in Zagreb.

Mamma Mia! Here We Go Again
(Ol Parker; 2018; pictured above right) Vis plays a Greek isle in this sequel.

The Weekend Away
(Kim Farrant; 2022; pictured below right) Thriller set in Split about a holiday gone wrong.

Faraway
Faraway (Vanessa Jopp; 2023) Romantic comedy set on a Croatian island.

How The War Started On My Island
(Vinko Brešan; 1996) Dark comedy about the 1990s Croatian War of Independence.

COLLECTION CHRISTOPHEL/LEGENDARY ENTERTAINMENT/UNIVERSAL/ ALAMY STOCK PHOTO ©

NETFLIX/PAKT MEDIA/ALBUM/ ALAMY STOCK PHOTO ©

FOLLOW

Croatia Honestly
(croatiahonestly.com) Stories and recipes by anthropologist and writer Andrea Pisac.

Croatia
(croatia.hr) Official website of the Croatian National Tourist Board.

Croatia Week
(croatiaweek.com) News from Croatia in English.

DNA Croatia
(dnacroatia.com) Follow Digital Nomad Association Croatia for interesting events.

Total Croatia News
(total-croatia-news.com) English-language daily news.

ZAGREB

CULTURE | CITY LIFE | HISTORY

Experience Zagreb online

SKALA
1
STREET FOOD

ZAGREB
Trip Builder

Zagreb is an understated charmer with a slow-burn vibe. Wander the Upper Town and Lower Town to see historic landmarks, stop by quirky museums, take in Zagreb's vibrant street life and coffee culture, and roam its many forest parks.

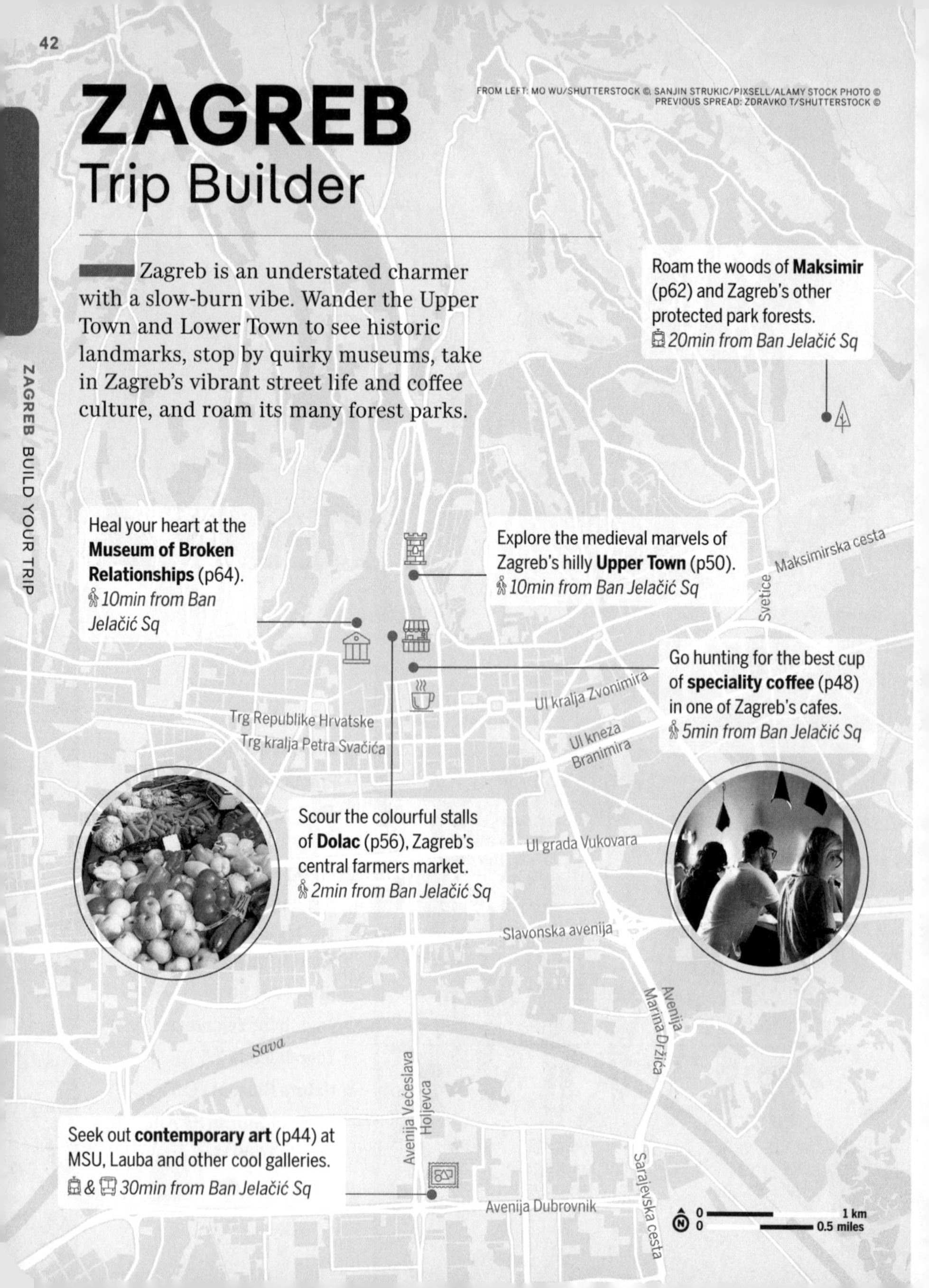

Roam the woods of **Maksimir** (p62) and Zagreb's other protected park forests.
20min from Ban Jelačić Sq

Heal your heart at the **Museum of Broken Relationships** (p64).
10min from Ban Jelačić Sq

Explore the medieval marvels of Zagreb's hilly **Upper Town** (p50).
10min from Ban Jelačić Sq

Go hunting for the best cup of **speciality coffee** (p48) in one of Zagreb's cafes.
5min from Ban Jelačić Sq

Scour the colourful stalls of **Dolac** (p56), Zagreb's central farmers market.
2min from Ban Jelačić Sq

Seek out **contemporary art** (p44) at MSU, Lauba and other cool galleries.
& 30min from Ban Jelačić Sq

Practicalities

ARRIVING

Zagreb Airport has an airport bus (one-way ticket €8) that runs regularly from Zračna Luka Franjo Tuđman to the main bus terminal. Local bus 290 runs to Kvaternikov trg every 35 minutes and costs €0.80.

MONEY

Most places accept cards for payment, but it's worth having some cash just in case.

FIND YOUR WAY

The Tourist Information Center on Trg Bana Jelačića gives out heaps of useful free brochures, maps and tips.

WHERE TO STAY

Area	Pro/Con
Upper Town	Best for ancient vibes and heaps of history. Mind the steep cobblestone streets.
Lower Town	Plenty of hotel options around the city centre. Convenient to the train and bus terminals.
Outlying neigbourhoods	More lodging options are popping up beyond the centre if you want workaday vibes.

EATING & DRINKING

Zagreb has a small but burgeoning restaurant scene, ranging from tiny, cash-only eateries and traditional taverns serving continental cuisine to swanky brunch spots and fine-dining restaurants.

Must-try štrukli (baked cheese dumplings; pictured top left) Le Bistro at Hotel Esplanade or La Štruk on Skalinska (p57)

Best cup of espresso Cogito or Express (p49)

Best wine shop and tastings Bornstein (p57)

GETTING AROUND

WALK

Zagreb is great for walking, especially if you stick to the Lower Town and Upper Town, where distances are manageable.

TRAM

The blue ZET trams are fun to ride and go to most attractions beyond the centre. Buy your ticket from the driver or at a kiosk and then validate it at one of the yellow machines on board.

JAN–MAR
Cold and grey but the least crowded season.

APR–JUN
Sunny, breezy days of blooming flowers and street happenings.

JUL–SEP
Hot, humid days but pleasant nights.

OCT–DEC
The city prepares for Advent as temperatures cool.

01 THE CAPITAL'S Contemporary Art

CULTURE | CREATIVITY | GALLERIES

Tap into Zagreb's palpable creative energy that's driven by a vibrant independent art scene and a clutch of powerhouse institutions, as well as a host of ambitious creators and curators. The city has a variety of places where you can check out home-grown art, as well as frequent visiting exhibitions by regional and international artists.

How To

Getting around Zagreb's art museums and galleries are scattered around town, but all are easily accessible by public transport.

When to go Most are closed on Mondays; admission to MSU is free on the first Wednesday of every month.

Art therapy Check out the annual Artupunktura, a platform for art and culture that puts on an amazing roster of events and art around Zagreb every autumn.

Art in a former mosque On Trg Žrtava Fašizma, the **Croatian Association of Artists (HDLU)** is housed in one of the few architectural works by Ivan Meštrović, a striking circular pavilion. It's a must-visit on the art circuit of Zagreb and puts on a busy and diverse programme of exhibitions and events throughout the year. The building itself has had several fascinating incarnations, including a stint as a mosque in the 1940s; people in Zagreb still call it the 'Old Mosque'.

Worth the trek Don't miss the exhibits at the **Museum of Contemporary Art (MSU)** housed in a blocky city icon across the Sava in Novi Zagreb. It displays both solo and thematic group shows by Croatian and international artists in its 17,000-sq-metre space. The packed year-round schedule features film screenings, theatre, concerts and performance art. The annual Summer at MSU, typically from mid-June through mid-July, features a lively roster of events. Check out the dates at *msu.hr*.

Edgy, contemporary art **Lauba**, the House for People and Art, displays a private art collection in a former textile-weaving mill in an industrial area of Črnomerec in western Zagreb, providing an insight into Croatian contemporary art from the 1950s to today. It hosts a dynamic roster of events, and rotating exhibits change frequently inside the industrial-chic space. **Bez Naziva** (Without Title) is a cool on-site cafe-bar.

Left Museum of Contemporary Art
Below left Lauba

Where to Find New Trends

Galerija SC (Studentski Centar)
Showcases work by young artists.

Galerija Miroslav Kraljević
Explore experimental art practices on the outer edge of Zagreb's Design District.

Galerija Modro
An outstanding display of Croatia's contemporary art in the Upper Town.

Galerija Šira
Features work from students at the Academy of Fine Arts Zagreb in the heart of the Lower Town.

Kranjčar Gallery
Rotating exhibits of Croatian contemporary art, from video and painting to sculpture and photography, steps from the cathedral.

VN Gallery
Frequently changing displays of art in different formats and media in the western part of town.

Trotoar Gallery
Contemporary art by local and regional creators.

02 QUIRKY Museums & Art

OFFBEAT | CULTURE | EXHIBITIONS

Zagreb might not have world-famous, big-hitter museums, but for its relatively small size, the city has an exceptional variety of unusual museums worth checking out. They cover all sorts of niche phenomena, from mushrooms and cannabis to hangovers and selfies, catering to travellers with oddball interests. Zagreb also has its own solar system you can seek out.

MATIJA HABLJAK/PIXSELL/ALAMY STOCK PHOTO ©

How To

Getting around Many of Zagreb's museums are scattered around the city centre. The museums further afield are all reachable by tram, bus or a combination of the two.

When to go The museums have varied opening hours, so it's best to check their websites before you head out.

Sweet tickets At the Museum of Chocolate, your entry ticket comes in the shape of a sample box of chocolates.

DENIS LOVROVIC/AFP VIA GETTY IMAGES ©

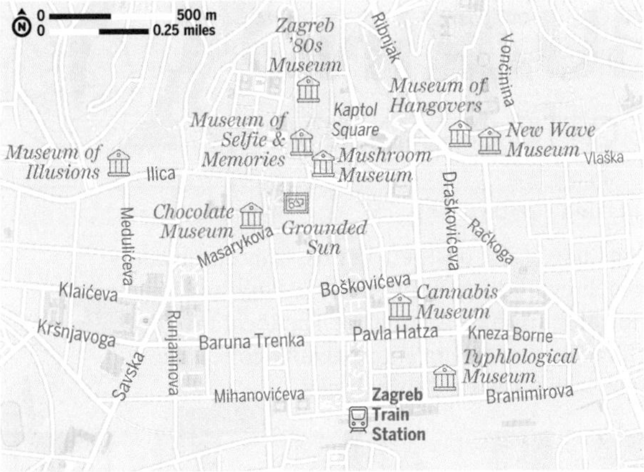

Nature's delights Check out the interactive exhibits at the **Chocolate Museum**, and learn the difference between hemp, cannabis and marijuana (which is illegal in Croatia) at the **Cannabis Museum**. Afterwards, indulge in a fungi feast for the eyes and see the collection of more than 1200 freeze-dried mushrooms – some poisonous – on display at the **Mushroom Museum**.

The gift of seeing At the **Typhlological Museum**, admire artwork made by people with visual impairments, visit a dark room and learn about Braille. Get twisted at the **Museum of Illusions**, where the Slanted Room and the Mirror of Truth are among 70-plus intriguing exhibits, hologram pictures, puzzles and educational games that offer a fun mental workout.

Music and fun The **New Wave Museum** takes you on a musical journey back to Zagreb's golden era in the late 1970s and 1980s when the city had a happening punk and rock scene. Have heaps of fun posing and snapping photos at the **Museum of Selfie & Memories** and then read the drunken tales on display and play darts while wearing drunk goggles at the **Museum of Hangovers** (best visited as a group).

Travel back in time at the four-room **Zagreb '80s Museum**, devoted to the city's golden decade, with heaps of memorabilia on display (Commodore 64 and Atari, anyone?) and interactive exhibits.

Left Museum of Illusions
Below left Cannabis Museum

Zagreb's Solar System

It started with *Grounded Sun*, the golden, sphere-shaped sculpture made by renowned Croatian artist Ivan Kožarić in 1971 and placed on Bogovićeva as a landmark. In 2004, artist Davor Preis created metal scale models of the planets in the solar system, using *Grounded Sun* as the centre, and placed them in relative distances at nine locations around the city.

Tracking down the planets of the *Nine Views* art installation is a fun quest. The placements of the planets around the city centre are all within easy walking distance.

Find Mercury at Margaretska 3, Venus at Trg Bana Josipa Jelačića 3, Earth at Varšavska 9 and Mars at Tkalčićeva 21.

03 BUZZING Coffee Scene

FOOD AND DRINK | CAFE CULTURE | LOCAL LIFE

When Zagreb residents have time on their hands, they can usually be found at a cafe. Pretty much everything happens over *kava* (coffee), from business and gossip to catchups and first dates. The local love of coffee was the perfect platform for the rise of the specialty coffee scene in Zagreb, which has become one of the city's big draws.

SANJIN STRUKIC/PIXSELL/ALAMY STOCK PHOTO ©

How To

Getting around Most of these cafes are in the city centre, a stroll away from the main square.

Zagreb Coffee Bites Check out the Instagram page of @zagrebcoffee bites, which organises meetups and walks around the love of specialty coffee.

The Saturday peak Don't miss *špica,* the local tradition of people-watching while sipping coffee between 11am and 2pm on Saturdays. Grab one of the prime pavement tables along Bogovićeva, Preradovićeva or Tkalčićeva.

SANJIN STRUKIC/PIXSELL/ALAMY STOCK PHOTO ©

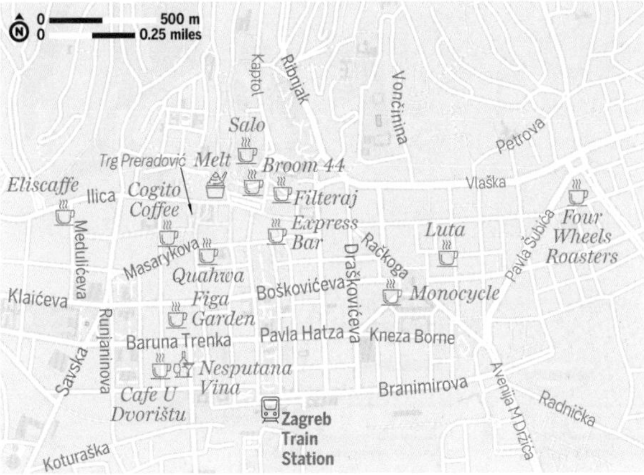

Coffee culture From bean to cup of *kava*, coffee has always been deeply ingrained in Croatian culture and social lives. And then specialty coffee took off. Among the first kick-starting the movement was **Eliscaffe** by barista Nik Orosi on Ilica, which roasts its own 100% arabica beans and serves a mean *triestino* (a Trieste-style large macchiato in a glass).

Local roasters to look out for **Cogito Coffee** is Croatia's top boutique roaster. Artsy **Cafe U Dvorištu** is devoted to sourcing in-season fresh coff ee beans and seeing the process all the way through to that delicious cup of coffee you'll drink at one of its four Zagreb locations. Another roastery and coffee shop worth visiting is **Quahwa**, tucked away in a courtyard off Teslina. It serves up some of the finest arabica in Zagreb, from super strong lattes to traditional Turkish coffee. Also worth checking out for its premium-quality coffee is **Four Wheels Roasters** on Martićeva.

Zagreb's top spots for specialty coffee

Express Bar (Petrinjska 4) Tiny but packs a punch; find it steps away from Bana Jelačića.

Luta (Radoslava Lopašića 14) In Zagreb's happening Design District.

Monocycle (Kneza Mislava 17) Petite corner cafe with views of the Croatian Association of Artists (HDLU).

Figa Garden (Gundulićeva 39) Cosy hideaway in the city centre.

Filteraj (Vlaška 10) A plant-based, zero-waste cafe.

Left Street cafe
Below left Barista Nik Orosi, Eliscaffe

Coffee & Food Pairings

While people in Zagreb traditionally drink coffee on its own, I have been particularly excited about how the specialty coffee scene is interacting with the growing local food and wine industry. Here are some places to check out.

Melt is the spot to enjoy tasty vegan gelato paired with top coffee.

Broom 44 has started roasting its own beans.

Salo is a farm-to-table bakery where the quality of coffee matches the beautiful food made with locally sourced ingredients.

Nesputana Vina wine shop shares its courtyard with Cogito Coffee HQ in downtown Zagreb, a perfect place to enjoy great coffee and some of Europe's best natural wines.

■ **Recommended by Matija Powlison Belković**
co-owner of Cogito Coffee
@cogitocoffeeroasters

04 THE MAZE of Medieval Zagreb

HISTORY | ARCHITECTURE | WALKING

Though Zagreb reveals its historic layers like an onion, the city started with two hilltop medieval settlements, Kaptol and Gradec. For whiffs of the ancient past, roam remnants from Zagreb's early days, starting at its historic heart.

IVANSMUK/GETTY IMAGES ©

How To

Getting around The Upper Town is spread across two hillsides connected by a string of staircases and passageways. Wear good walking shoes.

When to go The gas lamps are lit manually at dusk every day and light up the streets.

Night skies Zagreb Observatory, at the top of the medieval Popov Toranj tower, has amazing night views of the city, and it's open for visits on Wednesday nights.

MIKHAIL MARKOVSKIY/SHUTTERSTOCK ©

Wow-Worthy Views & Cannon Blasts

Take in a sweeping 360-degree view of the city and ponder Zagreb's roots from the panoramic viewpoint atop **Lotrščak Tower**, built in the mid-13th century to protect the south city gate from invasions. Since 1877, a cannon has been 'fired' from the tower every day at noon, allegedly to commemorate a day in the mid-15th century when a cannon blast warded off Turks camped across the Sava River. Today, locals set their watches by the blast, and visitors get startled.

ALEX CIMBAL/SHUTTERSTOCK ©

Walk Through an Ancient Gate

Light a candle and honour a loved one at medieval **Gradec**, a dark soulful shrine inside the **Stone Gate** that oozes serenity and calls for a pause on your Upper Town wanderings. According to legend, a great fire in 1731 destroyed every part of the wooden

Stroll a Former Stream

Walk along Tkalča, as locals call Tkalčićeva, a charming pedestrian road that winds uphill from Trg Bana Jelačića, with pastel-coloured town-houses and bustling cafe terraces. Imagine a pretty stream lined with watermills running in its place, which once separated the settlements of Kaptol and Gradec in the Middle Ages.

Above left St Mark's Church (p52)
Left Gradec shrine, Stone Gate
Above Lotrščak Tower

gate except for the painting of the Virgin and Child, which was created by an unknown 17th-century artist. People believe that the painting possesses miraculous powers, and they come regularly to pray and leave flowers as an offering. Square stone slabs are engraved with thanks and praise to the Virgin Mary. On the western facade of the Stone Gate is a statue of Dora, the hero of an 18th-century novel, who lived with her father next to the Stone Gate.

Sacral Pit Stops

Zagreb has places of worship aplenty, and it's fascinating to discover their ancient roots. Alongside **Zagreb Cathedral** (currently closed for repairs after the 2020 earthquake), the 13th-century **St Mark's Church** on its namesake square is one of the city's iconic sights. Check out its showpiece, the colourful glazed tiled roof, with the medieval coat of arms of Croatia, Dalmatia and Slavonia on the left side and the emblem of Zagreb on the right.

Witches, Ghosts & Skeletons

The mace on the Stone Gate prevents witches from flying into the old town. It's said that the mysterious Black Queen lurks in secret passages underneath St Mark's Church. Park Grič hides dozens of skeletons, and there used to be a cemetery here. The most gorgeous mansion on Demetrova is home to a ghost lady. Beware when you pass by the Capuchin stairs, or you could hear the sound of witches' laughter.

These legends are a tiny part of mysterious local lore that makes the Upper Town a perfect setting for an evening walk.

■ **By Iva Silla** *creator of Secret Zagreb tours and gamified activities and host of the tips-filled podcast* Croatia Underrated, @secretzagreb

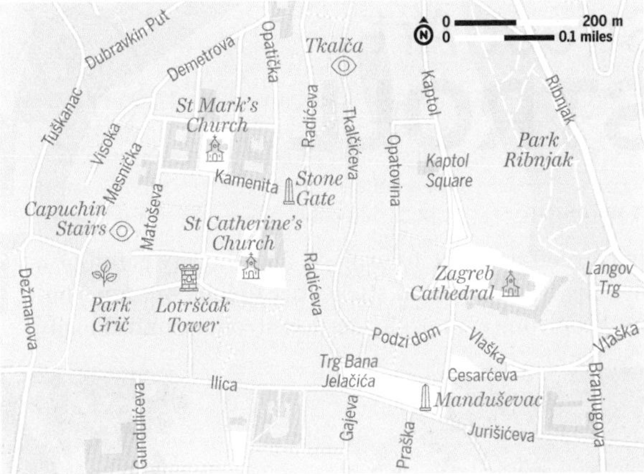

Far left Stone Gate, with mace on the roof
Below Manduševac fountain

A stroll away from St Mark's, the stunning **St Catherine's Church** was built in the 17th century by Jesuits. Although scorched by fire and reconstructed by Austrian architect Herman Bollé after the massive 1880 earthquake, the facade of this single-nave, baroque beauty still gleams. The interior contains a fine altar dating from 1762. Look up to spot the 18th-century medallions depicting the life of St Catherine on the ceiling of the nave.

Toss a Coin for Good Luck

Manduševac, a fountain on Trg Bana Jelačića, is named after Manda, a beautiful girl who, according to local lore, once gave water from this ancient spring to a knight who returned from battle thirsty. The knight asked the girl to scoop up some water for him (*zagrabi*, in Croatian), and so Zagreb was named. See all those coins in the fountain? They are wishes for good luck tossed in by passersby.

05 Street-Art STROLL

CREATIVITY | STREET LIFE | WALKING

Zagreb has a booming street-art scene to explore, and the city is full of amazing murals, graffiti, stencils, paste-ups and sticker art to look out for. The pieces don't last forever, but keep your eyes peeled as you stroll around the city.

DAVOR VISNJIC/PIXSELL/ALAMY STOCK PHOTO ©

Trip Notes

When to go Every summer, the colourful Art Park Festival (pictured above) takes over Park Ribnjak with music, ping-pong and street art created before your eyes.

Get involved Book a walking tour or sign up for a graffiti workshop with street artist Krešimir Golubić, aka Leon GSK (leongsk.com).

Festivals The annual Okolo // Around brings public art installations and urban interventions to the streets of Zagreb for about 10 days in August.

Street-Art History

Zagreb was first splashed with street art in the 1980s and became the first city in communist Eastern Europe with a scene. Today, check out work by Lonac, Zagreb's top street-art muralist.

Zagreb Street Art Festival brings international artists in September.

By Krešimir Golubić, aka Leon GSK
pioneer of graffiti and street art in Croatia
@leon_gsk; @zagrebstreetartguide

01 Don't miss the street-art feast at **Opatovina**, a tiny Upper Town park. Many local and international artists have left their marks, but Bare's sleeping Gulliver mural is the star.

02 The **Zakmardijeve Stube** stairs leading to Stross from Radićeva are known as Punk Rock Street, a street-art hall of fame featuring pieces by local greats, such as Fishes Invasion and yo.pecador.

04 **AKC Medika** is a must-see on Pierotti if you're into alternative urban culture and art. It has clubs, studios, an anarchist library, galleries and heaps of great street art.

03 Take a stroll on the 'carpet' of **Mala Martićeva**, a cool strip in Zagreb's Design District, where artist Boris Bare spray-painted colourful floor murals emulating the tilework he found on Zagreb doorways.

05 Though slightly fading, the huge murals at **Studentski Centar** are some of the best in Zagreb, painted by legends of the city's street-art scene, such as Lonac, Sarme, Chez and Lunar.

06 ZAGREB for Epicureans

FOOD | WINE | TASTINGS

Bring along an empty stomach and discover Zagreb's tastiest spots for food and drink. The city has a small but vibrant scene fit for epicureans on the lookout for edible and drinkable delights. Dig into Zagreb's local bites and booze at the city's restaurants, eateries and bakeries, and during its many food and drink festivals.

MO WU/SHUTTERSTOCK ©

How To

When to go Food markets are especially exciting in spring and summer when it's a merry feast of berries, which are also sold from wooden kiosks set up across the city.

PLACe Market Check out the night street-food market that springs up at Dolac in spring and autumn.

Wine fest Check out Vinski Grad (Wine City), an outdoor festival that takes over Park dr. Franje Tuđmana every June.

WANDERING VIEWS/SHUTTERSTOCK ©

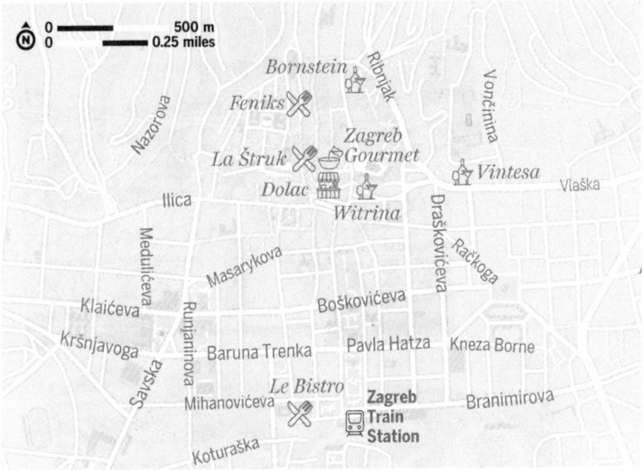

A feast of food and colours Indulge your senses at **Dolac**, the bustling central farmers market dotted with red parasols and stalls overflowing with garden-fresh fruit and veg. The 'belly of Zagreb' has bright pops of colour and is a field day for photo ops. The main part is on an elevated square, and the street level has indoor stalls selling meat, dairy and flowers.

Learn to make štrukli This iconic Croatian dish of cottage cheese-filled dumplings is traditional for Zagreb and the Zagorje region. **Zagreb Gourmet** offers culinary workshops in its space on Opatovina, up the stairs from Dolac. A class includes hand-rolling dough and a short visit to the market while the *štrukli* are in the oven. Don't feel like rolling dough but want to try some *štrukli?* Check out **La Štruk** around the corner on Skalinska, where you can try all sorts of varieties, or **Le Bistro** restaurant at Hotel Esplanade, which has served this staple since 1951.

On the wine front For tastings and mingling over vino, check out **Vintesa**, an independent wine shop tucked away in a courtyard off Vlaška. **Bornstein** is the oldest wine shop in Zagreb and has a bar set in a historic cellar. Don't miss Saturday morning tastings organised at **Witrina**, off the main square, with guest winemakers and food producers.

Left Dolac market
Below left Mini *burek*

The Lure of Bakeries

Bakeries in Zagreb are a one-stop shop for comfort food, from sweet and savoury pastries to pizza and *burek* (heavy pastry stuffed with meat or cheese). Bakeries can be found everywhere and exude a quaint, old-world charm. Ask for or point to your pastry of choice from a glass counter overflowing with baked goods. Eat this breakfast on the go or share it with friends over coffee.

Zagreb locals frequent bakeries around the clock. A morning visit to Dolac market is not complete without a piece of *bučnica* (savoury pumpkin pie) from Kuraž, while late-night drinks are best soaked up with a greasy *burek* from Feniks (Radićeva 10) at 3am.

■ **By Andrea Pisac** *anthropologist, travel writer and author of three bestselling cookbooks on Croatian cuisine, @andreapisac, facebook.com/CroatiaHonestly*

Zagreb **ICONS**

01 Šestine umbrella

This iconic red umbrella harks back to the 18th-century folk costumes from the Šestine area below Medvednica; you'll see them all over Dolac.

02 St Mark's rooftop

This colourful glazed tiled roof shows the medieval coat of arms of Croatia, Dalmatia and Slavonia, as well as the emblem of Zagreb.

03 Licitar Hearts

Zagreb's most iconic souvenir, these tradi-tional, heart-shaped, red ginger-bread cookies are exchanged as keepsakes.

04 Zagreb Cathedral

The twin spires of Zagreb Cathedral, Croatia's largest sacral building, have soared over the city for eight centuries.

05 Zagreb funicular

The blue Zagreb funi-cular has connected the Lower Town and Upper Town since 1890. The ride takes 64 seconds and has fun views.

06 City trams

When they first started running in 1891, Zagreb's trams were horse-drawn. Electricity has powered the bright-blue icons since 1910.

07 Zrinjevac Pavilion
The 19th-century Music Pavilion on Zrinjevac is the stage for many concerts and events.

08 Ban Jelačić on his horse
Zagreb's main square owes its name to Ban Jelačić, the 19th-century *ban* (governor) who proudly presides over it from his horse.

09 Croatian Naïve Art
Pop into the Croatian Museum of Naïve Art to check out the colourful and often dreamlike paintings of this unique genre.

10 Old Mosque
One of the few architectural works by Ivan Meštrović, Croatia's most famous sculptor, this striking circular pavilion is known as the 'Old Mosque'.

07 Nature HIDEOUTS

PARKS | GARDENS | OUTDOORS

Take a break from Zagreb's urban delights to immerse yourself in one of the city's many green spaces. Explore gorgeously manicured parks and gardens, the leafy main cemetery and lakeside hideaways, and roam its semi-wild forest parks beyond the city centre.

SERHAT ÄÄDAÄ/ANADOLU AGENCY VIA GETTY IMAGES ©

How To

Getting around Nextbike, a bike-share system available 24/7, lets you hire a bicycle from 20 locations around the city. Get more details at nextbike.hr.

When to go You can wander Zagreb's parks and gardens year-round, but spring is the best season to visit, when the city's flora comes to life.

Flower power Catch the annual FloraArt Zagreb in mid-May, an international garden show that brings fantastic floral creations to Park Bundek.

WANDERING VIEWS/SHUTTERSTOCK ©

Verdant City-Centre Hideaways

Roam the gorgeous little **Botanical Garden** in the heart of the city, steps from the main train station on Marulićev trg. Its maze of meandering paths is perfect for serene strolls and meditation. Laid out in 1892, the Botanical Garden has an English-style arboretum, a greenhouse with giant water lilies, a flower parterre and a pretty larch-wood bridge.

Zrinjevac is the locals' most beloved go-to for green breaks right in the city centre, close to Trg Bana Jelačića. This tree-lined square is a popular hangout during sunshine-filled weekends, and it has pop-up cafe stalls during spring and summer, as well as during Advent. It's part of the Green Horseshoe (also known as the Lenuci Horseshoe), a U-shaped series of seven city squares with parks.

DEYMOSHR/SHUTTERSTOCK ©

Wilderness on the City's Edge

Looming over the city from the north, Medvednica Nature Park is a patch of wilderness criss-crossed by more than 70 hiking trails and numerous mountain huts. Covered by dense forests of silver fir, Pannonian beech and sessile oak, this beloved nature escape is known to locals as Sljeme, after its highest mountain peak (1035m).

Above left Larch-wood bridge, Botanical Garden
Above Zrinjevac
Left Mirogoj Cemetery (p62)

Serene Cemetery

One of the most beautiful cemeteries in Europe, **Mirogoj** is a monumental place, designed in 1876 by Austrian-born architect Herman Bollé, who created numerous buildings around Zagreb. Walk around this final resting place of some 300,000 souls, which resembles an open-air art gallery with its maze of leafy lanes shaded by spruce, chestnut and maple trees. It's particularly poignant to visit on All Saints' Day (1 November), when people visit their loved ones who rest here and thousands of candles twinkle in the night.

Park Perfection

Roam the woods and lakes of **Maksimir** to blend in with locals. A 15-minute tram ride east of Trg Bana Jelačića, this peaceful wooded enclave covers 18 hectares and is a favourite stomping ground. Opened to the public in 1794, Maksimir was the first public promenade in southeastern Europe. It's

Lost in the Woods

Zagreb has 17 protected forest parks of different shapes and sizes spread across different city neighbourhoods. Check out Tuškanac-Dubravkin Put-Cmrok Meadow, which stretches from the Upper Town, and Dotrščina, with its antifascist memorial park that adjoins Maksimir and Grmoščica in the western suburbs.

For an unexpected pocket of wilderness, visit the protected Savica Lakes north of the Sava River, a wetland area with a series of swampy lakes between two bridges, Most Mladosti and Domovinski Most. Roam the walking trails and find the ornithological station, where you can spot more than 30 bird species.

Far left Savica Lakes
Below Jarun beach

landscaped like an English garden, with alleys, lawns, a series of pretty lakes and thick woods to get lost in. Sing a song inside the Echo Pavilion and check out the rustic Swiss Cottage house. Inside the park, the Zagreb Zoo has a modest collection of the world's fauna and public daily feeding times for pelicans, sea lions, capuchins and African lions.

Lakeside Retreats

Explore **Jarun**, known as the 'Sea of Zagreb', in the southern section of the city. It's a popular getaway for residents at any time of the year, but especially in summer, when the clear waters of its artificial lake are ideal for swimming. You can also take in the greenery while cycling or rollerblading on its many paths.

Enjoy lakeside fun and games on the lovely patch of greenery that is **Bundek** in Novi Zagreb. The park has two lakes: the Big Lake is for swimmers, while the Small Lake is a nature reserve. Check out the rollerskating paths, playgrounds, a floating stage for up to 2500 visitors and heaps of pop-up festivals by the lake.

■ **By Olinka Vištica**
co-founder of the Museum of Broken Relationships
@brokenships

A Tale of Broken Hearts

WITNESS MEMENTOS LEFT AFTER A RELATIONSHIP ENDS

Artists Olinka Vištica and Dražen Grubišić started the wonderfully weird Museum of Broken Relationships after their romantic relationship ended. Now on display in the string of all-white rooms are donations from around the globe that tell the stories of romances that withered to broken family connections, from the hilarious to the heartbreaking.

Left Museum entrance
Centre & Right Exhibits

FINN STOCK/SHUTTERSTOCK ©

Love and relationships entered the museum world in an era when so much of our private lives were in the public eye. The Museum of Broken Relationships displays a seemingly random collection of anonymous contributions from around the world. These exhibits, often banal trinkets, are accompanied by stories of the people who donated them, and all symbolise the end of a relationship. They function as triggers of memory, launching an emotional process of making meaning out of these objects.

When I look back at the museum and the space it has covered from just an abstract idea – barely a sentence on a scrap of paper – to an almost 3300-piece collection of objects and stories coming from every corner of the world, I feel proud and humble. People often tell me, 'Oh, it's such a simple and universal idea. No wonder it has taken root'. It's true on the one hand. On the other, in this world that often looks like a factory of instant happiness, it took courage to openly and directly use difficulty, loss and pain as a trace element and a key to connecting fellow humans.

I could tell you about the exhausting work of at least 10 people, entangled in fish lines and colourful paper cranes, trying to hang 1000 paper birds in the hope of visually telling the story of an unrequited teenage love in Mexico City. When the person behind the story came to the exhibition, the rainbow of cranes brought tears to her eyes.

I could have never imagined a sex toy as banal as a dildo from Bloomington, Indiana, would produce such

JULIE MAYFENG/SHUTTERSTOCK ©

PAUL PRESCOTT/SHUTTERSTOCK ©

a stir in the visitors centre of the European Parliament in Brussels, another surprising space for the museum to pop up. Conspicuously named Exhibit 37, it was almost removed but then remained a silent and coy witness to the importance of good sex in marriage.

In Amsterdam once, I found myself in the flat of a man I'd never met before. Suffering from severe illness, he entrusted me with a huge painting that represented three men in an intricate and complicated threesome that lasted for years. I will never forget the weight of the painting and the beauty of the scene as we were carrying it down the canals. I learned of the man's passing just a couple of days after the exhibit opened. The ending sentence of his story – 'Don't let death stop you from travelling' – still echoes.

> These exhibits, often banal trinkets, are accompanied by stories of the people who donated them, and all symbolise the end of a relationship.

In the quiet evening hours, just before we close the museum, I often take a last glance at its familiar objects. It is as if they return my glance, with a gentle caution not to take my own struggles too seriously. Even in the darkest of stories, there is life, such as the narrative accompanying the dog collar light from Berlin. Its concluding lines may appear as a simple instruction to the curator, but for me, they take on a deeper meaning: 'Hang it blinking, as it reminds me of a heartbeat. And the battery can be exchanged.'

On Full Display

Since the project started as a travelling exhibit back in 2006, it has been shown in 63 cities and 34 countries, and its collection now features 3330 artefacts and stories from all over the world.

The items on display range from a below-knee prosthesis from Zagreb; rubber gloves from Seoul, South Korea; a plastic Godzilla with beaded necklaces from Mexico City; an unopened birthday present from Germany; and a dead sprig of mint in a glass from Australia.

08 Chasing City VIEWS

SCENERY | ROOFTOPS | PANORAMAS

With its many hills and a mighty mountain lording over it from the north, Zagreb has an impressive variety of places where you can survey the urban scene. Seek out some of the most spectacular panoramas of the city to take in all its glory, from city promenades and rooftop bars to mountaintop vistas.

ZDENEK MATYAS PHOTOGRAPHY/SHUTTERSTOCK ©

How To

Getting around You can take public transport (tram, bus or cable car) to many scenic spots, and you can also walk around and even hike up to Sljeme.

When to go Every season has its own appeal, and views are fantastic, but breezy summer and early autumn evenings are particularly great.

Cable car cost A one-way ticket to the top of Sljeme costs €9.95. A return ticket is €16.59.

ZDRAVKO T/SHUTTERSTOCK ©

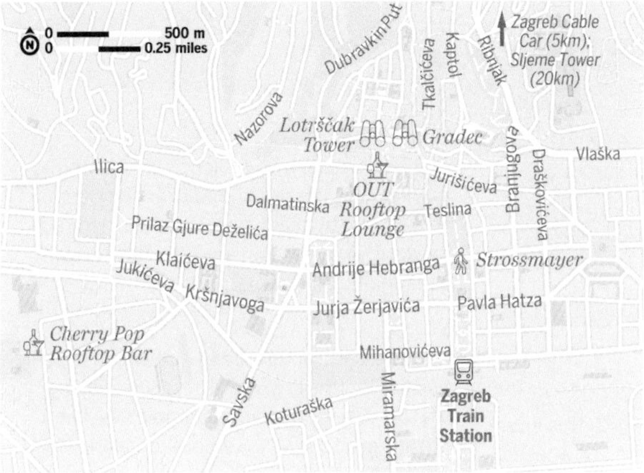

Supreme city views In the Middle Ages, Gradec and Kaptol were two, often feuding, hilltop settlements that gave rise to Zagreb as we know it today. These age-old settlements form the Upper Town, the neighbourhood that offers the most scenic vantage points for catching the panoramas of the city spreading out below. Among the best spots is the **Strossmayer** promenade, or Štros as locals call this leafy path that was the city's first public walkway, today lined with chestnut trees and benches. The bench with the statue of Croatian writer Antun Gustav Matoš sitting wistfully is a great place to unwind and take in the vistas. The viewpoint from **Lotrščak Tower** is another stunner, as is the **Gradec** plateau, just behind St Catherine's Church, stretching across red-tile roofs towards the cathedral.

Pair your panorama with a drink For poolside fun and craft cocktails with a side of dazzling city views, head to the **Cherry Pop Rooftop Bar** at the chic high-rise Hotel Zonar that opened in 2023 in the western neighbourhood of Trešnjevka. In the city centre, **OUT Rooftop Lounge** on Ilica, near Zagreb's main square, has a fun vibe, live music on some nights and a great vantage point for seeing the historic Upper Town rise up on one side.

Left View of St Catherine's Church, with Zagreb Cathedral
Below left Strossmayer promenade

View from the Mountaintop

Hop on the Zagreb cable car for a scenic 16-minute ride to the peak of Sljeme mountain. To get to the base, catch tram 14 from the main square, get off at the Mihaljevac stop and then take tram 15 to the last stop, where you can board the cable car.

At the mountaintop, check out the lookout atop the Sljeme Tower. At an altitude of 1118m, this open-air observation deck offers a 360-degree bird's-eye perspective of Zagreb below and the sloping verdant landscapes of Medvednica Nature Park.

Listings

BEST OF THE REST

Festivals & Events

Zagreb Advent
Catch Zagreb's Christmas market, which draws in crowds for street food, mulled wine, craft stores and live music. It's set up at various locations around the city centre from early December to January.

Animafest
Taking place every June since 1972, this international festival of animated film showcases creative animation screened in locations around the city, from parks and movie houses to the open-air Tuškanac summer cinema.

Q'art
This Ilica street festival started as a gathering of artists and creatives for a day of music, games, mingling, and selling their arts and crafts. The block party has now expanded to other neighbourhoods.

Dvorišta
For 10 days each July, a bunch of Upper Town courtyards (called *dvorišta*) of mansions and townhouses that are normally off-limits open their doors for live music, food and booze.

Subversive Festival
Over two weeks in May, Europe's activists and philosophers descend on Zagreb in droves for film screenings and lectures as part of the region's most progressive festival.

Local Flavours

Salo — €
A great little brunch spot, this bright bistro-bakery on Opatovina doles out artisan bread, small creative plates and specialty coffee. Open Wednesday to Saturday; 8am to 4pm.

Broom 44 — €
Right on Dolac, with tables spilling onto the market, this breakfast and brunch hot spot serves mostly plant-based dishes inspired by world cuisine, with ingredients sourced seasonally. Closes at 3pm daily.

Vinodol — €
Upscale central European fare with a modern twist. A longtime favourite with locals and visitors. Go for succulent lamb or veal and potatoes under *peka* (a domed baking lid).

Stari Fijaker — €€
Sample a range of old-school Croatian and central European staples while soaking up the atmosphere of yesteryear. Expect hearty fare; look out for lunchtime specials *(gableci)*.

Lari & Penati — €
Small and stylish bistro great for weekday meals, especially lunch. The menu mixes Croatian staples and international favourites. Closed Sundays and dinnertime on Saturdays.

Pod Zidom — €€
Upmarket bistro by Dolac market, with a focus on modern cuisine made using market-fresh seasonal ingredients. A great selection of organic wines. Closed Mondays.

LORDZG/SHUTTERSTOCK ©

Zagreb Advent

Mali Bar €€

Earthy-toned spot with a terrace that's all about seasonal small plates that are market-fresh and inspired by the Med, Middle East and Asia. It's a tiny place, so book ahead.

Delicious Desserts

Amelie

French flavours on Vlaška right below Zagreb Cathedral. Have a creamy cake at a table on the terrace or cosy up inside over macarons and hot chocolate.

Vincek

This *slastičarna* (patisserie) on Ilica has been a favourite for ice cream and cake since the 1970s. Vincek's outpost by the funicular dishes up health-conscious sweet treats.

Korica

This artisanal bakery has lip-smacking pastries and sandwiches and three branches around the Lower Town. The almond croissants and marble cakes are delish. It also serves coffee.

Craft Beer

Garden Brewery

Inside the huge glass atrium of an old red-brick factory in the industrial east of Zagreb, this craft brewery offers 20 taps fresh from the source, plus street food and guided tours on weekends.

Craft Room

This buzzy hot spot for lovers of beer has a fantastic range of local brews and grub, plus two outdoor terraces on Opatovina, up the stairs from Dolac market.

Mali Medo

Sister pub to Pivnica Medvedgrad, Croatia's largest craft brewery known for its tasty natural lagers, Mali Medo has a prime spot along Tkalča for house-brewed beers poured late into the night.

Vincek

Tours with a Twist

Bike Tours Zagreb

Sign up for the classic three-hour city tour on one of the orange bikes (biketours.life).

Walk with Tito

Sign up for a historical-figure-themed walking tour, following in the footsteps of Tito, the famous leader of Yugoslavia (walkwithtito.com).

Tesla Tour Croatia

Learn what inspired the brilliant inventor and visionary , Nikola Tesla, as you stroll through Zagreb checking out Tesla-related sites (teslatourcroatia.com).

Alternative Culture

Pogon Jedinstvo & Močvara

Get a sense of offbeat Zagreb at these adjoining independent culture venues on Sava's northern riverbank. They host everything from avant-garde music theatre performances to alternative music acts.

Urania

This former cinema on Kvaternikov trg has a Cogito coffee shop and a programme of cool cultural events, including film screenings, recitals, book launches, theatre and live music.

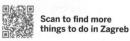

Scan to find more things to do in Zagreb

CONTINENTAL CROATIA

FARMLAND | WILDERNESS | HISTORY

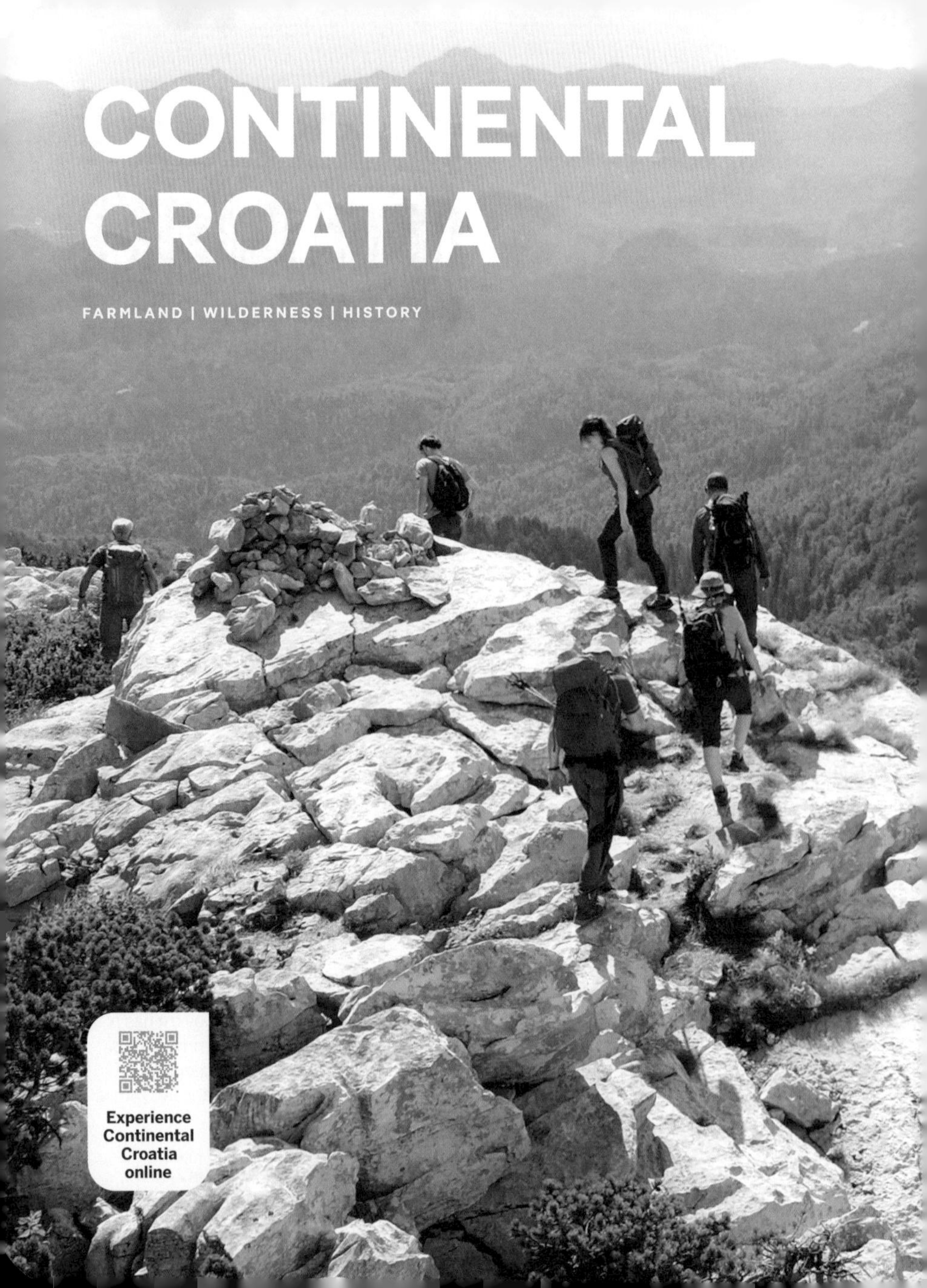

Experience Continental Croatia online

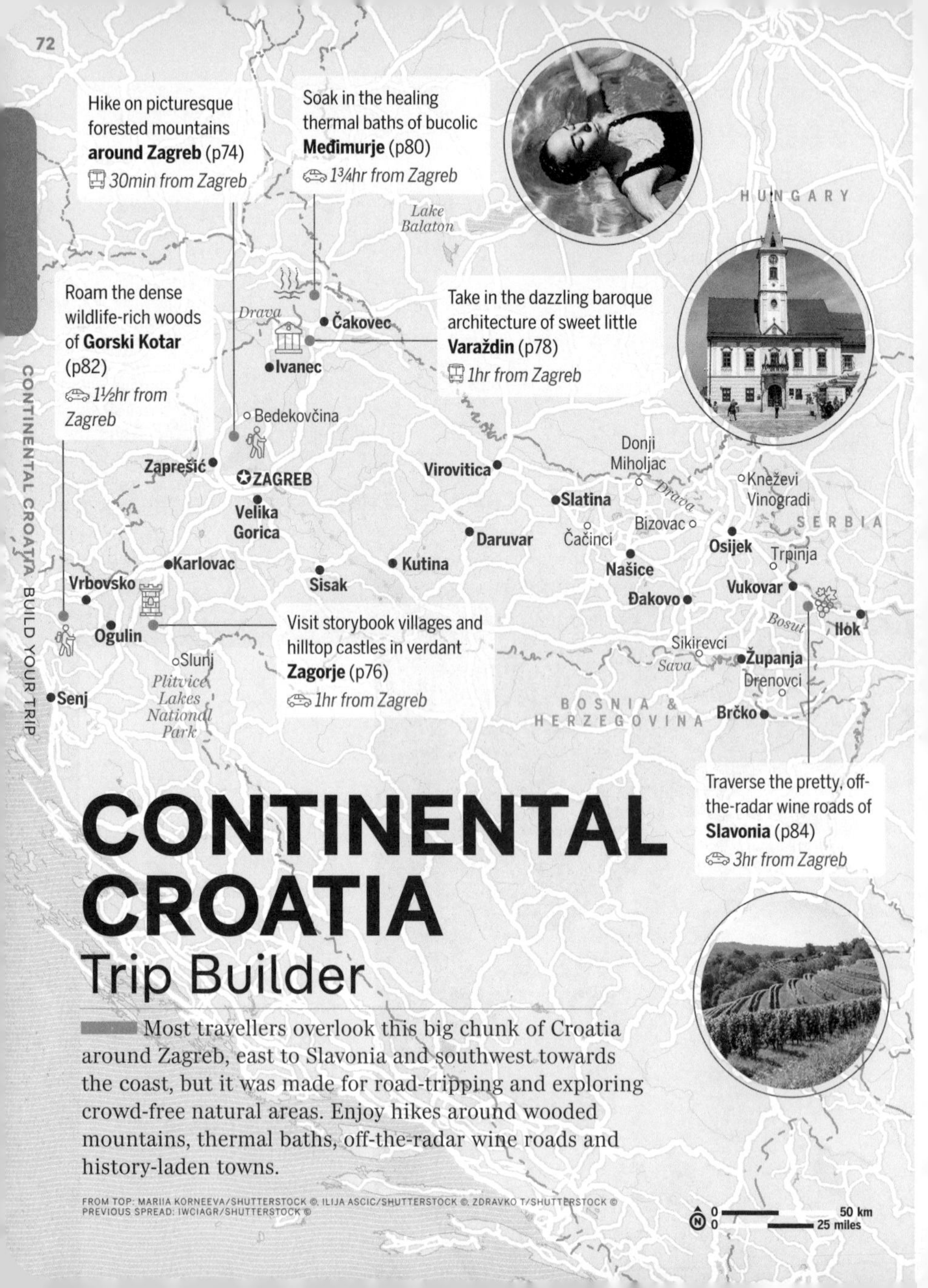

Hike on picturesque forested mountains **around Zagreb** (p74)
30min from Zagreb

Soak in the healing thermal baths of bucolic **Međimurje** (p80)
1¾hr from Zagreb

Roam the dense wildlife-rich woods of **Gorski Kotar** (p82)
1½hr from Zagreb

Take in the dazzling baroque architecture of sweet little **Varaždin** (p78)
1hr from Zagreb

Visit storybook villages and hilltop castles in verdant **Zagorje** (p76)
1hr from Zagreb

Traverse the pretty, off-the-radar wine roads of **Slavonia** (p84)
3hr from Zagreb

CONTINENTAL CROATIA

Trip Builder

Most travellers overlook this big chunk of Croatia around Zagreb, east to Slavonia and southwest towards the coast, but it was made for road-tripping and exploring crowd-free natural areas. Enjoy hikes around wooded mountains, thermal baths, off-the-radar wine roads and history-laden towns.

Practicalities

ARRIVING

Zagreb Airport is the biggest in Croatia, convenient for most destinations in this region.

Osijek Airport is well-placed for direct arrivals to Slavonia in the eastern stretch of the country.

MONEY

Most places accept cards for payment, but cash is still king in more rural areas.

CONNECT

In most areas, wi-fi is widely available at cafes, restaurants and lodgings but can be spotty in regions near neighbouring countries.

WHERE TO STAY

Town	Pro/Con
Varaždin	A good base for exploring Međimurje and Zagorje, but you'll need a car.
Osijek	Heaps of accommodation; great for visiting wine country.
Sveti Martin na Muri	Home to the area's thermal bath resort.
Fužine	On Bajer lake in Gorski Kotar; has a lovely hotel and apartment rentals.

GETTING AROUND

Bicycle Cycling is increasingly popular, especially in Slavonia and Međimurje. Slavonia has some excellent long-distance options: the 80km Pannonian Peace Trail; a 140km-long stretch of the Euro Velo 6 Danube route; and the Amazon of Europe Bike Trail along three rivers.

Car Hiring a car is the best way to explore the region. Some roads are windy and can be tricky to navigate.

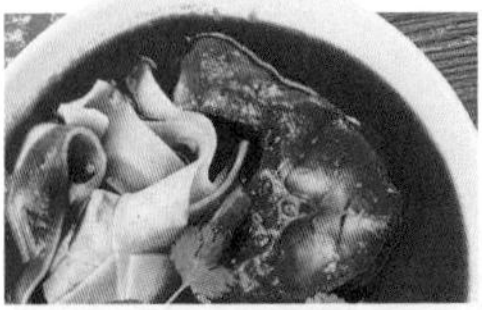

TOP: FANFO/SHUTTERSTOCK © BOTTOM: IVICA9/SHUTTERSTOCK ©

EATING & DRINKING

Each region in continental Croatia has its own specialties, from *patka* (duck) with *mlinci* (baked noodles) in Zagorje to spicy *fiš paprikaš* (freshwater fish stew with paprika; pictured top left) in Slavonia and the forest-to-plate food of Gorski Kotar with its wild mushrooms and game.

Must-try štrukli Grešna Gorica (p76)

Best graševina wine Ilok Ilok Wine Cellar (pictured bottom left; p87)

MAR–MAY Great time for hikes as nature bounces back to life.

JUN–AUG Blissfully crowd-free because most people head to the coast.

SEP–NOV Harvest time in the wine regions.

DEC–FEB Leafy hikes outside Zagreb or snow-sledding in Gorski Kotar.

09 Hiking Beyond ZAGREB

NATURE | OUTDOORS | TREKS

The Croatian heartland surrounding Zagreb is strewn with charming towns, delightful farm restaurants and spectacular pockets of nature that are perfect for hiking. Scale forested mountains, such as the imposing Medvednica, which looms over Zagreb from the north; explore the picturesque wine microregion of Plešivica; and roam the Žumberak-Samobor Highlands Nature Park.

GORAN SAFAREK/GETTY IMAGES ©

How To

Getting around The areas around Zagreb are well connected by bus. For more spontaneity, you'll need a car.

When to go Each season has its charms. Weekends are the busiest times, so be prepared to wait at restaurants and huts.

Mountain meals Join Zagreb locals for a lunch of bean stew and strudel at one of the 20 mountain huts peppering the slopes of Medvednica. Runolist, Grafičar, Grofica and Puntijarka are favourites.

OPIS ZAGREB/SHUTTERSTOCK ©

Left Brisalo Waterfall, Žumberak-Samobor Highlands Nature Park
Below left Medvedgrad castle

Forest hikes, medieval forts and caves Looming above Zagreb to the north, mighty **Mt Medvednica** offers a beloved nature escape from Zagreb. Roam this protected nature park that's covered by dense forests of silver fir, Pannonian beech and sessile oak, and which has more than 70 hiking trails (the Bliznec and Miroslavec educational trails are popular) and 100km of cycling paths. Check out **Veternica cave** (open by guided tour on weekends), home to 18 protected species of bats, fossils and weirdly shaped stalagmite formations. Stop by the fortress of **Medvedgrad**, built in 1254 to protect Zagreb from Tartar invasions, which had more than 150 masters through its rich history. The visitor centre opened in 2021 and is a great spot to learn about this allegedly haunted fort.

Roam the wild highlands Immerse yourself in the pristine nature of **Žumberak-Samobor Highlands Nature Park**. Carpeted with meadows and forests, it has river canyons, waterfalls, medieval forts, remains of Celtic cemeteries, paragliding spots, rock-climbing areas and scenic villages. The well-marked trails are lined with mountain huts and restaurants, but most open at weekends only. Consult the park website (pp-zumberak-samoborsko-gorje.hr) for information on routes or stop by the tourist office on the main square of Samobor, the closest town, for detailed hiking information.

While you're in Samobor, try a *kremšnite* (custard pie), which draws in day-trippers from Zagreb. **U Prolazu** patisserie has the best in town.

Vineyards of Plešivica

Half an hour from Zagreb, Plešivica may be Croatia's smallest wine region, but it delivers top-quality bottles. Numerous family-owned wineries, such as Šember, Tomac and Jagunić, take pride in their sparkling wines and also produce riesling, pinot noir and sauvignon blanc.

In a tranquil rural area above the town of Jastrebarsko, the slopes of Plešivica (779m) are also an attractive hiking destination, with a network of trails encompassing the Samobor hills. Have an active getaway while savouring local flavours served in spots from small farms and inns to the Michelin-starred Korak restaurant and winery.

■ **Morana Zibar**
TV personality, trivia buff, and food and wine writer; @moranazibar

10 Storybook Villages & CASTLES

HISTORY | ARCHITECTURE | SCENERY

The bucolic Zagorje region provides rural escapades on Zagreb's doorstep. The landscape of tiny villages squirrelled among medieval castles, vineyards, cornfields and verdantly forested hills was made for easygoing road trips. Whether you want to feast on hearty cuisine at rustic restaurants, get a taste of village life or tour ancient castles, you're in for an offbeat treat in Zagorje.

GORAN_SAFAREK/SHUTTERSTOCK ©

How To

Getting around Having a car is a must while exploring Zagorje. Beware of the winding, hilly and narrow roads.

When to go Josip Broz Tito, the former president of Yugoslavia, was born in Kumrovec. Every year for his birthday on 25 May, devotees flock to the village.

Hilltop meal Have a traditional lunch at Grešna Gorica, a rustic restaurant known for its tasty mainstays (order the *štrukli*) and views of Veliki Tabor castle.

SERGEY-73/SHUTTERSTOCK ©

Find fairy-tale castles The Croatian aristocracy began building fortified castles in the region to stave off threats from the Turks in the 16th century. The best-preserved of them is the pentagonal **Veliki Tabor**, perched on top of a hill. The golden yellow castle-fortress has everything a medieval master could want: towers, turrets, and holes in the walls for pouring tar and hot oil on the enemy. Worth a detour is **Trakošćan Castle**, with three floors of exhibits and 87-hectare grounds landscaped into a romantic, English-style park with an artificial lake.

Get a taste of 19th-century village life In the Sutla River valley village of Kumrovec near the Slovenian border, the **Staro Selo (Old Village) Museum** is a recreation of a 19th-century village, showcasing 30 restored houses and barns made of pressed earth and wood. A stream bubbles through the idyllic setting, and the open-air ethnographic museum presents a vivid overview of peasant traditions and village life in the late 19th and early 20th centuries. These *hiže* (traditional Zagorje huts) are filled with furniture, mannequins, toys, wine presses and baking tools that evoke the region's traditional arts, crafts and customs.

Pay respects to Croatia's communist past **Kumrovec** was the birthplace of Josip Broz Tito, one of the world's most illustrious leaders. His house contains original furniture, letters from foreign leaders and memorabilia, with a life-sized bronze sculpture outside.

Left Veliki Tabor
Below left Staro Selo (Old Village) Museum

Europe's Largest Neanderthal Fossil Site

Go way back to humanity's roots in Krapina, home to the Museum of Krapina Neanderthals.

In 1899, an archaeological dig in a cave on the Hušnjakovo hill unearthed findings of human and animal bones from a Neanderthal tribe from 100,000 BCE to 35,000 BCE. This brilliant museum is built on the site of the fossil haul, the largest ever found in Europe, and explores the history of the universe, Earth and humanity through a series of fun, high-tech exhibits.

Outside the museum, you can walk up the leafy hill where the remains were found, today marked by a sculpture of Neanderthals wielding clubs.

11 A FEAST OF Baroque Architecture

ARCHITECTURE | HISTORY | LANDMARKS

Soak up the extraordinarily refined 18th-century baroque buildings in the spruced-up historic centre of Varaždin. Roam this showcase of scrupulously restored baroque architecture and well-tended gardens and parks, bequeathed to the city when it was Croatia's capital. Many of Varaždin's aristocratic mansions and elegant churches have been renovated as part of the town's longstanding bid to become a UNESCO World Heritage Site.

How To

Getting around You can walk to most sights and attractions in Varaždin, and this small town is about 1½ hours by bus from Zagreb.

When to go Every August, Špancirfest (spancirfest.com) enlivens the town's parks, streets and squares with music, street performances, theatre, creative workshops, traditional crafts and contemporary arts.

Lunch by the ramparts Have a meal at Bedem by the Old Town ramparts. The weekday *gableci* (traditional lunches) are excellent value.

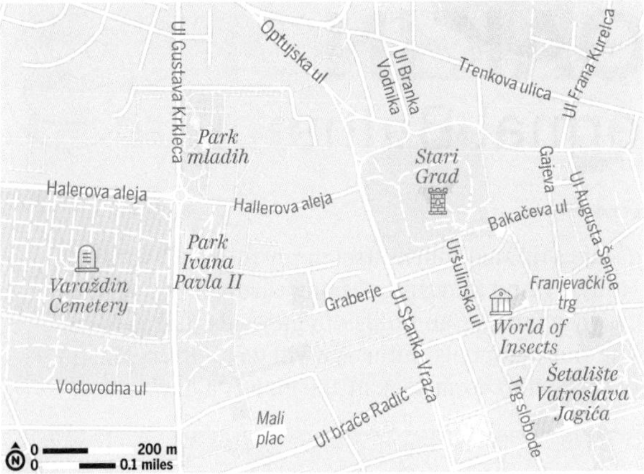

Visit the castle-fortress The gleaming whitewashed fortress of **Stari Grad** (Old Town) is a stunning gem of medieval defensive architecture, surrounded by a manicured park. Construction began in the 14th century, and the present Gothic–Renaissance structure dates from the 16th century, when it was the regional fortification against the Turks. The museum houses a hotch-potch of furniture, paintings, watches, glassware, decorative objects, insignia and weapons amassed over centuries and displayed throughout 30 exhibition rooms. Much more interesting than the historic collection inside, though, is the architecture. Enter the sprawling fortress via a drawbridge and wander around to view the archways, courtyards and chapels.

Travel back in time through music **Varaždin** is famous for its baroque music festival, Varaždin Baroque Evenings, which takes place over two weeks in September (sometimes spanning into early October). The 53rd edition took place in 2023. Local and international orchestras play in the cathedral, churches and theatres around town. For info, tickets and more, visit *vbv.hr.*

Check out World of Insects This entomological collection, housed in the classicist **Hercer Palace** built in 1791, comprises nearly 4500 exhibits of bug life, including 1000 insect species. It's well set out to spark a child's interest in the natural world, with beautifully displayed examples of insect nests, habitats and reproductive habits. Audioguides are available.

Left Varaždin's whitewashed fortress
Below left Hercer Palace

Spectacular Resting Place

A 10-minute stroll west of Stari Grad takes you to Varaždin Cemetery, a serene horticultural masterpiece first established in 1773 and redesigned in 1905 by visionary Viennese architect Hermann Helmer. Meander amid tombstones, avenues and promenades lined with more than 7000 trees, including maple, boxwood, magnolia, beech and birch. The park architecture is remarkable, with its cypresses arranged into geometrical shapes in the style of French parks. Check out the *Angel of Death* monument by Robert Frangeš Mihanović, a beautiful representation of the deceased parting from the living.

12 SOAK IN Thermal Baths

NATURE | WELLNESS | CYCLING

The undulating landscapes of Međimurje stretch northeast of Varaždin towards the borders with Hungary and Slovenia. Cycling through this fertile corner of patchwork fields, teensy villages and hills of vineyards makes for a great countryside escape. The thermal pools in the spa village of Sveti Martin are the area's highlight and are perfect for a soak at the end of a day's ride.

GORAN_SAFAREK/SHUTTERSTOCK ©

How To

Getting around You need a bicycle or car to explore Međimurje. Public transport is virtually nonexistent.

When to go Visit for Martinje on 11 November, the feast of St Martin. Celebrate food and drink along the Međimurje Wine Road, which has close to 30 tasting rooms and cellars.

Going green In 2023, Međimurje received the coveted Green Destinations title recognising its sustainability efforts, the first in Croatia and the fourth in the world.

ZORAN PAJIC/SHUTTERSTOCK ©

Healing waters The village of Sveti Martin, Međimurje's main destination, is home to **Terme Sveti Martin**, proclaimed as the first 'healthness' resort in Europe, combining health and wellness. It is also Croatia's first bike resort, with more than 700km of trails in the area. You don't need to stay at the resort to visit its series of outdoor, indoor, and thermal pools and aquapark; day tickets are available. There are also tennis courts, forest trails, shops, restaurants (Falat serves an amazing breakfast with food from local farms) and a wellness centre.

The pinnacle of cycling The wooden lookout on **Mađerkin Breg**, unveiled in 2022, serves as an info point on cycling in the area, which is known for its incredible scenery. Located in the undulating wine country of Štrigova, the lookout offers a spectacular panorama, with views of four countries from the top: Austria, Slovenia, Hungary and on clear days even Slovakia.

Rudolf Steiner's influence The offerings of Terme Sveti Martin are inspired by the life and work of philosopher, social reformer, artist and founder of anthroposophy Rudolf Steiner (1861–1925), who was born in Croatia. His spiritual-scientific teachings inspired the Waldorf education system, and he also founded the biodynamic approach to farming. Visit the **Dr Rudolf Steiner Centre** (centar-rudolf-steiner.com) in Donji Kraljevec to learn more about his legacy. His birthplace is also open to visitors.

Left Aquapark, Terme Sveti Martin
Below left Mađerkin Breg

Where to Eat in Međimurje

Goričanec
An idyllic setting with a lake, horse riding, loads of outdoor seating in a verdant setting and great traditional dishes. €

Mala Hiža
Foodies from Zagreb travel to this restaurant in Mačkovec village for its creative takes on local recipes. €€€

Terbotz
Lovely family-run restaurant and winery on a picturesque hilltop in Železna Gora. €

Le Batat
The healthy dining restaurant at Terme Sveti Martin serves wholesome food with locally sourced ingredients. €€

Make sure you try the local dessert specialty, *Međimurska gibanica*, a hearty layered cake packed with nuts, fresh cheese, apples and poppy seeds. All of the restaurants above serve *gibanica*.

13 THE WOODS of Gorski Kotar

HIKING | WILDLIFE | OUTDOORS

Exploring the mountainous wilderness of Gorski Kotar is a delight. Often called the 'green lungs of Croatia' – about 85% of its surface is forested – this region is home to bears, wolves, the endangered Eurasian lynx and abundant birdlife. Though an increasingly popular nature retreat for city dwellers from Zagreb and Rijeka, it remains off the radar for most international visitors.

How to

Getting around Having your own wheels is a must.

When to go Gorski Kotar is a four-season destination: a winter wonderland for snowy walks and sledging and a cooling summer escape for hiking and rafting its string of lakes, crystal-clear rivers and cascading waterfalls, and caving around the karst formations.

Forest goodies Vagabundina Koliba, a mountain shelter restaurant on a forest road, serves amazing forest-to-plate food, starring foraged wild plants and game meat.

Into the deep forest

Relatively isolated and rarely visited, despite being only 32km northeast of Rijeka, **Risnjak National Park** (np-risnjak.hr) covers 63 sq km and rises to 1528m at its highest peak, **Veliki Risnjak**.

The park offers gorgeous hiking, the landscape links the Alps with the Balkan ranges and is thickly forested with beech and pine trees, and is carpeted with meadows and wild-flowers. The bracing alpine breezes make it the perfect getaway when the coastal heat and crowds become overpowering.

Most of the park is virgin forest, with only a few settlements. The starting point for the Leska Path, an easy and shaded 4.2km trail, is the park information office, west of the village of Crni Lug.

Allow about two hours to complete the route. You

Hiking, Risnjak National Park

pass clear streams, forests of tall fir trees, bizarre rock formations, a deer feeding station and a mountain hut with a picnic table.

Wildlife watching Risnjak National Park is a sanctuary for three charismatic mammal species: brown bear, wolf and Eurasian lynx (a fluffy-eared, medium-sized wild cat). The area is one of the last refuges in the country for the lynx (*ris* in Croatian), which gives its name to the park. All three animals are difficult to spot, and you need to visit with a guide or visit for several days for the best chance.

Gems of Gorski Kotar

With heaps of natural beauty and cultural attractions, Gorski Kotar is a real treasure box if you're into pristine nature and local life.

The Lokvarka Cave is a must-see, and this imposing grotto welcomes visitors into its subterranean world. Hike to the deep, blue spring of the Kupa River, an enchanting turquoise wonder.

For offbeat local food specialties, such as fried frog legs and dormouse goulash, head to Hotel Bitoraj, a cosy hotel restaurant near Bajer lake in the little town of Fužine.

■ **Jelena Holenko Pirc** *experience designer, tour guide and founder of Gorski Kotar–based Lynx and Fox agency; @lynxandfox*

14 Scenic Wine Roads OF SLAVONIA

VINEYARDS | CELLARS | HERITAGE

Grape vines have been cultivated in Slavonia, the mostly flat agricultural heartland of Croatia for thousands of years. Check out the burgeoning wine roads of Slavonia, a region bordered by three major rivers (the Sava, Drava and Danube) stretching east towards Hungary and Serbia.

MARIO KRPAN/GETTY IMAGES ©

How To

Getting around Buses connect the bigger towns in Slavonia. To get to the smaller villages around Baranja, you need your own wheels.

When to go Catch the best of the harvest in autumn.

Fit for royals The old wine cellars of Iločki Podrumi (ilocki-podrumi.hr) are well worth a look. Its dry white *traminac* was served at the coronation of Queen Elizabeth II.

Call ahead It's best to make sure someone is on-site to show you around.

VEDRANA2701/SHUTTERSTOCK ©

Slavonian Wine Primer

White wines made from local grapes, including *graševina,* are the most renowned, justifiably so. Earthy reds are also produced along the wine roads of Slavonia, primarily from *frankovka (blaufränkisch),* merlot and cabernet sauvignon.

ROBERT ANIC/PIXSELL/ALAMY STOCK PHOTO ©

The Ancient Roots of Croatian Wine

Visit **Kutjevo** (kutjevo.com), a winery in the town of the same name, on a guided tour of its medieval wine cellar dating from 1232, formerly part of a Cistercian abbey. Nearby are two of Slavonia's top wineries: **Krauthaker** (krauthaker.hr), whose *graševina* and sweet wines regularly win top awards, and **Enjingi** (enjingi.hr), one of Croatia's leading eco-producers, with winemaking experience dating back to 1890. Also stop

Wine Activities

Wine & Bike Tour Erdut On the second weekend in September, enjoy a bicycle race and concerts around the scenic vineyards.

Vinski Maraton This late September marathon starts and ends in the Baranja village of Zmajevac, a fun race with wine tastings along the traditional wine roads.

Above left Kutjevo Vineyards
Left Enjingi Vineyards
Above Kutjevo wine

by the **Sontacchi Winery** in the centre of Kutjevo, where two brothers produce a stellar pinot noir and cabernet franc, in addition to other wines.

Visit the 'Wine Mother'

A small triangle in the far northeast of Croatia at the confluence of the Drava and Danube rivers, Baranja stretches east of Osijek towards Serbia and north towards Hungary and the town of Beli Manastir. It's thought that the name Baranja is derived from the Hungarian word for 'wine mother', and its scenic *surduci,* as the traditional wine roads are called, are lined with wineries. Grape cultivation has been revived on the gentle hills around Kneževi Vinogradi, mainly in the villages of Zmajevac and Suza. Traditionalist in its approach to winemaking, **Gerštmajer** (gerstmajer.com) offers tasting tours of its cellar and 11 hectares of vineyards. Just down the hill is the area's biggest producer, **Josić** (josic.hr), which has a fine-dining restaurant

Hot Pairing

The food of Slavonia is spicier than in any other region of Croatia, and much of it features liberal amounts of paprika and garlic. The hotness of the food is thanks to the Hungarian influence prevalent in northeastern Croatia. In addition to its star dish, *fiš paprikaš* (freshwater fish stew spiced with paprika) the most famed foods of Slavonia are the cured meats, especially *kulen*, a paprika-flavoured sausage cured for nine months and usually served with cottage cheese, peppers, tomatoes and *turšija* (pickled vegetables). These spicy treats pair well with sharp Slavonian whites, such as *traminac* and *graševina.*

Left *Kulen* (paprika-flavoured sausage)
Below left Ilok wine cellars

on-site in an atmospheric space with a vaulted ceiling. Meat is the menu's strong suit. Try the duck *perkelt* stew and pair it with the *graševina* wine. On the main road in nearby Suza, **Kolar** (suzabaranje.com) offers a restaurant, shop and wine tastings in its century-old cellar. **Vina Belje** (vinabelje.hr) in Kneževi Vinogradi has ancient cellars and a gorgeous viewpoint amid its vineyards.

Head East for a Wine Feast

Slavonia boasts ancient cellars in the town of Ilok at **Ilok Wine Cellar** (ilocki-podrumi.hr), and a 30-minute tour takes you to the underground cellar with its oak barrels. Also nearby is **Vina Papak** (vinapapak.com), with a tasting room surrounded by pretty vineyards.

The wineries in Erdut along the Danube are also worth visiting, especially **Erdutski Vinogradi** (erdutski-vinogradi.hr), where a visit includes a stop at the old cellar that dates from 1730 and a delightful walk under a vine-covered passageway. Smaller **Brzica** features a shaded tasting area under a walnut tree with marvellous river views. In Dalj, north of Vukovar, **Vina Antunović** (vina-antunovic.hr) is headed up by the area's only female winemaker, known for her award-winning *graševina*.

Listings

BEST OF THE REST

Landmarks of Slavonia

Tvrđa

This baroque quarter of Osijek, the capital of Slavonia, is a lived-in complex of cobblestone streets, spacious squares and stately mansions. It's also home to the Museum of Slavonia, which showcases the region's history, and the Gloria Maris museum, dedicated to seashells and marine and freshwater life.

Church of St Peter & Paul

This red-brick, neo-Gothic church's 90m-high tower is surpassed in height only by the cathedral in Zagreb and dominates downtown Osijek. Built in the 1890s, the interior has 40 elaborate stained-glass windows in Viennese style and vividly coloured frescoes by Croatian painter Mirko Rački.

Kopački Rit Nature Park

Situated 12km northeast of Osijek, this park is one of Europe's largest wetlands and is home to more than 290 bird species and rich aquatic and grassland flora. Visit the interpretation centre, stroll the wooden board-walks and take a boat tour of Sakadaško lake.

Ilok

Surrounded by the vine-growing hills of Fruška Gora, famous for viniculture since Roman times, the town of Ilok on the border with Serbia features the well-preserved Odescalchi Palace high above the Danube; today, the palace houses the city museum.

Đakovo Cathedral & Lipizzaner Horses

The provincial town of Đakovo, 35km north of Osijek, has an impressive neo-Romanesque cathedral that's decked out tip-to-toe in colourful frescoes. Find an illustrious heritage of Lipizzaner horses at Ergela, the state stud farm that can be traced back to the 16th century. The stallion station is in the heart of town, while another is in Ivandvor, a few kilometres away.

Vučedol Culture Museum

Located 5km down river from the town of Vukovar, this state-of-the-art museum covers one of Europe's most significant archaeological sites and provides an introduction to the Chalcolithic-era Vučedol Culture, which flourished between 3000 BCE and 2500 BCE.

War Memorials of Vukovar

Visit the poignant reminders of the infamous 1991 Battle of Vukovar, including the former water tower reopened as a museum, the stirring Place of Remembrance, Vukovar Hospital 1991 and the haunting Ovčara Memorial, about 6km out of town.

Slavonia's Arts & Crafts

Pottery Classes in Suza

In the pretty village of Suza in Baranja, Daniel Asztalos offers hands-on pottery classes at his 100-year-old steam mill. Sign up for a workshop on traditional Baranja ceramics on the Asztalos Keramika Facebook page.

Kopački Rit National Park

Land Art by Nikola Faller
Look out for the mesmerising Four Seasons land art project by Nikola Faller, who has been running the Slama Land Art summer festival in Slavonia for nearly two decades. Arrange a tour of his art studio on Facebook (facebook.com/slama.land.art3).

Đakovački Vezovi
A great time to be in Đakovo is the first weekend in July for the annual Đakovački Vezovi (Đakovo Embroidery), which features a Lipizzaner horse display and a folklore show of dancing and traditional songs.

Flavours of Slavonia & Baranja

Čarda Kod Baranjca €
No-frills eatery near the Drava known for its freshwater fish dishes, such as *fiš paprikaš* and *perkelt* stew featuring catfish, carp or perch.

Čingi Lingi Čarda €€
In Bilje village, a 10-minute drive from Osijek, this airy, barn-like restaurant serves hearty regional plates of freshwater fish and meats by the lakeside.

Citadela €€
Roadside spot in Vardarac, with huge portions of traditional Baranja foods. Try the *perkelt od podolca* (local beef stew).

Kovač Čarda €
This Hungarian-run simple eatery by the road in Suza is known for Baranja's best and spiciest *fiš paprikaš*.

Piroš Čizma €€
Slavonian dishes prepared with a twist in the village of Suza. This spot doubles as a hotel.

Baranjska Kuća €
A big menu of traditional Baranja dishes in the lovely village of Karanac, with a chestnut-tree-shaded backyard that has an ethnographic museum.

ALEN GUROVIC/NURPHOTO VIA GETTY IMAGES ©

Church of St Peter & St Paul

Traditional Restaurants around Zagreb

Gabreku 1929 €€
A local classic in the town of Samobor, run by the same family since the 1920s and famed for its 40 types of sweet and savoury *palačinke* (crepes).

Bolfan Vinski Vrh €€
Great restaurant in a beautiful hilltop *klet* (cottage), with sloping vineyards and some of Zagorje's best views.

Vuglec Breg €€
Rural retreat and restaurant serving up Zagorje specialities, such as *purica s mlincima* (slow-roasted turkey with baked noodles), on a terrace with panoramic vistas.

Kod Đurđe €
Roadside restaurant near Krapinske Toplice serving simple Zagorje traditional mainstays prepared with care; open for lunch only.

Cycling Routes in Slavonia

Amazon of Europe Bike Trail
This trail runs along the Mura, Drava and Danube rivers, which together form a Unesco Biosphere Reserve (aoebiketrail.com).

Scan to find more things to do in Continental Croatia

ISTRIA
HISTORY | ARCHITECTURE | FOOD & DRINK
Experience Istria online

Cycle or hike the scenic **Parenzana Trail** (p98)

1¼hr from Pula

Discover the exquisite old town of **Rovinj** via its fascinating maritime history (p104)

45min from Pula

ISTRIA
Trip Builder

To get to know Istria, you must take it slow. Take time to soak in the atmosphere of its medieval towns and sublime landscapes of undulating hills. Afterwards, head to its olive groves and wineries to delight your taste buds.

Explore **Brijuni National Park**, islands that were once off-limits (p96)

15min from Fažana

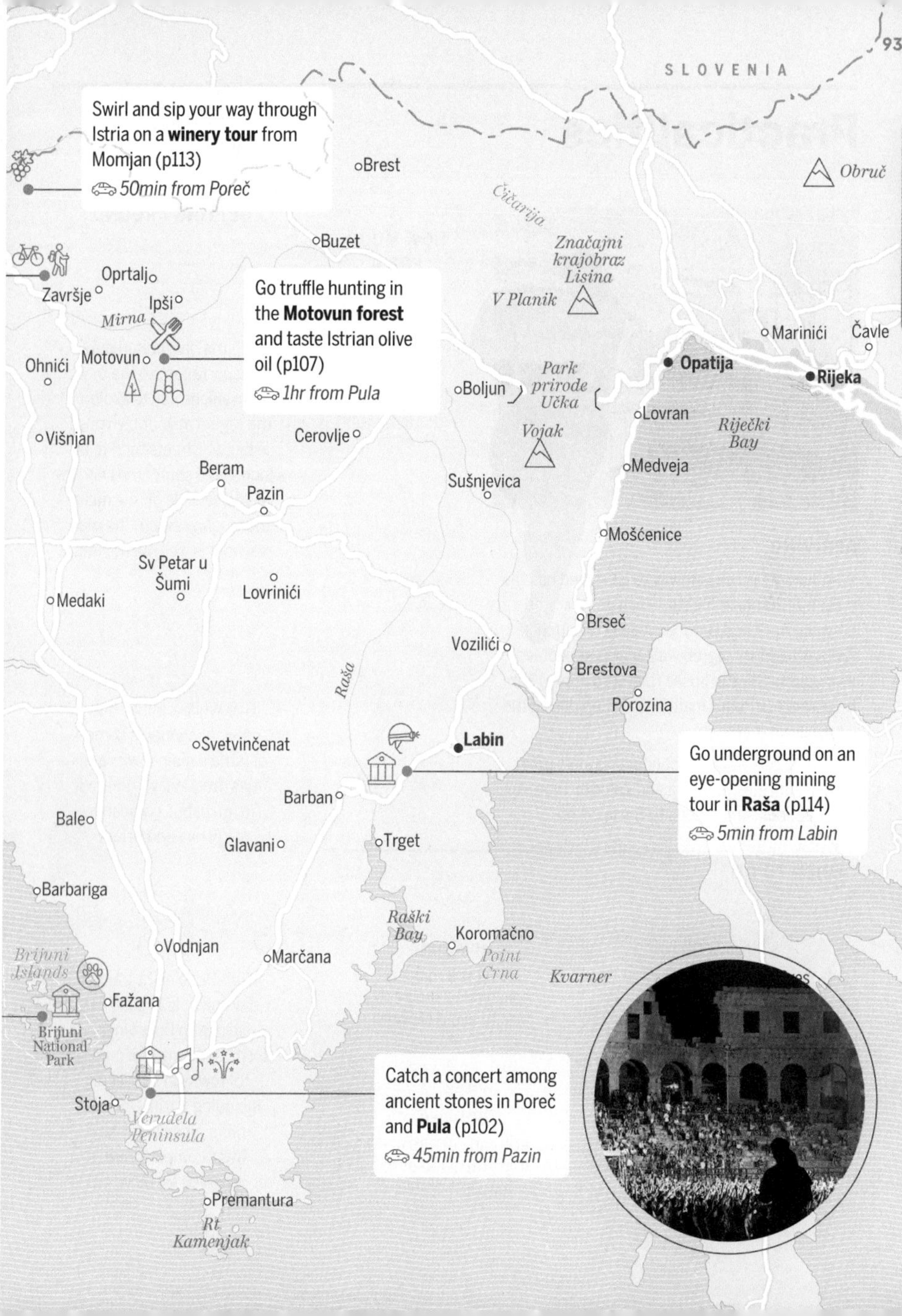

Swirl and sip your way through Istria on a **winery tour** from Momjan (p113)
50min from Poreč

Go truffle hunting in the **Motovun forest** and taste Istrian olive oil (p107)
1hr from Pula

Go underground on an eye-opening mining tour in **Raša** (p114)
5min from Labin

Catch a concert among ancient stones in Poreč and **Pula** (p102)
45min from Pazin

Practicalities

OPIS ZAGREB/SHUTTERSTOCK ©

ARRIVING

Pula Airport is the gateway to Istria and has the most international flights, which generally operate between April and October. A daily Croatian Airlines flight to Zagreb via Zadar is scheduled year-round. Shuttle buses (pictured above) link the airport to Pula's main bus station during the peak summer season.

A limited bus network connects Istria's main towns and cities to Rijeka and Zagreb; there are no direct rail connections to these cities.

HOW MUCH FOR A

***bijela kava* (cafe latte)**
€2

glass of *malvazija* wine
€2

dish of pasta with truffles
€18

WHEN TO GO

JAN–MAR
Sunny days and cool temperatures perfect for cycling and hiking.

APR–JUN
Spring is a magical season and the best time to avoid crowds.

JUL–SEP
Summer is peak season, while September is an ideal time to visit.

OCT–DEC
Autumn colours and the grape and olive harvests entice.

GETTING AROUND

Car Istria has limited public transportation, so the most convenient way to explore the region at your own pace is by car. Streets tend to be winding and sometimes narrow if you venture off the main thoroughfares, but the road network is well maintained.

Bus While a public bus network connects some of Istria's main towns and cities, frequency is limited. The main bus companies are Arriva and Brioni.

Train Up to eight trains a day link Pula in southern Istria with Buzet in the north, stopping at a number of towns in between, including Pazin. On some trains, a special 'Bike & Train' compartment is reserved for bicycles.

EATING & DRINKING

As a crossroads of cultures, Istria's regional cuisine is a mix of gastronomic influences. Tuck into a bowl of *maneštra,* a hearty vegetable soup reminiscent of Italian minestrone, followed by a plate of handmade fresh pasta called *fuži* or *njoki* (gnocchi; pictured top right). Sauerkraut *(kiseli kupus)* is a traditional staple going back to Austro-Hungarian times, as are *palačinke* (crepes; pictured bottom right). Don't miss the chance to sample a dish garnished with shavings of black or white truffles, a local delicacy, and doused with the exquisite extra virgin olive oil produced here.

Must-try truffle-infused tasting menu
Restaurant Zigante (p107)

Best olive oil tasting
Brist (p109)

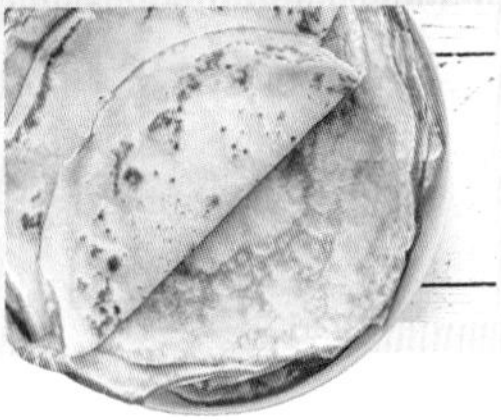

CONNECT & FIND YOUR WAY

Almost every town, especially popular tourist spots, have a free public wi-fi service. You can also connect to hot spots at most hotels, cafes and restaurants. Many mobile operators offer SIM cards for tourists with generous data plans at a reasonable price. Beware of spotty connections during the summer tourist rush when networks become saturated.

SCENIC ROUTES

Driving Istria's Ypsilon motorway saves time, but the region's secondary roads are much more scenic and are toll free.

WHERE TO STAY

From budget rooms to luxury villas with pools, a variety of accommodation options are on offer in Istria in urban, rural and seaside settings.

City	Pros/Cons
Pula	Istria's biggest city with a seaside location and good transport links.
Poreč	A busy tourist town of crowded beachside resorts.
Rovinj	This romantic and picturesque coastal town is easy to navigate on foot.
Motovun	A fairy-tale hilltop town, but you need your own transport.
Pazin	A central Istrian town that's low on tourist sights but well connected to buses and trains.
Labin	A lovely hilltop town close to beaches in Rabac but a bit far from other tourist spots.

MONEY

You can pay by debit and credit card at most hotels and restaurants, but some cafes and bars don't accept card payments. Have some cash on hand just in case.

15 An Island ESCAPE

ISLANDS | NATIONAL PARK | DAY TRIP

The clutch of 14 pine-scented islands and islets that make up Brijuni National Park is entirely car free. They were completely off-limits until 1983 when they became a national park. This open-air museum has plenty to explore: Roman ruins and archaeological sites, rocky beaches pocked with dinosaur footprints, a safari park of exotic animals and a museum dedicated to former Yugoslavian leader, President Tito.

How To

Getting there Brijuni National Park is a 15-minute ferry ride from Fažana – the fare is included in the entrance ticket.

Getting around Hire a bicycle or electric golf cart or catch a guided tour on the tourist train.

When to go You can visit the national park year-round, but fewer ferries run from November to March.

Tip The Brijuni Pocket Guide is an app covering all the park's attractions.

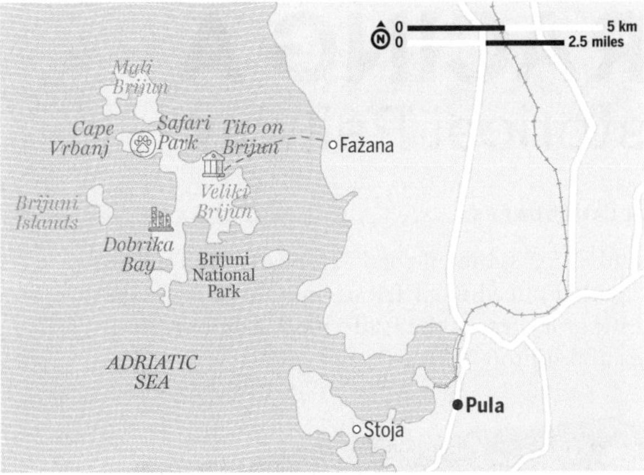

Animal farm After arriving at the dock, head through landscaped parklands past towering umbrella pines to the northern end of Veliki Brijun island. Grazing on the vast lawns of this 9-hectare **Safari Park** is a posse of animals gifted to President Tito by various heads of state. African ostriches rub shoulders with South American llamas, zebras from Guinea, Somalian sheep and Indian holy cows. You can also spot strutting peacocks and Lanka the Indian elephant, a gift from Prime Minister Indira Gandhi in 1974.

Track dino prints On nearby **Cape Vrbanj** looms a life-sized replica of a theropod, a reminder that dinosaurs were the islands' oldest inhabitants. Look out for their prints permanently etched into the rocky beach, as well as on the southern coves of Cape Ploče, Cape Kamnik and Cape Trstike.

Age-old stones On the edge of **Dobrika Bay**, the intriguing remains of a fortified Byzantine *castrum* (encampment) cover a stone-strewn rectangular plot covering 1 hectare. Search among the ancient stones to spot age-old olive presses, brick ovens and wine cellars.

Tito's legacy At the **Tito on Brijuni** exhibition, a collection of more than 200 photographs document President Tito's time on the island. Captured in black and white are the heads of state and dignitaries he hosted: Winston Churchill, Queen Elizabeth II and Che Guevara, as well as Sophia Loren and other film stars.

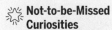

Left Safari Park, Veliki Brijun
Below left Fossilised dinosaur footprints, Cape Vrbanj

Not-to-be-Missed Curiosities

- Check out the dark-green vintage 1953 Cadillac Eldorado parked outside the museum – President Tito used this to cruise around his island home.
- At the bird park, say hello to Koki, the talking yellow-crested cockatoo, a gift from Tito to his grand-daughter Aleksandra, and one of the island's most famous residents. He may ask you *'Kako si?'* ('How are you?') or drop a few Croatian swear words.
- Look out for a plaque in the museum commemorating the signing of the historic Brijuni Declaration with Indian Prime Minister Jawaharlal Nehru and Egyptian President Gamal Abdel Nasser in 1956, which paved the way for the establishment of the Non-Aligned Movement.

16 TRACING A Historical Railway

HIKING | MEDIEVAL TOWNS | LANDSCAPES

Brilliant for hikers and cyclists, the off-road Parenzana Trail follows the former route of a railway that once linked Trieste in Italy to Poreč on Istria's western coast. This itinerary tracks the trail's most scenic section through verdant landscapes and hilltop towns.

Z. CIZIC/SHUTTERSTOCK ©

Trip Notes

Getting there Use a transport service (parenzana.net/en/services/transport-service) to get you to your starting point and pick you up at your destination.

Getting around The trail winds downhill from north to south, making this direction easier than the reverse.

Lighting Take a headlamp or torch for the tunnels that are not lit.

Bike type For cyclists, a mountain bike is ideal because of the mostly rocky, unpaved paths.

A Heritage Rail Trail

The Parenzana Trail (pictured) takes its name from the former railway whose route it traces. Most of the 123km-long Parenzana Railway runs through Croatia before passing through a small part of Slovenia and on to Muggia outside Trieste, Italy. The railway had a short life. It was inaugurated in 1903 during the Austro–Hungarian Empire and discontinued in 1935.

02 From the sign marking where Završje station once stood, take a short detour uphill to explore the tiny hilltop town of **Završje** (pictured left), once a bustling market centre thanks to the railway.

03 From the site of the former station, leave the trail for a 3km uphill trek to the heart of **Oprtalj**, a lovely hill town of handsome palazzos, stone gateways and an 18th-century Venetian town loggia.

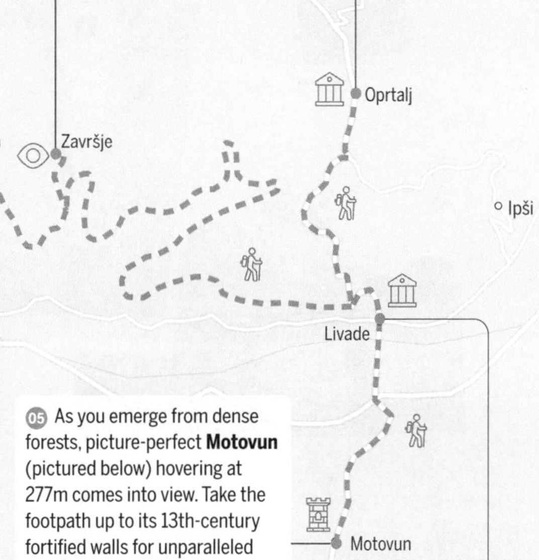

01 Begin in **Grožnjan** (pictured above), an artists' town perched at 293m, the trail's highest point. Wander its cobblestone lanes lined with immaculately restored stone houses and art galleries.

05 As you emerge from dense forests, picture-perfect **Motovun** (pictured below) hovering at 277m comes into view. Take the footpath up to its 13th-century fortified walls for unparalleled views of the Mirna River Valley.

04 After a long zigzagging descent to **Livade**, break your journey at the Parenzana Museum and learn about the railway's intriguing history. Refuel at rustic Konoba Dorjana and tuck into plates of Istrian pasta.

TYPICAL ISTRIAN
Architectural Elements

01 Škure (window shutters)
These brightly painted slatted window shutters typical of the Mediterranean can be adjusted to control light and airflow.

02 Kažun
A small cylinder-shaped stone structure with an open doorway served as a shelter for farmers working in their fields.

03 Kampanil (bell tower)
Bell towers are every Istrian town's most visible landmark. They typically stand completely separate from the church.

04 Loža (loggia)
These covered porches date back to Venetian times and are found near town gates or on public squares.

05 Dry stone walls
Stone walls demarcating fields and other property lines were built using the dry stone technique, which doesn't require mortar.

06 Venetian palazzi
Dating from the 14th and 15th centuries, Venetian palazzi are embellished with Gothic features, such as pointed arches and bifora windows.

07

06

08

09

10

07 Defensive fortifications
Hilltop towns were fortified with defensive walls and towers made of stone. Motovun still has its walls intact.

08 Stone wells
A town's well was not only a water source but also a meeting place. The stone wells on the squares of Svetvinčenat and Vižinada are surviving examples.

09 Frescoes
The interiors of the churches built during the Middle Ages were decorated with brightly coloured frescoes depicting biblical stories.

10 The lion of Venice
Gracing many age-old gateways and facades is the winged lion of Venice, a symbol of the Venetian Republic.

17 MUSIC AMID Ancient Stones

WORLD HERITAGE | ARCHITECTURE | MUSIC

Some of Istria's architectural treasures have become sublime venues for summertime concerts. In Poreč, the 5th-century Episcopal Complex of the Euphrasian Basilica is famous for its glittering mosaics of gold leaf and is one of the best surviving examples of Byzantine art. Pula's Roman amphitheatre dates from the 1st century and is exceptionally well preserved.

How to

Getting there You need your own transport to Poreč and Pula. Arrive early to secure parking.

When to go Visit in July, August or September. Concerts begin at 8pm or 9pm.

Booking tickets Tickets for concerts at the Euphrasian Basilica can be bought at the entrance or online (rezervacije-poup.hr). To book tickets for Pula's amphitheatre, visit Eventim (eventim.hr) and choose 'Arena Pula' under 'Lokacije' to see upcoming concerts.

Byzantine treasures The magnificent centrepiece of the UNESCO World Heritage–listed **Episcopal Complex of the Euphrasian Basilica** is the basilica itself, particularly its semicircular apse decorated with beautiful gold-leaf mosaics. This treasure of Byzantine art serves as the splendid stage backdrop for a series of weekly classical concerts from July to September, showcasing orchestras and quartets, as well as piano and guitar recitals. Arrive well before the concert to admire the mosaics up close and take a self-guided tour of the rest of the complex. Venture into the lapidarium and adjacent courtyard to admire exquisite floor mosaics dating from the 4th and 5th centuries. Next, head up the church's 16th-century bell tower to take in the spectacle of the sunset over the rooftops of Poreč's old town.

A majestic Roman relic Pula's best-known and most beloved landmark is its 1st-century sea-facing

IVANA VRNOGA/SHUTTERSTOCK ©

Roman amphitheatre, known locally as the **Arena**. Its age-old 30m-high limestone walls constructed of three tiers of arched windows once had enough space for 20,000 spectators, who gathered here to watch bloodthirsty Roman gladiators in action. Today, the amphitheatre is an exceptional big-ticket concert venue open to the sky that seats a crowd of 5000 among its ancient stones. Tom Jones, the Arctic Monkeys, 2Cellos, Simply Red and Robbie Williams are just a few of the big-name acts who have performed here in recent years.

More Exceptional Concert Venues

Cave Romane is an ancient Roman quarry near Pula that supplied the stone used to build the Roman amphitheatre. Today, a stage is set between its 40m-high man-made cliffs, creating a magical setting for concerts, theatre performances and film screenings.

Pula's 1st-century Small Roman Theatre was given a breath of new life in 2023 as an open-air stage. Its semicircular auditorium seats up to 1600 for concerts and performances.

During the Dvigrad Festival, the sounds of classical music resonate across stone ruins and the remains of St Sophia's Basilica in Dvigrad, a hilltop settlement abandoned during the bubonic plague.

Arena ruins

18 Rovinj's Maritime HERITAGE

HISTORY | MUSEUMS | OUTDOORS

Rovinj's sublime old town was once a separate island floating off Istria's west coast before it was joined to the mainland in 1763. This Venetian-flavoured town of pastel-coloured facades was the centre of an important fishing industry in the 17th century. Explore Rovinj through the lens of its maritime history to understand the significance of the sea on the town's socio-economic development.

How To

Getting here Rovinj can be reached by bus from most major towns.

Getting around Rovinj's old town is closed to cars and is entirely pedestrian only.

When to go Set out early to see fishers landing their catch. You'll also avoid the summer heat and crowds.

Tip Download the Batana Walk app and explore 20 sights related to Rovinj's maritime heritage. (Look up 'Batana Walk' in your app store.)

Rovinj Port You won't spot any yachts in Rovinj's compact **port** on the edge of its old town: the vessels moored here are humble fishing boats, a sign that this tradition is very much alive. Look closely and you may see a batana bobbing in the waters – this small, flat-bottomed wooden boat is a symbol of the town's maritime heritage.

Batana Eco-Museum This small **museum** celebrates Rovinj's traditional fishing boat through multimedia exhibits. Watch video projections of a batana floating out to sea as fishers banter in the local dialect and then return to shore with their catch. On display are maritime objects and tools donated by town residents, and a timelapse video reveals each stage of the batana-building process.

Old shipyard Follow the shoreline south past the Maestral Sailing Club towards the **ACI Marina** to find the **Old Shipyard**.

It's where batanas and medium-sized boats were built until the late 1940s. Today, the site is protected for its maritime heritage, and wooden boats are still repaired here.

Rovinj Traditional Boat Regatta During this two-day regatta in June, the waters off Rovinj's old town are full of traditional wooden boats decked out with colourful sails. Crews from Croatia, Slovenia and Italy show off their navigation skills during a race to nearby **St Catherine's Island**.

Epic Boat Trips from Rovinj

I recommend a day trip to Brijuni National Park, an archipelago of islands about an hour from Rovinj by boat. It's a national park, but it also has a lot of fascinating history.

Venice is just across the Adriatic Sea and is an interesting day trip. Boats make the trip there every day during the summer.

Sunset tours by boat are a popular option. These last for about two hours and sail around the archipelago near Rovinj, including the nearby islands of St Catherine and St Andrew. Sunset is the perfect time because this is when there are lots of dolphins around.

■ **By Kristina Omerović** *assistant front office manager at Grand Park Hotel Rovinj*

Rovinj port

19 A Taste of ISTRIA

FOOD | LOCAL FLAVOURS | TASTINGS

The most precious fruits of Istria's soil are the white truffles growing in dense underground forests, as well as the olives pressed each autumn for oil. A visit to Istria is not complete without a taste of these gastronomic delights.

ALISTAIR HEAP/ALAMY STOCK PHOTO ©

How To

Getting around Public transportation is limited in Istria. You need your own transport to explore at leisure.

When to go Black truffles grow year-round, while the highly prized white truffle (Magnatum Pico) makes an appearance between October and January only. To taste exquisite freshly pressed olive oil, visit when the harvest is underway in October and November and the olive crop is processed within 24 hours.

MARCO MAYER/SHUTTERSTOCK ©

A World Truffle Record

It was in the forests surrounding Motovun that the world's largest white truffle was unearthed in 1999. This event earned a mention in the Guinness Book of World Records for Giancarlo Zigante and his dog Diana, whose nose sniffed out the 1.31kg truffle. This discovery sparked the launch of Zigante Tartufi, a line of specialised truffle products and a chain of shops, as well as **Restaurant Zigante** in Livade, where you can sample a truffle-infused tasting menu. Stop by between October and January for a chance to taste the pungent Magnatum Pico, which grows in only a few regions of Europe.

ALLOVER IMAGES/ALAMY STOCK PHOTO ©

Hunt for Buried Treasure

Join a hunt for elusive tubers in the depths of Motovun forest with Miro and his dogs

Mark of Authenticity

Istrian olive oil has had PDO (Protected Designation of Origin) status on the EU level since 2019. This designation means that olive oil with this label has been entirely produced and processed in Istria and not mixed with oils from other regions or countries.

Above left Water dog sniffing out truffles
Left Truffle sauce from Restaurant Zigante
Above White truffles

Bela and Nera at **Miro Tartufi** (miro-tartufi.com). Watch as his specially trained hounds show off their truffle-hunting skills. After they catch a whiff of a strong-smelling tuber growing 25cm underground, Miro takes over to carefully dig up the precious delicacy. After the hunt, Miro's wife, Mirjana, welcomes you to the family home with platters of truffle-infused delights: dishes of homemade pasta, artisanal sausage and cheese, and scrambled eggs, all seasoned with generous shavings of white or black truffles.

Visit an Olive Grove

Look for the green signs marked with 'Cesta Maslinova Ulja – Olive Oil Roads', which point you in the direction of local producers welcoming visitors to their family-run groves. Stroll among the olive trees while learning about the cultivation and olive-oil-making process, followed by a tasting of exceptional olive oils.

B10 Istrian Fusion (b10.hr) in Kostanjica entices with a tasting room overlooking the rolling hills of the Mirna River Valley, a

Truffle & Olive-Oil Events

Each November in Vodnjan, Istravirgin (dmmu.info) is Croatia's biggest olive-oil event, celebrating the harvest with cooking demos and opportunities to sample freshly pressed oils.

The New Olive Oil Festival gathers local producers in Kanfanar each December for tastings and a competition for the season's best olive oils.

Learn how to whip up truffle-infused dishes and watch a truffle-hunting demo at Zigante Truffle Days, which take place over five weekends in September and October in Livade

The highlight of Buzet's Subotina Festival on the first Saturday of September is a massive omelette prepared with more than 2000 eggs and 10kg of truffles.

Left Olive oil on bread
Below Tasting, House of Istrian Olive Oil

FROM LEFT: ANNA SHEPULOVA/SHUTTERSTOCK ©, HOUSE OF ISTRIAN OLIVE OIL PULA ©

magnificent sight. Nearby in the hamlet of Ipši, **Ipša** (ipsa-maslinovaulja.com) is a family estate of olive groves and vineyards. In the middle of the property stands a handsome stone house that has been transformed into an elegant tasting room.

Further south near Vodnjan, Paul and Lena of **Brist** (brist-olive.hr) invite travellers on tours of their family groves, followed by a guided alfresco tasting experience under their trees.

At **Chiavalon** (chiavalon.hr), olive enthusiasts can learn about each stage of the production process at its state-of-the-art olive mill while sampling its monovarietals and blends.

Pula's Olive Oil Museum

At the excellent **House of Istrian Olive Oil** (oleumhistriae.com), get insights into the history and development of olive-oil production in Istria.

Through a series of well-designed interactive exhibits, you'll learn about the olive-oil trade during Roman times, the taxation system imposed by the Venetians and discover olive oil's many health benefits. Round off your visit with an expert-led tasting of a few high-quality Istrian extra virgin olive oils and then stock up on your favourites at the on-site shop.

Istria's Exquisite Olive Oil

STRIVING FOR QUALITY OVER QUANTITY

Istria has a long tradition of olive oil production, spanning more than 2000 years. During Roman times, olive oil was not only an everyday staple but also an important trade commodity. Today, Istrian olive oil is still on kitchen tables as well as on the map when it comes to quality.

Left 1600-year-old olive tree
Centre Olives
Right Olive-oil tasting

NINO MARCUTTI/ALAMY STOCK PHOTO ©

A 1600-year-old olive tree with a sprawling canopy is one of the natural attractions of Veliki Brijun island, part of Brijuni National Park off Istria's southwest coast. This age-old tree that's a symbol of the Mediterranean still bears fruit, but more importantly, it's a testament to Istria's long olive-oil tradition.

Olive-oil production has seen a renaissance in Istria in the past 25 years thanks to agricultural incentives and local investments. Compared to 350,000 olive trees and three mills two decades ago, Istria now has groves with more than 1.8 million olive trees and over 30 mills across the peninsula. Today, more than 100 producers in the Istrian region make extra virgin olive oil, and the vast majority are made up of small family-owned operations.

While Croatia can't compete with olive-oil heavyweights such as Spain or Greece, the EU's largest producers, the country's extra virgin olive oil packs a big punch when it comes to its high quality. Over the years, Istrian olive oil producers have won numerous awards from international competitions, and Istria has been recognised by the Flos Olei olive-oil guide as the 'World's Best Olive Region' for seven years in a row.

Istrian olive oil also enjoys PDO (Protected Designation of Origin) status at the national and EU levels. To meet the high demand for a gourmet product susceptible to adverse climatic conditions, producers in some countries import olive oil, which is then mixed with local oil to increase quantity. A PDO

ATLANTIDE PHOTOTRAVEL/GETTY IMAGES ©

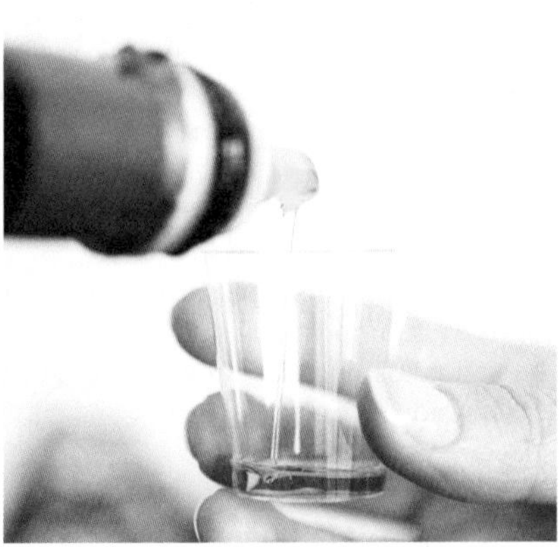

JUICE FLAIR/SHUTTERSTOCK ©

designation ensures that the olive oil in the bottle has been entirely produced and processed in the region indicated on the label.

Each olive variety has its own nuances that can be discerned and appreciated by the palate. Growing in Istria's rich soil are several native olive varieties, such as *Istarska bjelica*, *buža*, *črnica*, *drobnica*, *karbonaca* and *rošinjola*. Istrian olive oil tends to have fruity notes with a notable bitterness and sharpness that hints at a high-quality extra virgin olive oil rich in health-boosting polyphenols.

Istrian olive oil tends to have fruity notes with a notable bitterness and sharpness

Istria's reputation for high-quality olive oil combined with its beautiful landscapes and warm hospitality make it an ideal destination for olive-oil tourism. This form of gastro-tourism has seen a rise in the past decade as more people learn that a good extra virgin olive oil can be tasted and savoured much like a quality wine. Similar to visiting a winery, epicureans can visit a family-run olive farm, walk among the groves and learn about olive production before sitting down for an expert-led tasting. Look for the green 'olive oil road' signs on Istrian roads that point in the direction of local producers.

Olive oil is at its best just after it's pressed. Visit during the olive harvest in October and November for the opportunity to sample the season's new oil fresh from the press.

What Makes Quality Olive Oil?

The production process influences an olive oil's quality. An early harvest is favoured to preserve high polyphenol content.

Olives are generally picked just as they're starting to turn purple and are ideally harvested by hand. The crop must then be processed within 24 hours, using a modern mechanised mill that does not heat the oil higher than 27°C.

20 A WINE Wonderland

VINEYARDS | DRINKING | LANDSCAPES

Istria's landscapes covered with endless rows of vineyards hint at its status as an important winemaking region. Swirl and sip your way through the peninsula one glass at a time by stopping at family-run wineries in bucolic countryside settings.

JAZI/GETTY IMAGES ©

Trip Notes

Getting around Wineries are located in remote areas not served by public transportation. You need your own wheels to get around. Look for the brown 'wine road' signs pointing the way to local wineries.

When to go Most wineries are open year-round. Some close during harvest time in September.

Costs A wine-tasting experience costs €30 to €100 depending on the length of the tasting and the number of wines sampled.

Don't miss Istria's native Istarska *malvazija* and *teran* wines.

Vinistra Wine Fair

Vinistra is a premier wine event each May in Poreč, showcasing Istria's rich viticultural heritage. Taste the best Istrian wines, including Istarska *malvazija*, the white grape that can take the form of a crisp summer white, a full-bodied orange wine or a dessert wine.

By Goran Zgrablić
EatIstria cooking class and wine tours, @eatistria

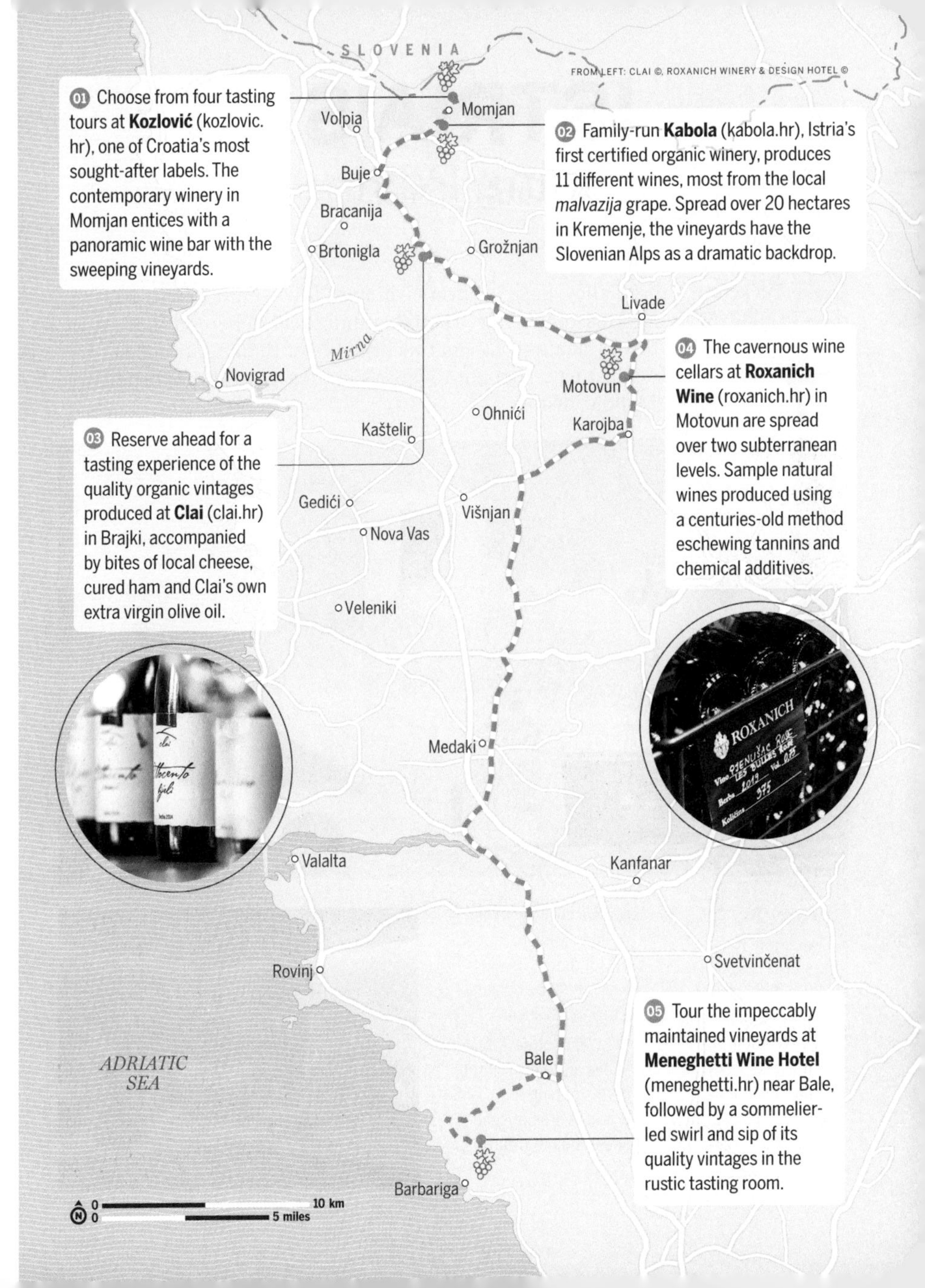

FROM LEFT: CLAI ©, ROXANICH WINERY & DESIGN HOTEL ©

01 Choose from four tasting tours at **Kozlović** (kozlovic.hr), one of Croatia's most sought-after labels. The contemporary winery in Momjan entices with a panoramic wine bar with the sweeping vineyards.

02 Family-run **Kabola** (kabola.hr), Istria's first certified organic winery, produces 11 different wines, most from the local *malvazija* grape. Spread over 20 hectares in Kremenje, the vineyards have the Slovenian Alps as a dramatic backdrop.

03 Reserve ahead for a tasting experience of the quality organic vintages produced at **Clai** (clai.hr) in Brajki, accompanied by bites of local cheese, cured ham and Clai's own extra virgin olive oil.

04 The cavernous wine cellars at **Roxanich Wine** (roxanich.hr) in Motovun are spread over two subterranean levels. Sample natural wines produced using a centuries-old method eschewing tannins and chemical additives.

05 Tour the impeccably maintained vineyards at **Meneghetti Wine Hotel** (meneghetti.hr) near Bale, followed by a sommelier-led swirl and sip of its quality vintages in the rustic tasting room.

21 ISTRIA'S Mining Past

HISTORY | HERITAGE | MUSEUMS

Tucked in a lush valley, Raša is Istria's youngest town, built in only 547 days in 1936–37 under Mussolini's rule. Though mining ceased here in 1966, this former mining town remains a fascinating example of Italian rationalist architecture. It's also a lasting testament to Istria's mining past, an important part of its social and labour history.

How To

Getting here Raša is in eastern Istria, a 5km drive west of Labin. A few buses stop here on the way to and from Pula and Labin, but services are limited.

Opening times Museum opening hours vary by season. Check the Arsiana website (arsiana.hr) for details. Mining tours must be booked a day in advance.

Tip Wear comfortable shoes and warm clothes on the mining tour. Temperatures are noticeably cooler below ground.

Step into a miner's house Dominating Raša's town square is the **Church of St Barbara**, the patron saint of miners, designed to resemble an overturned coal wagon, embellished with a bell tower that looks like a miner's lamp. Look out for a stairway on the other end of the square climbing up to the mining museum located above a row of shops. Inside the **Miner's House 'Arsia'**, multimedia exhibits take you back to Raša's mining days through images, sounds, film, and a collection of mining tools and objects. The modest interiors of a typical miner's house have been replicated in two rooms decorated with period furniture, everyday objects and a coal stove.

A day in the life of a miner Don a hard hat and headlamp and head into the dark tunnels of Raša's defunct coal mine where more than 10,000 miners once toiled in three shifts. A three-hour guided **Kova Experience Tour** (*kova* is the Istrian dialect word for 'mine') takes you underground to explore a 1.5km-long section of a mining tunnel. Get a glimpse of the miners' difficult working conditions and see the crumbling remains of the railway, heavy machinery and lift that transported the coal above ground. You'll also hear about the mine's milestones and major events, including the tragic explosion in 1940 that took the lives of 185 miners.

Left Raša coal mine tour
Far left Church of St Barbara
Below left Miner's House 'Arsia'

A Town Built for Miners

Both of my grandfathers worked in Raša's mine – every family has someone who worked there. Raša was inaugurated as a new mining town in 1937 during the time Istria fell under Italian rule.

The town was built as a planned settlement with everything the miners and their families would need: a square, a town hall, a church, a hospital, a school, a cinema, a swimming pool, sports grounds and residential quarters.

Its heyday was in 1942, when 10,000 miners were employed here and a record 1.1 million tonnes of coal was produced. Mining started to decline in the 1960s, and the mine eventually closed in 1966.

■ **By Jasmin Mahmutović**
director of the Raša Tourist Board, @visitrasa

Listings

BEST OF THE REST

Summer Cultural Festivals

Pula Film Festival

Pula's 1st-century Roman amphitheatre transforms into a cinema under the stars during this annual nine-day film festival started in 1953.

Dance & Non-Verbal Theatre Festival

The medieval town of Svetvinčenat sets the stage for performing arts with its massive Morosini-Grimani Castle, age-old town square and Venetian loggia becoming the backdrops for performers from across Europe.

Jazz is Back

The cobbled lanes and stone houses of charming Grožnjan resonate with the sounds of jazz every summer. Over two weeks, nightly concerts by international musicians draw music lovers to this hilltop town.

Labin Art Republika

A two-month-long programme of concerts, documentary film screenings, art exhibitions, comedy shows and family events keep Labin's historic old town buzzing all summer long.

Gastro Events

Festival of Istrian Maneštra

Istria's beloved *maneštra* is celebrated every June at this annual festival in lovely Gračišće. Teams of local chefs cook up their versions of this hearty soup of vegetables, grains and pulses on wood-fired stoves.

Festival of Istrian Pasta

Each July, food lovers flock to this gourmet festival in Žminj to sample different types of fresh homemade pasta typical to Istria, such as *fuži*, *njoki* and *pljukanci*.

Summer Festival of Istrian Prosciutto

Tinjan hosts three days each July dedicated to Istrian *pršut* (cured ham). Visitors queue up to taste this local delicacy, join the wine tastings and take in nightly concerts.

Sweet Istria

In August, you can satisfy your sweet tooth at Slatka Istra (Sweet Istria) in Vižinada with *fritule* (fritters), *cukerančići* (sugar biscuits) and *kroštule* (fried pastry), just a few of Istria's traditional sweets and pastries.

Istrian Grappa Fair

The tiny town of Hum brings together producers of Istrian *rakija* (grappa) each October. Honey, sour cherry, walnut and mint are just a few of the different flavours to sample and savour.

Local Museums

Memo Museum

Take a nostalgia trip at this quirky museum in Pula, where you can get hands-on with retro relics, such as rollerskates, typewriters, cassette players, toy trains and the iconic Zastava 750 car.

Fritule (fritters)

Ecomuseum Vlaški Puti

This interactive museum in Šušnjevica showcases the history, cuisine and culture of the Istro-Romanian community and Vlaški, their native tongue, through a collection of images and video.

Kažun Park

At this open-air park near Vodnjan, learn about the technique of dry-stone building and *kažun*, cylinder-shaped structures made entirely of stone that once served as shelters for agricultural workers.

Istrian de Dignan Ecomuseum

A collection of rooms spread over a sprawling townhouse in Vodnjan is filled with curiosities and fascinating mementos from times past, including metal and wooden tools, household objects and artisans' workshops.

Tiskara Antico

Step off Motovun's main square into a medieval printing house. Watch a demonstration of traditional hand-printing on handmade paper using a replica of a Gutenberg printing press.

Outdoor Adventures

Pazin Cave

Head underground and explore Pazin's mysterious cave on a three-hour guided caving adventure. You descend 100m through limestone caverns and across bridges made of huge boulders to an underground lake.

Pazin Zip Line

Zip 50km an hour above the treetops and get a bird's-eye view over Pazin's famous abyss 100m below on this thrilling zip-line experience.

Istra Kayak

Get close to the rocky coastline of Cape Kamenjak nature park on a kayak tour. Local guides show you the way to hidden caves, coves, nearby islets and secret beaches.

GORAN_SAFAREK/SHUTTERSTOCK ©

Pazin Zip Line

Adrenalin Park Kringa

Kids of all ages will enjoy the challenge of reaching new heights on aerial obstacle courses of elevated tracks of ropes and planks. For an adrenaline boost, try the giant swing.

Escape Castle Svetvinčenat

Explore the medieval towers and unlock the hidden chambers of Morosini-Grimani Castle on this family-friendly adventure game. Use virtual reality to defend the castle against invaders and forge your own sword.

Hiking Trails

Trail of the Seven Waterfalls

Follow magic forest paths that lead over bridges, through stone hamlets, across riverbeds and past rapids created by the Mirna and Draga Rivers to seven scenic waterfalls.

Stjepan Hauser's Trail

From Rakalj on Istria's eastern shores, this path (named after one of the musicians of 2Cellos) opens onto panoramic sea views as it traces the coastline southwards.

Scan to find more things to do in Istria

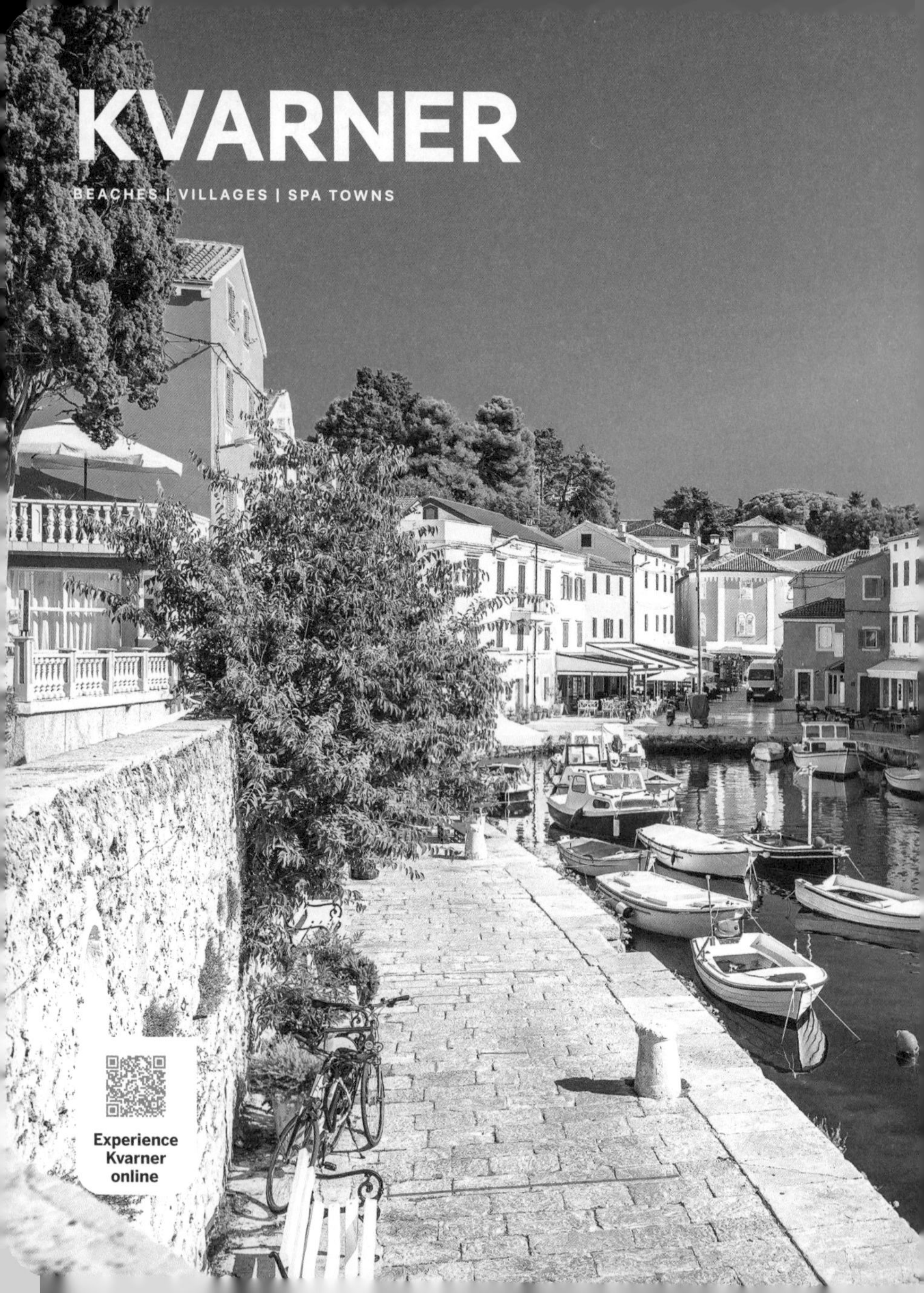
KVARNER
BEACHES | VILLAGES | SPA TOWNS
Experience Kvarner online

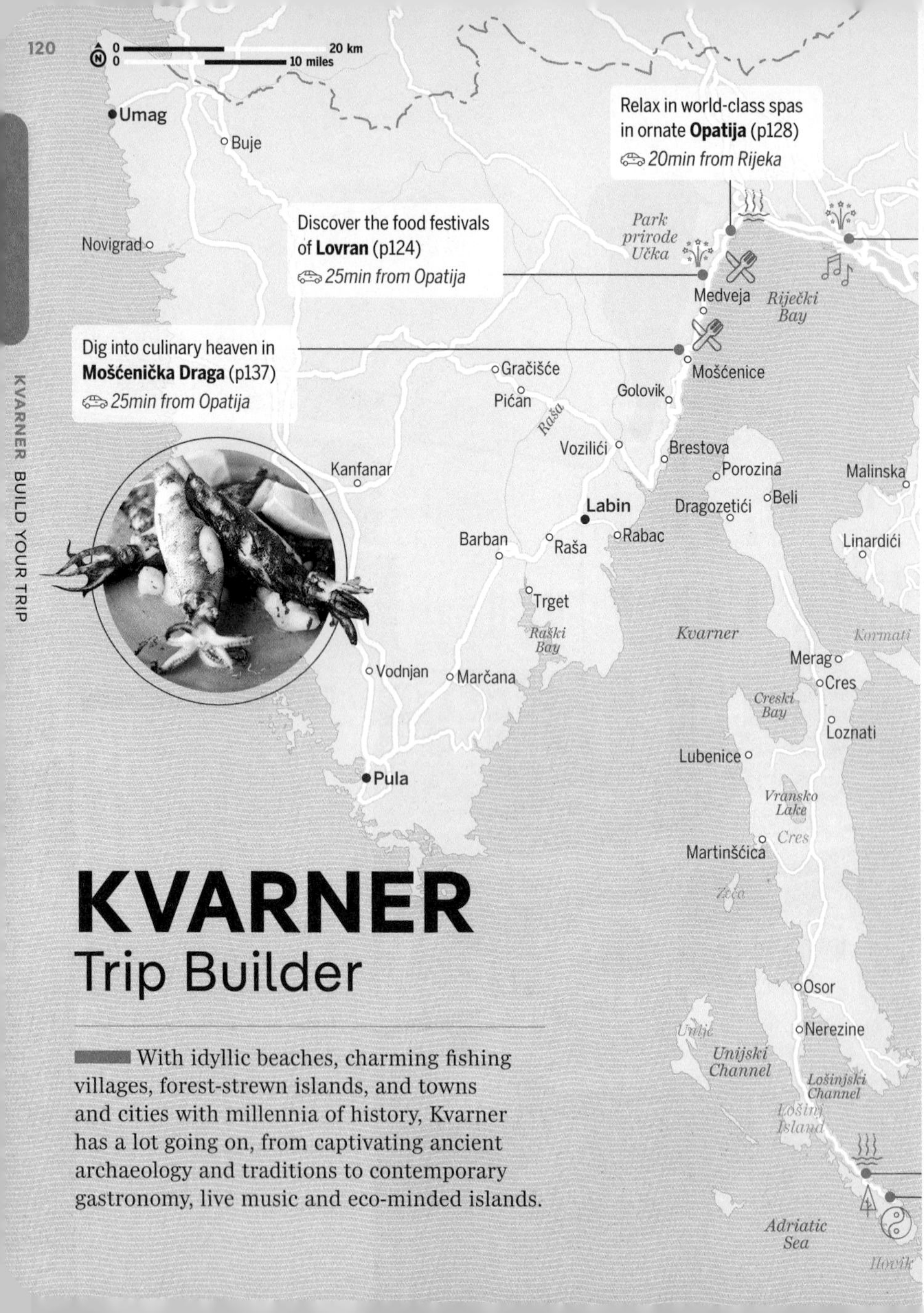

KVARNER
Trip Builder

With idyllic beaches, charming fishing villages, forest-strewn islands, and towns and cities with millennia of history, Kvarner has a lot going on, from captivating ancient archaeology and traditions to contemporary gastronomy, live music and eco-minded islands.

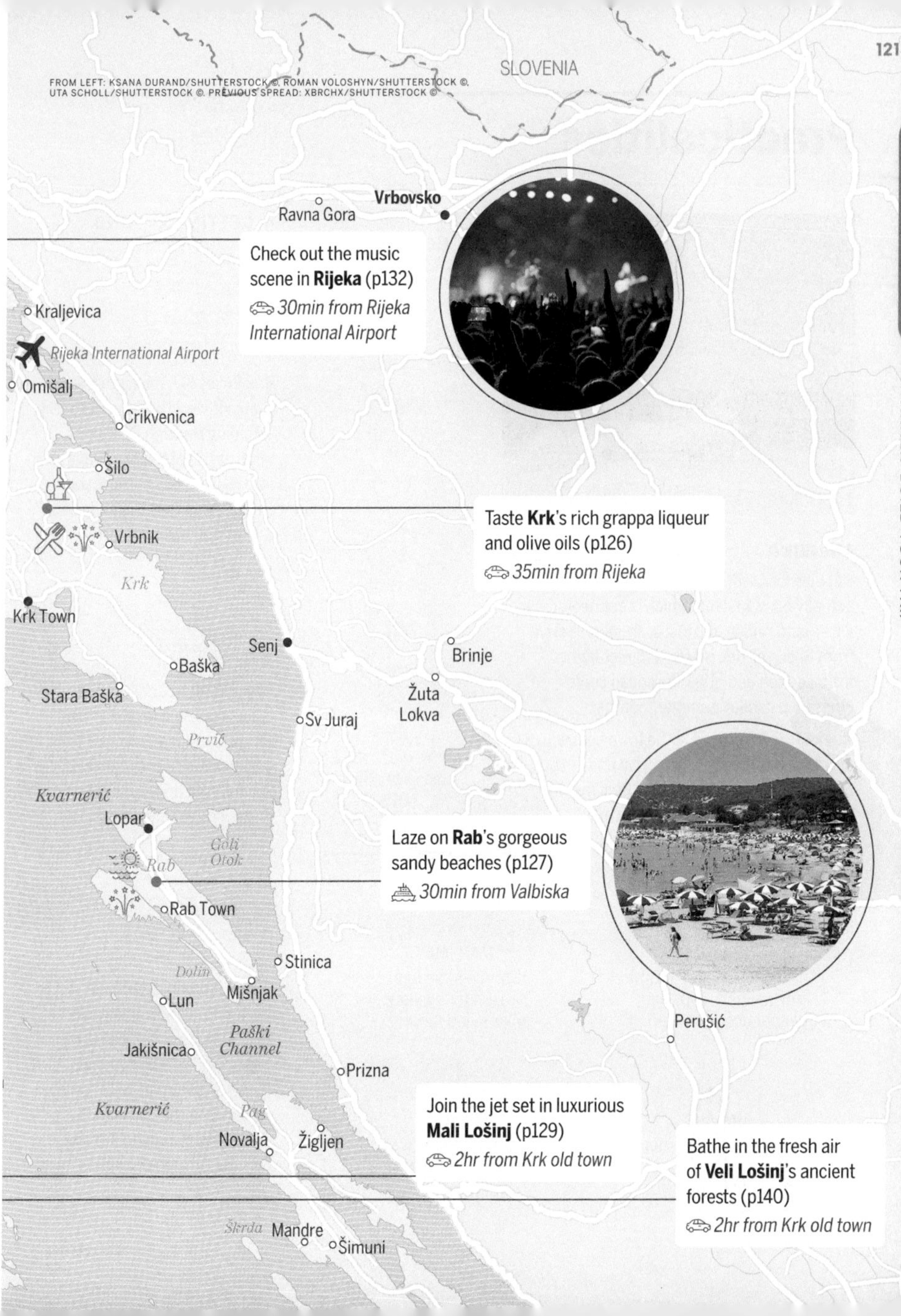

Check out the music scene in **Rijeka** (p132)
30min from Rijeka International Airport

Taste **Krk**'s rich grappa liqueur and olive oils (p126)
35min from Rijeka

Laze on **Rab**'s gorgeous sandy beaches (p127)
30min from Valbiska

Join the jet set in luxurious **Mali Lošinj** (p129)
2hr from Krk old town

Bathe in the fresh air of **Veli Lošinj**'s ancient forests (p140)
2hr from Krk old town

Practicalities

ARRIVING

Rijeka International Airport (pictured) is actually on Krk Island, which is connected by a free land bridge and just a 35-minute drive from Rijeka or Krk old town. Direct flights from London and other European capital cities land in peak summer months.

Rijeka Bus Station is in the town centre, and long-haul buses from Arriva and Flixbus arrive from Zagreb, Zadar and Split, as well as from further-flung European cities.

HOW MUCH FOR A

bottle of olive oil
€7

plate of *pljukanci pasta*
€12

bottle of *Vrbnička žlahtina* wine
€15

WHEN TO GO

NOV–FEB
Off season is a great time for wellness trips and cheaper accommodation.

MAR–MAY
Spring is the best season for cyclists, hikers and foodies.

JUN–AUG
Summer is busy, hot and sticky; head to the coast to cool down.

SEP–OCT
Best for beach lovers: the days and seas are still warm.

GETTING AROUND

Bus Buses link Rijeka to the Opatija Riviera, with services running through Opatija, Lovran and Mošćenička Draga. From Rijeka's bus station, you can also head to the islands of Cres and Lošinj via Krk.

Car Hiring a car or moped is a great way to explore the islands, particularly Krk, which is connected to the mainland by a toll-free bridge, so it's an easy drive from Rijeka.

Ferry Jadrolinija ferries link Krk to the islands of Cres and Rab. From Cres, you can drive to Lošinj via a bridge that crosses the Roman-built canal separating the two islands. The islands were historically one stretch of land.

EATING & DRINKING

Aside from open-minded, cool-kid Rijeka, which is Croatia's third-largest city, the Kvarner region doesn't have many urban areas. It's a predominantly rural area with historically rich towns surrounded by farms and their readily available local produce. As a coastal county, it's also awash with fishing villages, so expect fresh, seasonal plates from restaurants and cafes across the mainland and islands. The area's main wine producer is the island of Krk, which has been growing local grape, *Vrbnička žlahtina* (pictured top right), in the vineyards outside of Vrbnik for millennia.

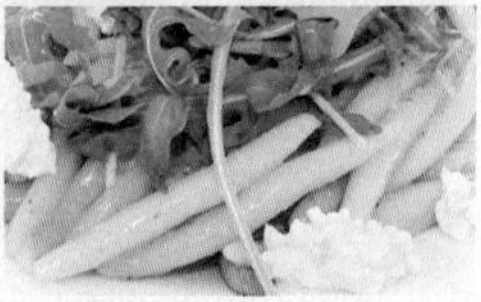

Best food festivals
In Lovran on the Opatija Riviera (p125)

Must-try pljukanci pasta
Konoba Nono (p143)

CONNECT & FIND YOUR WAY

The free public wi-fi in Rijeka covers the downtown area and part of the hilltop area of Trsat. You can also find free wi-fi in Cres old town, Krk old town, Opatija and Rab, including Rab old town and Lopar. Otherwise, get a local T-Mobile SIM card for data coverage.

WELL DRESSED

After you've visited the beach, cover up your swimwear before you wander around the old town centres to avoid offence.

WHERE TO STAY

If you're after some R&R, you'll find quaint hilltop cottages aplenty across Kvarner. But you're probably here for the sea, and holiday apartments, campsites and B&Bs await.

City	Pros/Cons
Rijeka	Top hotels, hostels and swanky yet affordable apartments on every corner.
Opatija	Ornate Habsburg hotels come at luxury prices in this bijou town.
Krk	Holiday apartments, campsites and a few lush boutique hotels.
Cres	Camping and campervans are big business. To stay within four walls, find apartments or B&Bs.
Mali Lošinj	Extremely posh luxury hotels and high-end apartments.
Veli Lošinj	Wellness resorts and B&Bs are dotted between holiday apartment rentals.

MONEY

Since the introduction of the euro in 2023, inflation has hit Croatia hard. While Kvarner is one of the cheaper corners of the country to visit, dining feels costly compared to previous years – just don't blame the proprietors.

22 FESTIVE about Food

HERITAGE | FESTIVALS | LOCAL FLAVOURS

If you're visiting Kvarner in spring, summer or autumn, graze on local treats at Kvarner's niche food festivals. Ancient Krk, the medieval wonder of Lovran and the Renaissance old town in Rab all have events that celebrate seasonal, traditional delicacies.

ALENA HAURYLIK/SHUTTERSTOCK ©

How To

Getting there & around Krk and the villages and towns of the Opatija Riviera are easily accessible by bus from Rijeka.

When to go Travellers are in the minority at the Lovran Asparagus Festival in April, which is put on for and by locals. July and August are busier, but Krk and Rab's local festivals predate the arrival of tourists by 400 years.

Be sure to try Krk grappa, a potent local liquor.

NEL PAVLETIC/PIXSELL/ALAMY STOCK PHOTO ©

NITR/SHUTTERSTOCK ©

Foodie Festival Season in Lovran

One of the highlights of the Riviera, **Lovran** is as picturesque as it is historically rich. The cobblestone lanes and streets pass humble buildings that date from the 1600s when Lovran was a walled city and sanctuary for people fleeing the invading Ottoman army. It's worth visiting for the quaint cafes, excellent restaurants and fascinating architectural features, such as the 'Turkish Head' donning a house opposite St George's Church, designed in 1722 to scare away unwanted visitors and ghosts. Also look out for the ancient Glagolitic script in St George's Church itself.

But the cherries on top are Lovran's three huge food festivals: the Lovran Asparagus Festival in April, Lovran Cherry Days in June

Sweet Treats

Though it has only 1000 residents, the medieval village of Volosko has one of Croatia's best bakeries. At Kaokakao Patisserie, pastry chef Anja Zulic creates a masterpiece: the divine Kaokakao cake, a dark chocolate-covered dome containing three layers of sponge and mousse – all chocolate flavoured.

Above left Asparagus
Left Cherries
Above Asparagus Festival

and Lovran 'Marunada' Chestnut Festival in October, which all take place in Liberty Sq. The Asparagus Festival sees the whole town watch a guest chef make a colossal asparagus omelette, using 1000 eggs and 30kg of asparagus collected from the nearby Ucka Mountain by 10 volunteers over three days. Attendees are then offered a free plate of what's perhaps the world's biggest omelette.

Ancient Delights on Krk

One of Krk's biggest celebrations of the year is **Lovrečeva**, an annual festival dedicated to the island's patron, St Lawrence. Taking place annually in mid-August, Lovrečeva marks its 500th year in 2024. A great food market is the backdrop of historical re-enactments, live music and folk dances at sites in and around Krk old town. Feast on delicious local products, such as Krk cheese, prosciutto,

Don't Forget the Dancing

As well as having a festive approach to food, Croatia keeps other strands of its intangible heritage strong. Krk's traditional dance of *tanac po staro* is on UNESCO's World Heritage list.

You can watch it on Easter Monday in the medieval town square of Omisalj, where local children proudly perform for the local community, donning their colourful ancestral attire, while tunes are played on the wooden sopile flute.

The villages of Kornić, Poljica and Vrh also have their own folk dance groups, performing throughout the year at events including Krk Music Fest, Lovrečeva and St Lawrence Day.

Left Dancers, Rabska Fjera
Below Chestnuts

homemade *šurlice* (noodles topped with goulash), white *žlahtina* wine and Krk grappa.

Don't miss the only hand-slicing prosciutto competition in Croatia. Keep an eye on the local tourism board's website for updates (tz-krk.hr/en).

A Saintly Affair in Rab

Established in 1364, the **Rabska Fjera** is the oldest and largest summer festival in Croatia, and it's worth timing your trip around it. This event takes place over the feast days of St James, St Anne and St Christopher (25 to 27 July). During the festival, the entire town goes back in time to the Middle Ages, complete with a food market packed full of stands selling *šulčići* (fried treats similar to doughnuts), *Rabska torta* (local cake made from marzipan, almonds and maraschino liqueur, traditionally baked in a spiral shape) and honey wine.

Don't miss the delicious seafood sold from the temporary fishing village of shacks and vendors on the beach.

Keep your ears peeled for *klapa* singers. Their style and songs are specific to Rab and the Kvarner region, and the deep liturgical a capella singing makes for a moving experience.

23 Time to UNWIND

SPAS | HEALTH | WELLNESS

Get decadent at Croatia's historic coastal resorts. The Austro-Hungarians selected mainland Opatija and the lush green island paradise of Lošinj during their tenure in Croatia as the ideal spots to set up health resorts. The legacy is still going strong more than 100 years later.

GORAN_SAFAREK/SHUTTERSTOCK ©

How To

When to go Spring and autumn are great times to visit Lošinj, as its microclimate sees sunny days that keep it warmer than neighbouring regions.

Costs Opatija is known for opulent hotels, but if your budget doesn't stretch to that, don't be put off. Holiday apartments in town have manageable rates, and food markets are affordable.

Top tip Opatija hosts an award-winning Christmas Advent market, known for its beautiful lights.

NEW AFRICA/SHUTTERSTOCK ©

Croatia's First Resorts

Opatija and Lošinj were quiet fishing villages and monastery towns until the Austrians built them up in the late 1800s, seeing their potential as seaside wellness destinations. The first spa resorts arrived on Croatia's coastline, they accidentally created the first tourism industry in Croatia.

XBRCHX/SHUTTERSTOCK ©

Spa Talking in Opatija

The Viennese royalty took convalescing, 19th-century wellness speak for getting some R&R, very seriously, and they gave their doctors an important assignment after the Habsburg empire lost Venice and its lido during a war in the 1860s: find a spot to build a new health resort.

Bijou Lošinj

Mali Lošinj is no stranger to international visitors. Centuries ago, holidaying Habsburg-era Austrians built luxurious villas in the suburb of Čikat, next door to Mali Lošinj. More recently, an influx of foreign investment has arrived, and the quaint pastel-coloured houses that line the port feel incongruous next to a hyper-modern marina packed with super yachts.

Above left Aerial view, Boutique Hotel Alhambra and Villa Elizabeth, Mali Losinj
Left Hotel Miramar
Above Spa experience

Opatija was selected for its fresh, salty air and year-round sun, with winter temperatures averaging 10°C.

Today's take on a wellness break is much more advanced than sunshine and sea air, and many hotels in and around Opatija have built iconic spa facilities. The **Miramar**, a heritage hotel that first opened its doors in 1876, has an indoor-outdoor seawater pool, and aqua aerobics, pilates and yoga are all included in the stay. Spa staff adopt a holistic approach to customer care that encourages guests to continue their newly found good habits even after they've checked out.

The **Ambassador Hotel** is a 1960s addition to the coast, with a swish spa that includes a Finnish sauna and Turkish bath. **Ikador Luxury Boutique Hotel and Spa** has gone all out, with a Himalayan salt room to relax in after a session in the steam room or Jacuzzi. You can also book a sound bath and have therapists soothe your soul with

Oldest in Opatija

Hotel Kvarner is the oldest hotel in Croatia and the northern Adriatic, as well as a symbol of Opatija itself, representing the arrival of the Austrian wellness resorts.

The neoclassical building was completed in 1885 and is perched on the waterfront next to the park and several royal villas. The ballroom is as grand as the day it was opened, with chandeliers and original cornices that make the perfect backdrop for its occasional use as a local theatre.

The hotel lobby rooms have a small museum dedicated to the ornate building's history, with a timeline that spans the walls and antique photography.

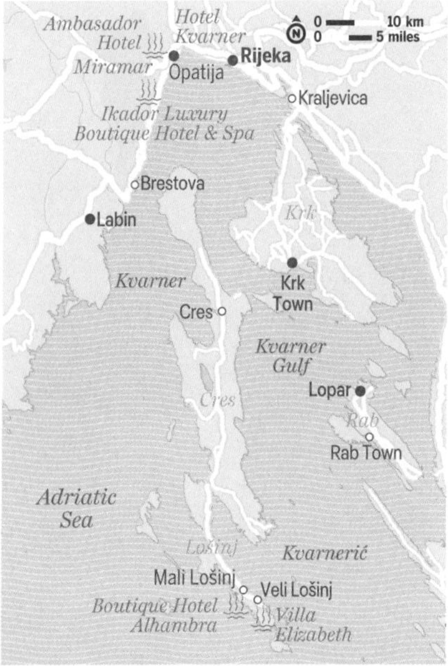

Left Hotel Kvarner
Below Forest, Lošinj

their rare crystal bowls, an instrument for sound healing.

Forest Bathing in Lošinj

Nicknamed the 'island of vitality', Lošinj has been a wellness destination for more than 100 years, and the first Habsburg-era health resorts were built on the island in the 1880s. But the island is also seeing the growth of more modern wellness trends, such as *shinrin-yoku*, the Japanese therapy of 'forest bathing'. It's proven to rejuvenate the immune system and lower blood pressure, reducing stress and promoting relaxation. Lošinj's dense pine forests are the perfect place for it. If the woods are calling, check out the health programmes at **Boutique Hotel Alhambra** and **Villa Elizabeth**, which offer forest bathing sessions with qualified therapists.

24 Rock Out in RIJEKA

MUSIC | LIVE GIGS | COMMUNITY

The busy port city of Rijeka was a music hub for generations of Yugoslavians, and the legacy lives on today. The city's vibrant live-music scene rocks on thanks to its flagship Ri Rock festival and a community of open-minded musicians and creatives.

VIGO MAVROVIĆ ©

How To

Getting here & around Rijeka airport is fully operational all summer, but if you're visiting in other seasons, take the three-hour bus from Zagreb. Rijeka's town centre is walkable.

When to go Ri Rock festival takes place every December, giving a platform to Croatian and Balkan acts, with the occasional international guest appearing too.

Gigs aplenty Pubs and bars in downtown Rijeka host live-music performances most nights of the week.

DARKY DARK/SHUTTERSTOCK ©

A Rocking Legacy

Theories abound as to why Rijeka was Yugoslavia's music capital. It could have been the Liverpool effect: Rijeka was also a busy port city where ships from the USA arrived with the latest rock LPs, so all genres from rock'n'roll to punk rock were more accessible for the youth of Rijeka. Or it could be all the empty warehouses following the city's industrial decline that begged to be used as rehearsal spaces and impromptu gig venues. Whatever the reason, 'yu-rock' (short for Yugoslavian rock) bands poured out of Rijeka across decades and genres, and the city is still considered Croatia's music capital, with new-wave punks Paraf, synth group Denis & Denis and noise rockers Grč still revered today.

MARILENA DRAGOSLAVIC/GETTY IMAGES ©

A Refined Museum

The Rijeka City Museum – Sugar Refinery Palace, a brilliant institution of local history, includes great exhibits on the origins and legacy of the city's music scene, tracing the cultural boom as far back as 1892 through to the punk scene that flourished in the 1970s and 1980s.

Above left Ri Rock Festival
Left Rijeka port
Above Youth Club (p134)

Flying with Let 3

Local institution Let 3, which translates as 'Flight 3', is beloved by rock fans in their hometown of Rijeka, and the band is still belting out raucous punk after 30 years. The often PVC-clad punk outfit was voted as Croatia's entry for the 2023 Eurovision Song Contest, where they performed the enjoyably provocative track 'Mama ŠČ!'. The song has thinly coded lyrics that berate Belarusian President Alexander Lukashenko for aiding Russia's invasion of Ukraine (coded because the Eurovision aims to be nonpolitical), which the band performed while launching faux nukes into the audience.

Going Live

If you want to watch live music in Rijeka, head to the **Youth Club** cafe and bar space. It has a welcoming, studenty vibe but is attended by people of all ages to check out the bands and live music. **Pogon Kulture**

Rijeka Will Rock You

I'm always telling people how cool Rijeka is and what's going on here. The city is full of little bars that the locals like to cruise to see which musicians are playing.

Everyone in Rijeka loves music. Go to as many shows as you can and you'll soon figure out the scene. Talk to people and they'll tell you what's going on.

Most of the live music organisations here also run associations to support LGBTQI+ causes or shelters for those escaping domestic abuse. Now that Let 3 are internationally known, Rijeka music is coming for you.

■ By Vinko Golembiowski
Vice President of Ri Rock, rirock.hr

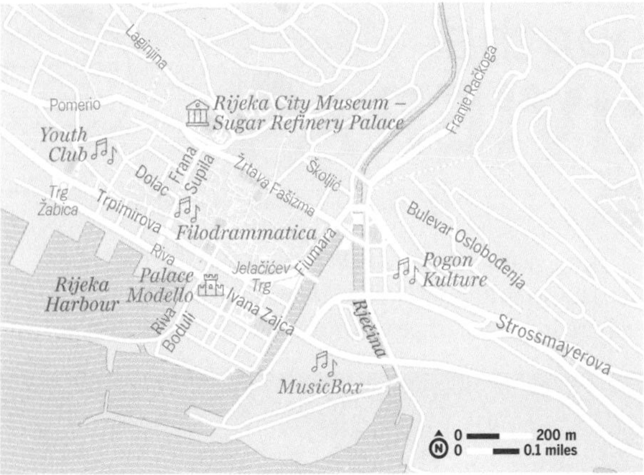

Left Let 3
Below Filodrammatica

is one of the larger spaces for gigs. It's a bit of a dive, but if you're in town when there's a show happening, it's a legit Rijeka punk experience. Ornate 19th-century ballroom **Filodrammatica** is hidden in plain sight, tucked away up some stairs off the main square.

Ri Rock

The Rijeka music scene is still thriving, nourished by the brilliant, award-winning **Ri Rock Festival** that has been going strong for more than four decades. The festival is a community-focused affair, booking pre-dominantly local artists from Rijeka and Istria, as well as a few bigger bands from the Balkans.

Alongside putting on the biggest annual rock festival in the city, the organisation also manages the Ri-Rock Academy music school, which teaches music to all ages, from kindergarten to the elderly, and **MusicBox**, a low-cost but top-quality rehearsal studio for young people to jam or get advice from the festival team. The festival also works with local charities such as SOS Rijeka, a centre promoting nonviolence and human rights, to keep safety and social justice at the forefront of the event.

25 Tour the RIVIERA

MEDIEVAL | RURAL | SCENIC

The small fishing ports and rustic hilltop villages along the Opatija Riviera are far less busy than their coastal counterparts in southern Croatia, making them the perfect getaway for travellers in search of peace, quiet and unspoilt charm.

XBRCHX/SHUTTERSTOCK ©

Trip Notes

Getting around Hiring a moped is a great way to get around this rural part of the country. The roads are smooth, and the views are spectacular.

When to go Spring, summer and autumn are perfect for exploring the Riviera villages. Beware of winter winds.

Eat your heart out The restaurants in these villages are incredible, particularly those on the water's edge. Pack your appetite.

Artistry Like No Other

In the village of Golovik, Mr Velčić presents his own backyard museum, Atelier Terrarium, at his two-floor studio. In his retirement, Velčić makes intricate 3D scenes carved from soft wood, featuring local flora and fauna and ethnographic scenes from bygone eras. To visit, call +385 91 507 8322 and bring a translator with you.

01 Pint-sized **Volosko** (pictured left) has a strong foodie scene, particularly around the harbour. Take in the cobbled streets and rustic vibes after a seafood feast at the excellent Trattoria Mandrać.

02 **Lovran** is a picturesque and historically rich medieval port town with interesting architecture, lanes full of old-world charm, and a great food scene.

03 The fishing village of **Mošćenička Draga** is tiny but densely populated. It has some of the best seafood restaurants in the country and a strong nautical tradition.

04 **Mošćenicea**, a medieval gated hilltop hamlet, is a charming village that's home to a perfectly preserved, horse-powered olive-oil mill, which is a real rarity. It's open from 11am to 3pm daily.

05 Built into the rocks, teeny clifftop **Brseč** is a humble village historically populated with agricultural workers. It's pure serenity, with just one shop and the world's smallest theatre.

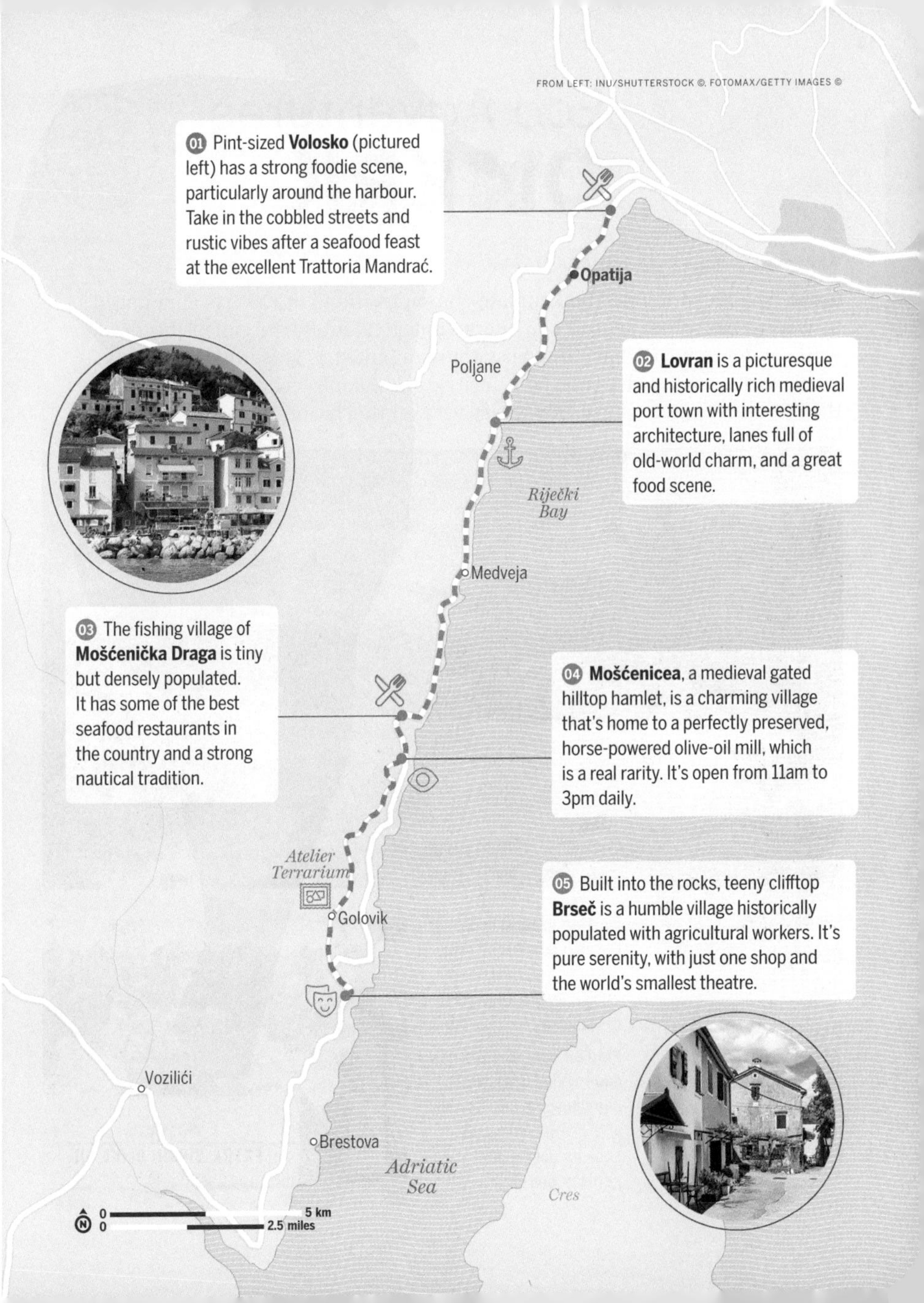

26 Eco Adventures ON KRK

GREEN | LOCAL STAYS | SUSTAINABLE

The green-minded and climate-conscious island of Krk has announced its goal to be carbon neutral and energy independent by the end of this decade while maintaining its booming, busy tourism industry. This initiative will be music to the ears of visitors who prioritise sustainable, eco-friendly travel, as the options for green stays grow every year on this beautiful island.

NINOPAVISIC/SHUTTERSTOCK ©

How To

Getting there It's easy to get to Krk without flying: buses head straight to Krk from Zagreb; from Rijeka, local buses head over the bridge connecting the island to the mainland.

Getting around Local buses run by Arriva drive up and down the island and serve the ferry port of Valbiska.

Find an eco-stay Krk has eco-minded B&Bs and camping or glamping sites with green credentials. Look for details on booking websites.

JAN GALLO/SHUTTERSTOCK ©

Left Wild sage
Far left Krk
Below left Olive oil, market stall

Leading the way to a greener Mediterranean Can an island with 20,000 inhabitants and 100,000 tourists in the summer become carbon neutral? The residents of Krk are working to find out. These islands have an ancient symbiotic relationship with nature – whether it be seasonal farming or using local herbs for healing – and are at one with their home.

Tour guides tell stories of the 1850 cholera epidemic on Krk, when wise locals kept a sponge full of vinegar under their noses and massaged local herbs such as peppermint, sage, lemon mint, thyme and pellitory of the wall to restart circulation – cholera was known as the 'blue death' for slowing the blood flow.

Today, the islanders are once again looking to nature for solutions. They are installing solar-powered systems and training locals to become solar installers. Keeping in line with the goal of zero emissions, the number of wind farms and turbines is increasing, with the aim of generating a mix of 60% solar power, 30% wind and 10% biomass by 2030. Krk is moving towards energy autonomy, hoping to reach it by 2030, and has become a role model for the whole Mediterranean region, showing that carbon neutrality and tourism can go hand in hand and needn't be mutually exclusive.

Living the Krk Life

I couldn't live anywhere else – we have such a good quality of life on Krk. We're a green island, with self-sufficient water use and are working towards becoming zero waste.

The nature is incredible: we have the richest biodiversity of any island in the Mediterranean, so we're mindful to preserve it and to consume biodynamic produce, like our sheep's cheese or olive oil. It's so safe and peaceful here, and it's ideal for families: our children and elderly are well taken care of.

It's easy to drive a scooter or walk to find a secluded, peaceful corner of the coast.

■ **By Slanica Peričić**
storyteller and Krk tour guide

27 Dolphin Watching IN LOŠINJ

WILDLIFE | NATURE | ADVENTURE

Fans of cetaceans will be glad to hear that the Adriatic Sea is home to bottlenose dolphins, which are carefully studied by the Blue World Institute in Veli Lošinj. This marine life organisation runs conscientious dolphin-watching trips in an ethical way. Dive into this delightful day out and mosey around the colourful, quaint seaside town of Veli Lošinj afterwards.

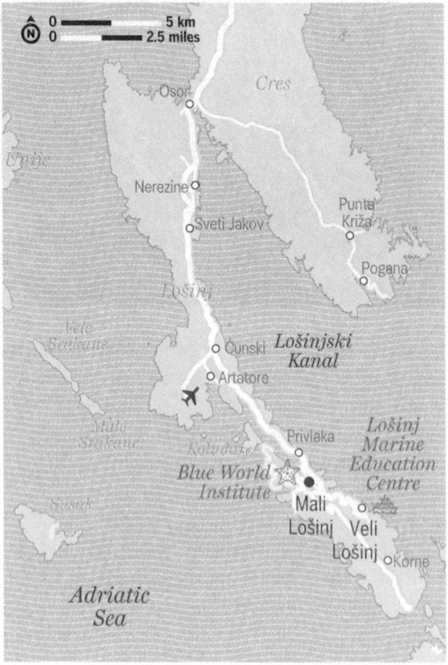

How To

Getting there Veli Lošinj is a small town at the southeasternmost point of Lošinj. By public transport, you can take a bus from Zagreb or Rijeka as far as Mali Lošinj.

Getting around Buses don't go beyond Mali Lošinj, so you'll need to hire a car, moped or local taxi between villages.

When to go The institute's dolphin-spotting boat leaves daily at 1pm from late spring through autumn.

Croatia's leading light in marine biology Founded in 1999, the **Blue World Institute** studies the bottlenose dolphin population of the Adriatic from Veli Lošinj, Vis and Murter using noninvasive photo identification methods, setting the example of ethical ways to interact with these beloved mammals.

A learning hub Since the opening of the **Lošinj Marine Education Centre** in Veli Lošinj in 2003, the passionate team has run seasonal dolphin-watching tours that cruise the east coast of Lošinj to see if any of the 200 local bottlenoses are in the mood to say hello. You'll know when they are: jumping is their form of socialising, and the dolphins communicate by banging their tail on the water.

Good practice To find a pod, skippers use binoculars (the institute does not use tracking devices, and the dolphins are completely wild) and follow fishing trawler ships just as the hungry, fish-seeking

Ethical Wildlife Watching

When you choose a dolphin-watching trip, ask questions. Nobody can guarantee that you'll see dolphins, so that's a sign not to go with them if they do. They'll be chasing dolphins, and that's not good.

We're not against companies running dolphin-watching trips – there are quite a few here in Lošinj that do it – but it should be done the right way.

Boats should approach dolphins sideways, not directly head on or from the back; keep a distance of at least 50m; maintain gentle behaviour; turn off the engine when near; and stay no more than 30 minutes with a pod.

■ **By Barbara Sucich**
educator at Lošinj Marine Education Centre, @dolphin watching.adriatic

dolphins do. The centre prints code-of-conduct leaflets that it distributes around the island at the beginning of the summer to remind other dolphin-watching tour leaders how to treat these finned friends with respect and care.

Money matters As well as paying for your excursion, the fee (adult/child €60/50) goes towards supporting the work of the marine biologists who also run a rescue centre for the loggerhead sea turtles that hibernate in Lošinj (not open to the public).

Bottlenose dolphin.

Listings

BEST OF THE REST

Buzzy Bars

Book Caffe Dnevni Boravak
Understated and effortlessly cool, this Rijeka cafe by day and bar by night is a favourite with locals for its welcoming ambience and great live music, including weekly jazz and open-mic events.

Celtic Caffe Bard
This fun, popular Irish bar next to the Cathedral of St Vitus in Rijeka hosts live music most nights of the week and serves the best range of craft beers.

Nemo Pub
Down-to-earth alfresco drinking by the river in Rijeka. Sip on beers, wines or an Aperol Spritz, served with love at reasonable prices.

Cafe Bar Triton
A Mali Lošinj institution, this vibrant waterfront bar hosts bands throughout the summer. It has the best cocktail menu on the island, and drinks are presented with flourish and care.

Cultural Hits

Museum of Apoxyomenos
One of the highlights of Kvarner, this wonderfully designed museum in Mali Lošinj houses an incredibly rare, truly stunning Greek bronze Apoxyomenos, which was pulled out of the sea perfectly preserved.

Maritime and History Museum of the Croatian Coast
This local history museum with a nautical twist is housed in a huge 19th-century palace in Rijeka. It has interesting temporary exhibitions as well as unexpected artefacts like a *Titanic* life vest.

Rijeka City Museum – Sugar Refinery Palace
Another local history museum in an interesting heritage building, this institution focuses on the arts, design and music from Rijeka, as well as the city's development.

Seafood Restaurants

Seafood Restaurant Feral €€
An enjoyably quirky fish restaurant with nautical decor and a homey vibe in Rijeka, serving huge portions at good prices.

Bistro Mornar €€
On the quayside downtown, Mornar is a Rijeka favourite known for its delicious fresh seafood, and is one of the best places to eat in the city.

Maslina €€
Tucked away in a small square off the Korzo in Rijeka, this great Italian restaurant serves squid ink spaghetti to die for and the best pizza around.

Bistro Yacht Club €€
A tiny seafood restaurant and down-to-earth gem in Opatija, with tables inside and a lucky few on the harbour's edge. Order the divine *bacalar bianco* (codfish paste with garlic) with the catch of the day.

Celtic Caffe Bard

Plavi Podrum €€€

This fine-dining spot in Volosko is an elegant treat, from the huge floor-to-ceiling windows to the haute cuisine dishes of unusual pairings with squid ink galore.

Ganeum €€

A cosy bistro in Lovran. Whether you go for shellfish, grilled fish or beef, you won't be disappointed.

Konoba Zijavica €€€

Preparing incredible fish plates is in the blood at one of Croatia's finest JRE restaurants (a French organisation that honours top young chefs). Chef Stiven's father has a fishing background, and his wife creates incredible sweets.

Konoba Pescaria €€

A traditional Croatian approach to freshly caught grilled fish, shrimp and more, served in huge portions at reasonable prices at this dockside spot in Mošćenička Draga.

Konoba Nono €€

Delicious calamari, delectable locally caught mussels and the best *pljukanci* (tube-shaped) pasta on the island; it's a struggle to choose what to order at this place in Krk Town.

Konoba Bonifacic €

Reserve ahead for a sea-view table at this great garden restaurant in Osor that specialises in grilled fish steak, mussels and langoustines.

Cool Cafes

Grad

On the Rijeka waterfront, Grad is a great place to sit outside with an espresso and a slice of the exemplary cake delivered fresh from Patisserie Kaokakao in Volosko.

Štriga

This cosy, booth-sized cafe at the top of Rijeka's canal basin is a local favourite, with an excellent coffee menu and indoor or outdoor seating to watch the world go by.

IVAN NEMET/SHUTTERSTOCK ©

Maritime and History Museum of the Croatian Coast

Academia Coffee House

In the heart of Rijeka's old town centre, this spot is a chic respite from the hubbub, serving the best coffee in the city and great snacks for sightseeing fuel.

Caffe Bar Mimoza

In a town full of bijou cafes and cake shops, Mimoza is a local secret in Opatija, serving great, cheap coffee on a sun-drenched balcony up the street from the town centre, where most tourists don't venture.

Krk Olive Oil

Utla Olive

The award-winning olive farmers at Utla in Malinska are happy to give you a tour of their olive groves, followed by an olive-oil tasting. You won't leave empty handed.

Nono Oleoteka

Located in Krk old town, the proprietors of one of the best restaurants on the island make their own olive oil at a press in their tavern. Grab a bottle before they sell out.

Krk Olive Oil 10-30-10

Divine olive oil grown and pressed by OPG (family farm) David Mrakovčić just outside the quaint village of Vrh. Drop him a line via the website to visit (ulje103010.com/103010-en).

Scan to find more things to do in Kvarner

NORTHERN DALMATIA
ANCIENT | ACTIVE | COASTAL
Experience Northern Dalmatia online

NORTHERN DALMATIA
Trip Builder

Northern Dalmatia has it all: ancient cities and towns, five national parks, incredible gastronomy and a sailing scene that travels to islets and coves. Yet the region is quieter than its southern counterparts, meaning this region's treasures are yours for savouring.

Sail to the crystal blue waters of **Ugljan** (p159)
1½hr from Zadar

Taste local produce flavoured by the landscape in **Zadar** (p150)
25min from Zadar International Airport

Marvel at the Renaissance architecture in serene **Šibenik** (p160)
30min from Zadar

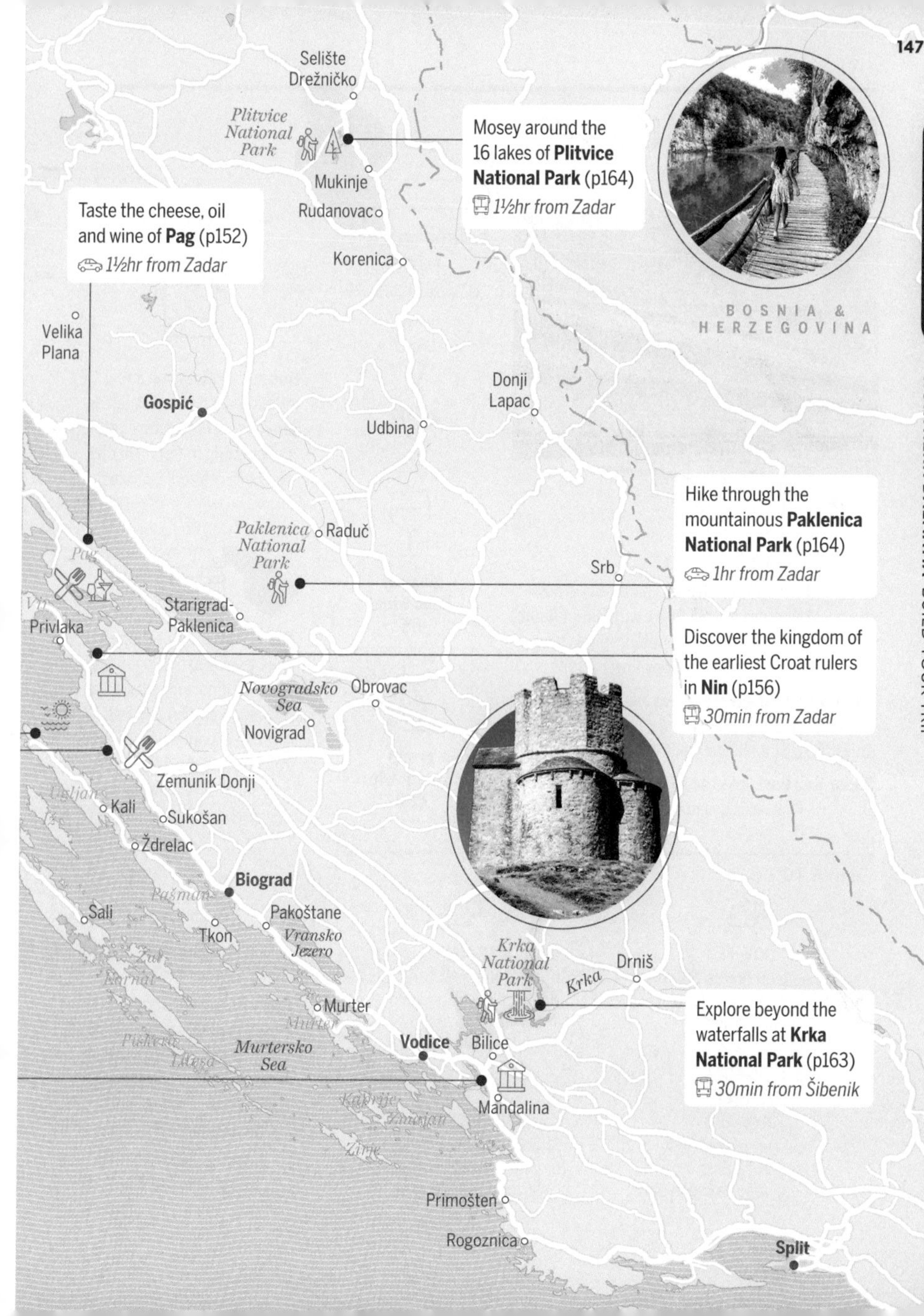
Mosey around the 16 lakes of **Plitvice National Park** (p164)
1½hr from Zadar
Taste the cheese, oil and wine of **Pag** (p152)
1½hr from Zadar
Hike through the mountainous **Paklenica National Park** (p164)
1hr from Zadar
Discover the kingdom of the earliest Croat rulers in **Nin** (p156)
30min from Zadar
Explore beyond the waterfalls at **Krka National Park** (p163)
30min from Šibenik
Selište Drežničko
Plitvice National Park
Mukinje
Rudanovac
Korenica
BOSNIA & HERZEGOVINA
Velika Plana
Gospić
Donji Lapac
Udbina
Paklenica National Park
Raduč
Srb
Pag
Starigrad-Paklenica
Privlaka
Novogradsko Sea
Obrovac
Novigrad
Zemunik Donji
Ugljan
Kali
Sukošan
Ždrelac
Biograd
Pašman
Sali
Tkon
Pakoštane
Vransko Jezero
Krka National Park
Krka
Drniš
Murter
Murtersko Sea
Vodice
Bilice
Mandalina
Primošten
Rogoznica
Split

Practicalities

ARRIVING

Zadar International Airport (pictured) is a 25-minute drive from the old town, with direct flights from London and other European capital cities landing in summer. Winter sees fewer flights.

Zadar Bus Station has Arriva and Flixbus services from Rijeka and Zagreb, most of which travel onwards to Šibenik and Split.

Zadar Sea Port links the islands of Ugljan, Dugi Otok and Kvarner's Lošinj by ferry.

HOW MUCH FOR A

gelato €2

glass of local wine €5

group sailing trip €50

GETTING AROUND

Bus Local buses link Zadar to other coastal towns, such as Šibenik and Primošten, before terminating in Split. Flixbus runs international services.

Car Hiring a car or moped is the best for exploring inland destinations, including Lika, Paklenica, Nin and Pag (which is connected to the mainland by bridge). Public buses from Zadar do not regularly serve these areas.

Ferry Boats link Zadar to the islands of Ugljan and Dugi Otok. Zadar is a huge sailing hub, and it's easy to arrange day trips or chartered boats. Šibenik also offers sailing trips and ferries to its nearby island of Zlarin.

WHEN TO GO

NOV–FEB
Off season brings quieter streets and cheap accommodation.

MAR–MAY
Spring is the best time for cyclists, hikers and sailors who like to dodge crowds.

JUN–AUG
Peak summer is busy, and temperatures soar in the cities; head to the islands.

SEP–OCT
Shoulder season is best for beach lovers, bringing warm days and seas.

EATING & DRINKING

Local chefs swear by the benefits of their 'Mare Monte' location between the sea and Velebit mountains. The geography lends the meats and cheeses a particular flavour, infused by salt from the sea and wild sage that grows among the grasses. The sea-to-table platters are particularly rich, as the smaller fish in the northern Adriatic have a tastier flavour than those further south. Consequently, Northern Dalmatia's gastro scene has some of the finest seafood and lamb in the country, with Michelin-listed restaurants and local food festivals gracing both Zadar and Šibenik.

Best pašticada beef
Tinel (pictured right top; p166)

Must-try scampi in truffle sauce
Foša (p152)

CONNECT & FIND YOUR WAY

Wi-fi Free wi-fi is available in public areas in Zadar and Šibenik.

Mobile phones Buying a local SIM card is a cheap and effective way to stay online. T Mobile, A1 and Telemach are solid network options and cost around €15 for 30 days of data. There's no mobile signal in the Velebit mountains and much of Paklenica National Park.

CONTEMPORARY ZADAR

The oldest city in Dalmatia has a happening cultural scene, from Banksy exhibitions to contemporary art festivals. Check *zadar.travel* to see what's on when you're in town.

WHERE TO STAY

Whether you're after rural solitude, metropolitan hustle and bustle, or seaside Renaissance towns, North Dalmatia is a prime location, with heritage hotels, holiday apartments, and weird and wonderful countryside stays.

City	Pros/Cons
Zadar	Reasonably priced boutique hotels and apartments throughout the old town.
Lika	Eco-stays are blooming in this rural, off-the-beaten-path county.
Nin	Family-friendly resorts and small B&Bs in this quaint historical town.
Plitvice	Interesting accommodation is sprouting up around Croatia's most famous natural sight, from tree houses to mountain lodges.
Šibenik	A beautiful and budget-friendly town to stay in, full of heritage hotels and holiday apartments.
Krka	The pretty village of Skradin at the foot of Krka National Park has great B&Bs and holiday apartments if Šibenik isn't close enough for you.

MONEY

You get more for your money in Northern Dalmatia compared to other parts of the country. Accommodation, restaurants and activities are comparatively more affordable than in the southern stretches of this region.

28 A Taste of 'MARE MONTE'

FOOD & DRINK | LOCAL EATS | RESTAURANTS

With delectable local produce that's flavoured by salty sea winds and wild sage that sheep graze on the rugged terrain, Northern Dalmatia's culinary secret ingredient is its *mare monte* location, nestled between the Adriatic Sea and the colossal Velebit mountains.

ANDREJ SAFARIC/SHUTTERSTOCK ©

How To

When to go Zadar is a vibrant hub of activity all year round, but the summer sailing season is undeniably glorious.

Sea to table Seafood in Northern Dalmatia is known for being mouth-wateringly delicious, so make reservations at top restaurants, such as Foša in Zadar.

Meat feasts Free-range sheep roam the rugged terrains of Pag and inland Dalmatia, grazing on salted grasses and sage as they go, making for tasty meat and cheese.

INAVANHATEREN/SHUTTERSTOCK ©

PROSTOCK-STUDIO/SHUTTERSTOCK ©

Zadar's Booming Food Scene

Zadar has always been a seafood hub, but its nascent fine dining and gastronomy scene is on the rise. Delicious cuisine has always been a Zadar selling point, thanks to the city's unique position between the sea and the Velebit mountains. But now with two Michelin-recommended restaurants, **Foša** and **Kastel**, and myriad mind-blowing seafood *konobe* (taverns), Zadar is finally getting the recognition it deserves as a culinary hotspot.

Head to the open-air food market **Pijaca**, which has been a trading hub in the city for centuries, and look out for a batch of food festivals that take place in Five Wells Sq, such as the Zadar Tuna, Sushi and Wine Festival in April or the Street Food Festival in September.

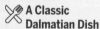

A Classic Dalmatian Dish

You'll spot *pašticada* on menus across Croatia, but it originates from Dalmatia (often called *Dalmatinska pašticada*). The braised beef takes lengthy preparation. It's pierced and filled with cloves of garlic, carrots and bacon, marinated overnight and then cooked in a sweet and sour sauce and served with gnocchi.

Above left Pijaca market
Left Sushi
Above Pag cheese (p152)

The Down-to-Earth Flavours of Pag

A long, thin island that nuzzles the Croatian mainland, **Pag** is wild in more ways than one. Its 60km that stretch from northwest to southeast are mostly tough, rocky terrain whipped by the infamous Adriatic north-northeast wind known as *bura*, giving *Wuthering Heights* vibes to much of the island. It's the *bura* that makes for such a great bounty of food.

Lamb is a popular dish, as the sea-salted wind makes for a flavoursome sage and grass dinner for the free-range sheep. Consequently, the lamb in the region tastes fabulous, as do the sheep's milk and the famous Pag cheese (a hard cheese sold at various ages of maturity, much like wine) and the sheep-milk ricotta. Pag's produce contains lots of omegas and vitamins.

Seaside Šibenik

Unlike many other Dalmatian coastal communities, Šibenik was not a Greek or Roman settlement. Croat King Petar Krešimir IV founded it in the 11th century, strategically

Regional Riches

The star of the Zadar region and our restaurant is the produce. We have truffles, saffron and good-quality Adriatic fish, which are smaller and tastier as they're less salty. We don't overcomplicate things. In my masterclasses, I explain we try to use every part of the fish; fish is not only the fillet. I've been head chef at Foša since 2016, and I've seen a lot of changes in the food scene in the city and the whole of Croatia. We're more open now, learning from international guest chefs and also sharing what we know internationally. We are very proud of the Zadar region.

■ **By Saša Began**
head chef at Foša
@fosarestaurant

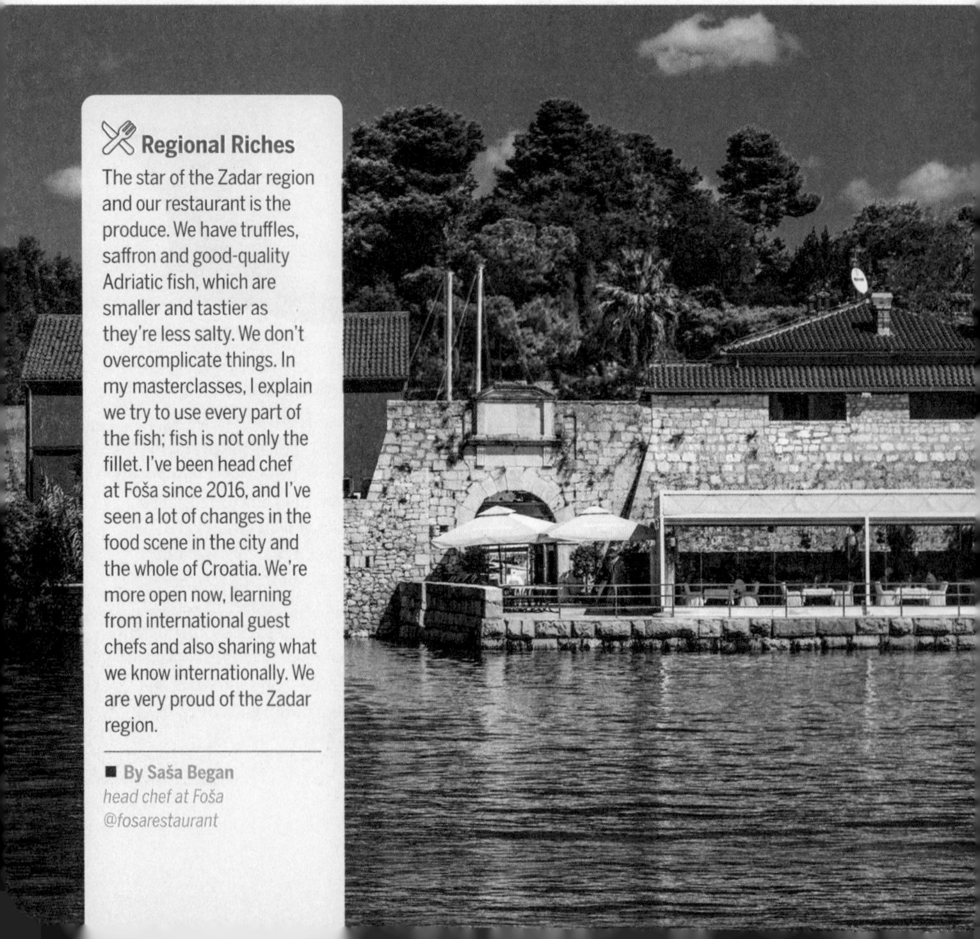

selecting the location for its defensive position in a sea inlet between Zadar and Split. Rich Croatian cuisine is served in this tiny Dalmatian city, which is full of stellar dining options. **Pelegrini**, a star of the foodie scene, has an astounding tasting menu full of modern twists on local cuisine, and Michelin-starred chef Rudolf Štefan uses local produce so fresh you can practically taste the sea air. Dining doesn't come any finer than this.

More humble but just as delicious, **Tinel** dishes up plates in a cute and cosy town-house. Traditional Croatian delicacies include *pašticada* (braised beef) and homegrown dried figs in wine for dessert. For old-school vibes, swing by **Restaurant Uzorita**, which grills fish on a traditional barbecue in the outdoor kitchen, and the catch of the day is roasted to your liking.

Left Foša restaurant
Below Grilled mackerel

29 Every Building Tells A STORY

ARCHITECTURE | HISTORY | CHURCHES

Dig into the fascinating depths of Northern Dalmatia's millennia-spanning history by checking out its jaw-dropping architectural treasures from Roman super-structures to humble churches and medieval cathedrals. The region's buildings tell a local story, no matter whether they date from the 1st or the 21st century.

IAN DAGNALL/ALAMY STOCK PHOTO ©

How To

Getting around Hiring a car or moped is the easiest way to travel between towns.

When to go These magnificent buildings can be admired at any time of the year.

Take a tour Zadar is a hub for excellent tour agencies, such as Art and Nature Travel (art-and-nature-travel.com) and Free Spirit Tours (freespirittours.eu/tours/free-walking-tour-zadar), which know every corner of the city and bring the past alive with boundless enthusiasm.

DVOEVNORE/GETTY IMAGES ©

Old Town Ramble

Zadar's old town is an absolute treasure trove of living history – where else can you find a cafe-bar in an 11th-century church on People's Sq, a bank in a medieval church and a tiny Romanesque church that now serves as a souvenir shop called **Galeria Sv Petar**, which sells gorgeous crafts by local artisans.

What's left of ancient Zadar – 80% of the city was flattened in World War II – has been meticulously preserved. Stunning 1970s modernist architecture, such as the **Archaeological Museum Zadar**, overlooks the best preserved 2000-year-old **Roman Forum** in the country, which neighbours a 21st-century creative masterpiece, the ***Sea Organ***.

Zadar is one of the oldest cities in the Adriatic, founded by the Illyrians in 1000 BCE, who named their metropolis Jader and made

TRABANTOS/SHUTTERSTOCK ©

Fortress on High

St Michael's Fortress in Šibenik feels like a *Game of Thrones* set, and the old town's thin alleys connect to wider lanes that flow up towards the peak of the hilltop fortress. Destroyed and rebuilt numerous times over the centuries, this citadel was first recorded as a church in 1066 and is now home to an open-air auditorium.

Above left Cafe-bar, Church of St Lawrence
Left Roman Forum
Above Stone heads, Cathedral of St James, Šibenik (p157)

it the capital of the Liburnia region, which stretched across Kvarner Bay to the north and encompassed its northern islands.

Knights of Nin

St Nicholas Church, a magnificent medieval structure on the hill as you approach Nin, has stood for 900 years and is much revered because the first Croatian kings were crowned inside. Sadly, the doors are locked, so you can't go in, but it's still impressive from the exterior. The 9th-century **Church of the Holy Cross** is another important monument of early Croatian architecture. It's one of Nin's icons and has remained untouched since its construction.

The Croatian kingdom's early heyday lasted from the 8th to the 13th century, and the dukes, kings and bishops of Nin played a huge part in forming Croatian identity, adopting Christianity and the Glagolitic alphabet and crowning the country's first rulers here. Consequently, local tourists and school trips head to this tiny peninsula town to marvel at the ancient churches.

Sounds of the Sea

Watching the sunset as a spectrum of colours twinkles under your feet and hypnotic tones float from the sea has become *the* blissed-out evening event synonymous with a trip to Zadar.

On the northwestern corner of the old town peninsula, the *Sea Organ* and *Greeting to the Sun* (pictured) are two much-loved sculptural installations by Croatian architect Nikola Bašić. They serve not only as serene spots but also mean a lot to Zadar locals, as the two sculptures have regenerated the waterfront, which was in a bad state for decades.

Zadar University students now relax here between lectures, alongside sunbathing and swimming tourists.

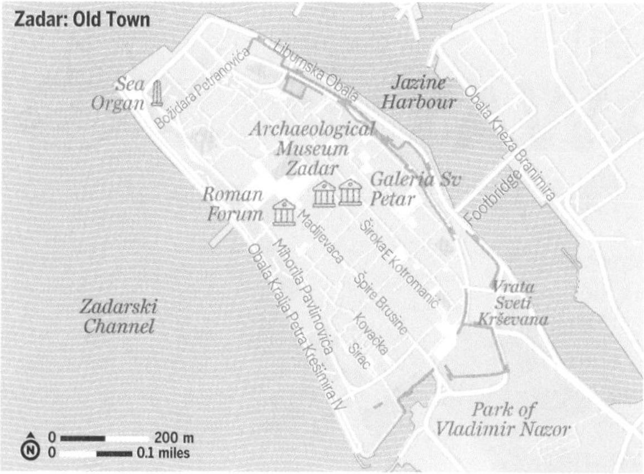

Left *Greeting to the Sun* sculpture
Below Cathedral of St James

Dazzling Šibenik

From the Riva, Šibenik's seaside promenade, stairs sweep up to one of the undisputed jewels of Dalmatian architecture, the **Cathedral of St James**. After 10 years of failed attempts by other builders, Zadar designer Juraj Dalmatinac was brought into the construction project in 1441, and his masterpiece is a jaw-dropping marvel of bright white stone mined from the nearby islands of Brač and Korčula.

Now a UNESCO World Heritage Site, the Cathedral of St James has a montage of architectural styles from different eras. Gothic and Renaissance features are piled on top of one another like a layer cake, and the cathedral was finally completed in 1536. Its most fascinating feature is the frieze of 71 heads that line the outer walls at the city end of the building. The portraits pull all manner of funny faces, from the hilarious to downright scary, and are caricatures of local 15th-century citizens.

30 Sail AWAY

BOATING | ISLANDS | ADVENTURE

Zadar has a long history of mercantile and naval sailing, but now a huge boom in nautical tourism has made the region and its stunning islands a hot spot for cruising the seas. Options abound for every experience level, and you can cruise around gorgeous islands with myriad beaches and coves to discover that are accessible only by sea.

How to

When to go June, July, August and September are prime sailing times.

Day trips Most first-time visitors go for day-long sailing tours with local skippers who lead large sailboats through the channels, stopping at islands to swim or stand-up paddleboard in the aquamarine waters.

Chartering a boat Zadar also has chartered sailing companies that run week-long trips and rent ships to experienced sailors, with a crew or unstaffed if you're fully licensed.

The bays of Dugi Otok Dugi Otok is the longest island in the Zadar archipelago, known for its dazzling beaches. Uninhabited **Veli Žal** is a favourite for its white sands, and **Veli Rat** is famous for its lighthouse surrounded by stunning pebble bays and fragrant pine trees. Secluded **Brbinjšćica** is perfect for diving and snorkelling, bookended by caves and cliffs that protect it from the waves of the open sea.

Zadar's nearest island Ugljan is a real beaut and easy to access by day-tripping ships or a short ferry ride. If you've chartered a boat for a longer sail, the cute port villages of **Preko**, **Poljana** and **Ugljan Town** are worth exploring, but it's the remote coves that are inaccessible by land that you'll want to glide to.

Ugljan's **Uvala Frnaza** bay is a truly spectacular inlet, and the otherworldly aquamarine hues beg you to dive in.

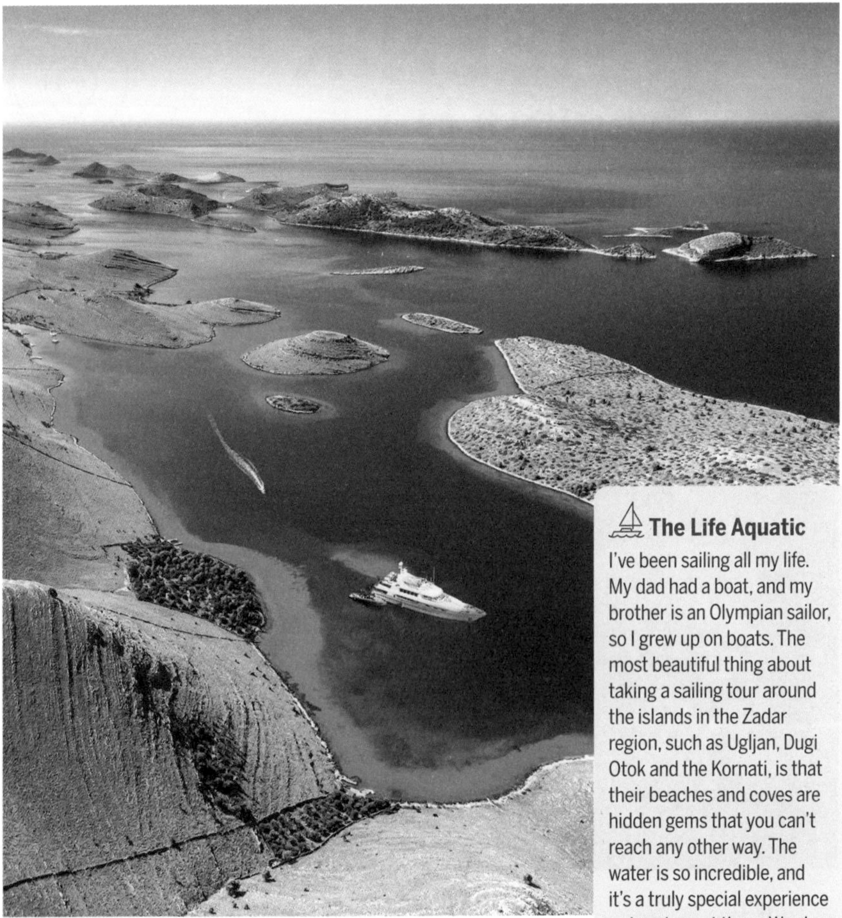

Float further afield A chartered trip from Zadar gives you time to reach the **Kornati**, an archipelago of 89 islands that make up the vast **Kornati National Park**. The rocky islets are sparse and uninhabited, but the reefs around them are home to legions of fish, corals, sponges and a rare, protected mollusc called Pinna nobilis (meaning 'noble pen shell'). Hire a boat through the park (np-kornati.hr) or from agencies in Zadar or Šibenik, which is closer.

The Life Aquatic

I've been sailing all my life. My dad had a boat, and my brother is an Olympian sailor, so I grew up on boats. The most beautiful thing about taking a sailing tour around the islands in the Zadar region, such as Ugljan, Dugi Otok and the Kornati, is that their beaches and coves are hidden gems that you can't reach any other way. The water is so incredible, and it's a truly special experience swimming out there. We also have many regattas, and people come from around the world to compete in them.

■ **By Anna Kostov**
co-owner of Zadar Adventure
@zadaradventure

Kornati National Park

31 ŠIBENIK Lights Up

ILLUMINATIONS | FESTIVALS | HERITAGE

See Šibenik's gorgeous Renaissance architecture and marbled paved streets shine, when the city centre is lit up by the lively, annual Light is Life festival. The festival, which gives a nod to the past while grounding the city firmly in the 21st century, illuminates the old town all evening and night on 28 August every year.

PHOTOPANKPL/SHUTTERSTOCK ©

How To

When to go Light is Life takes place on 28 August every year

Advance reservations Book accommodation in advance if you're attending Light is Life, as many Šibenikers who live around Croatia and elsewhere in Europe return to their hometown for this festival.

Chill with the locals Charming Šibenik has a population of 4000 and fortunately lacks the intense crowds of its Dalmatian coastal counterpart cities.

MATYAS REHAK/SHUTTERSTOCK ©

DUSKO JARAMAZ/PIXSELL/ALAMY STOCK PHOTO ©

Electric origins In 1895, Šibenik lit its streets with the remarkably modern invention of electricity. One of the world's first hydroelectric plants was built on the Krka River that year, the second of its kind following Nikola Tesla's structure at Niagara Falls. Tesla, who was born in the region, had offered his technology to the city of Zagreb, which declined his invention.

Local engineer Ante Šupak, who later became mayor, worked with his son to build the pioneering hydroelectric plant, the remains of which you can still see in Krka National Park, where a huge turbine wheel sits as a reminder that Šibenik became the third city in the world with an alternating current (AC) street-lighting system and the first with a complete system of production, distribution and transmission.

Light is Life today Every year, this momentous 1895 event is celebrated on the anniversary of the town's illumination: 28 August. During the Light is Life festival, Šibenik shines from fortresses to the seafront. Some years, small sailing boats are lit up in the bay, and the light show includes installations, sculptures and fireworks. Concerts and music on the Riva complete the party atmosphere. While the spectacle varies year to year, this festival is absolutely one to time your visit around.

Left Fireworks, Light is Life festival
Far left Hydroelectric plant, Krka National Park
Below left Old turbine, Krka National Park

More Festivals

International Children's Festival
Running for more than six decades, this annual festival in Šibenik takes place over two weeks in June and July and is the oldest festival in the world dedicated to kids' creativity.

SHIP
Across four days of music performances and industry talks in September, Šibenik becomes a stage for genre-spanning acts ranging from classical music to EDM.

Dimensions Festival
Music lovers from around the world flock to tiny Tisno for its summertime EDM festivals, including Dimensions and heaps of others hosted at the Garden Resort.

32 Park LIFE

LAKES | MOUNTAINS | WATERFALLS

Northern Dalmatia is home to five of Croatia's eight national parks. The most popular and accessible scenic spots are Paklenica's rugged mountain range and canyons, or the famously waterfall-laden deep-green oases of Krka and Plitvice.

How To

When to go Spring and autumn provide the best climates for hiking.

Take a tour Countless tour agencies visit Krka and Plitvice national parks. If navigation isn't your strong point, book a tour because the parks are huge.

Guided trek The terrain is tough going in Paklenica, so consider hiring a hiking guide. Zadar-based Mountaineering Association Paklenica (pdpaklenica.hr) helps maintain the park and knows it inside out.

Go With the Flow at Krka

Krka National Park is the second most visited in Croatia, and the park's star is its namesake Krka River, a 73km-long titan that has been the lifeblood of Dalmatia for millennia. Declared a national park in 1985, the 109-sq-km area includes seven waterfalls that cascade over 17 levels. The turquoise, greens and blues of Skradinski Buk waterfall take centre stage in social-media posts and press about the park, but nothing prepares you for seeing them in person. The breathtaking waters rushing 800m before crashing 46m down over the tufa rock formations truly are picture perfect.

With cycling and hiking trails, a handy fleet of boats that link the upper and lower ends of the river, dense green trees, and rare flowers that line the mighty river and falls, Krka National Park is truly marvellous to visit in any season.

Fairy-Tale Falls

'One of my favourite hiking trails in the whole park is the path around the Manojlovački waterfall. You can walk to the bottom of the waterfall and see so many different green colours in the water and the remains of the old watermills.'

■ **By Nikolina Lučić**
educator and interpreter at Krka National Park

Above left Skradinski Buk waterfall
Left Samograd Cave, Grabovača (p165)
Above Boat trip, Krka River

Pretty Plitvice

Croatia's busiest national park, **Plitvice Lakes National Park** is a true wonder of nature – if you visit in the shoulder seasons of spring and autumn, that is. Plitvice is exceptionally busy all summer, but for good reason. The 16 aquamarine lakes are stunning, and the interconnecting waterfalls – one of which, Veliki Slap, is Croatia's highest, at 62m tall – are an ethereal sight. The calcium carbonate in the rushing waters forms a bed of chalky white tufa karst underneath that makes the crisp blues dazzle.

Exploring the paved shores and boardwalks of these aquamarine lakes on foot takes six hours, but you can shave off a couple of hours by taking the park's free electricity-powered boats and connecting buses. Both services leave every half hour from the park's piers from April through October.

If you have just half a day to visit the park, prioritise the lower lakes canyon, known as Route A, to visit Veliki Slap (the Great Waterfall), a must-see from above, as well as a loop of the boardwalks through and beside the lakes.

Paklenica Pro

My favourite thing to do while trekking in Paklenica is to speak with the mountain villagers. They're so funny, and they share their wisdom about the area. The thing I love the most about being in the mountains or Paklenica Canyon is that you have no phone reception, and you're out of range for 24 or 48 hours. It's so peaceful. To get used to hiking, practice walking with 4kg in a backpack, as you'll need to make sure you're carrying 2L or 3L of water with you. Make sure you have a hiking app with offline maps you can save to your phone.

■ **By Dragan Jurjević**
hike leader at Hiking & Adventure Croatia; facebook.com/hikingadventurecroatia

Left Paklenica Canyon
Below Rock climbing, Paklenica National Park

Ain't No Mountain High Enough

The highest peaks of **Paklenica National Park** are Vaganski Vrh (1757m) and Sveto Brdo (1753m). These mountains make for an incredibly scenic backdrop, beloved by hikers and climbers alike, but take heed of the double terrain. The southern, sea-facing side of the mountains is dead hard underfoot and best visited with a guide if you're not a seasoned trekker. The northern Lika side of the range is softer, with grass and mossy ground. Research your route in a lot of detail before you hike or book in with experienced guides like Dragan from Hiking Adventure Croatia (facebook.com/hikingadventurecroatia).

With a grand size of 95 sq km, wild Paklenica sprawls across two counties: Zadar and Lika-Senj. The mighty Velebit mountain range passes through the park: anything south of the road between the seaside town of Karlobag to inland hamlet Gospic is the South Velebit region, formally considered Paklenica National Park.

The lush Lika region is an overlooked corner of Croatia. Aside from the infamous Plitvice Lakes, Lika is still off the beaten path, with only the most dedicated of hikers and ramblers stopping to connect with Croatia's wilder side. Stay a few nights in this nature-rich region and you'll find a lot to explore. Active travellers have loads of activities to dive into, from rafting or canoeing on the Gacka River, horse riding or cycling along the country roads with the Velebit mountains in view, or spelunking in the Grabovača cave complex near Perušić.

Listings

BEST OF THE REST

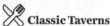

Classic Taverns

Konoba Tovar €

Tuck into delicious seafood at one of the most reasonably priced spots in Zadar. This traditional restaurant has a homey vibe and an excellent menu. Don't miss the mouthwatering mussels.

Restoran Konoba Martinac €€

Get a table on the terrace and choose from the extensive menu of freshly caught seafood and locally sourced meat dishes at this classy spot at the north end of Zadar's old city.

Tomislav €€

In the centre of Nin's old town, this charming spot with a large outdoor terrace serves traditional Croatian fare of braised meats with gnocchi, seafood and more.

Tinel €€

This homely restaurant (quite literally – it's in a house in Šibenik's old city) is beloved for its delicious menu of Dalmatian classics and warm, welcoming decor and staff.

Bijou Bars

Bastini Wine & Cocktail Bar

Hosts Bruno and Jakov are shaking up Zadar old town's drinking scene with delicious cocktails served on an elegant terrace up on the city walls, overlooking the marina below.

Colonna Bar & Caffe

One of Zadar's best-kept secrets, this airy outdoor spot with views of the column it's named after serves inventive cocktails made with fresh local ingredients, including the best negroni in town.

Jack Rabbit Slim's

This small terrace bar is tucked away in Šibenik's old town centre and pours delicious fruity signature cocktails as well as longstanding favourites made by charming mixologists.

Fine Dining

Foša €€€

Award-winning chef Saša Began insists he's not the star of this Michelin-recommended waterfront haven in Zadar, but his ingenious approach to fish in presentations both raw and cooked certainly is.

Kaštel €€€

Zadar's other Michelin-recommended spot is named after the 13th-century castle it sits within. It's a treat for the taste buds whether you go for the exceptional seafood or local lamb.

The Botanist €€

Zadar's only plant-based restaurant takes a fine-dining approach to vegan food, with beautifully presented plates of seitan so that vegetarians don't miss out on the exquisite flavours of traditional Dalmatian cuisine.

GORAN_SAFAREK/SHUTTERSTOCK ©

Burnum Roman Ruins

Pelegrini €€€

Local chef Rudolf Štefan has a Michelin star for a reason. This Šibenik restaurant is magnificent, from service to decor, and the seasonal tasting plates are divine.

Sail the Seas

Marlin Sailing

Veterans of the scene, Marlin offers single- and multiday sailing tours, as well as a sailing school to teach budding mariners the ropes.

Zadar Adventure Sailing

Join Anna on one of her small sailing boats to whizz around the Zadar channel and beat the crowds to the best swim spots. Lunch is included, and SUP boards are available on request.

Red Sails Boat Rentals Zadar

This ace company has a small fleet of speed boats for hire at reasonable rates (starting from €120 a day). For a little extra, a friendly skipper joins you to do the hard work.

Roam the Ruins

Roman Forum

Arriving in the 1st century BCE, the Romans built an extremely rare forum in Jadera (aka Zadar), with multiple shop sizes, two floors and a gallery – a Roman mall if you will.

Burnum Roman Ruins

Just off the road from Kistanje to Knin are the remains of the only Roman military amphitheatre in Croatia. The two magnificent white arches of a ruined aqueduct are just around the corner.

Roman Temple & Villa

The remains of prosperous Roman Aenona are striking in petite Nin old town, where the ruins of a temple and foundations of a large villa date from the 2nd century CE.

FABIAN JUNGE/SHUTTERSTOCK ©

Šibenik Museum

Mighty Museums

Archaeological Museum Zadar

This wonderful institution is humble in size, but it truly brings Roman Zadar to life. The museum is full of astounding sculptures of Roman leaders so large that you feel the imposing might of their empire.

Museum of Ancient Glass

Up in the Zadar city walls in an old heritage building, this glassware museum shows the sophistication of local artisans through the ages. It also runs workshops and has live glassmaking displays.

Solana Nin Salt Museum

Salt farming has never been explained in such a fascinating way, and to understand this ancient industry is to understand the wealth of Zadar and the region for centuries.

Šibenik City Museum

This beautifully curated local-history museum behind the cathedral is finicky to find but persevere as it's laden with treasures that outline the city's rich history.

Scan to find more things to do in Northern Dalmatia

SPLIT & CENTRAL DALMATIA

HISTORY | ISLANDS | WINE

Experience Split & Central Dalmatia online

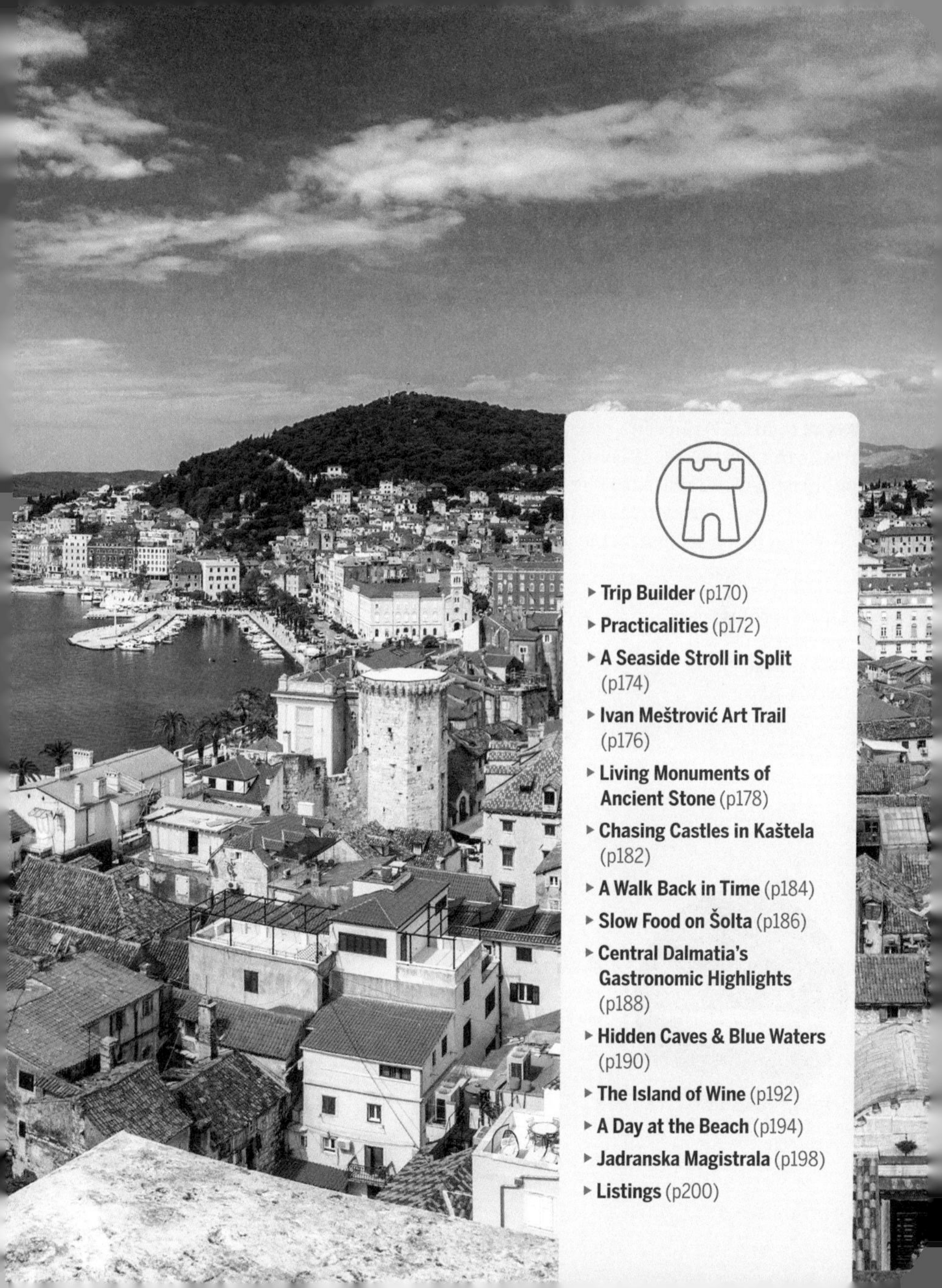

SPLIT & CENTRAL DALMATIA
Trip Builder

Central Dalmatia's towns and cities are treasure troves of heritage architecture and artworks adorning public spaces. Endless beaches and countless islands conceal scenic coves and natural wonders. Other big draws include excellent wine and many gourmet delights.

Cycle among the castles and vineyards of **Kaštela** (p182)
20min from Split

Explore living mini-cities protected by UNESCO, such as **Trogir** (p180)
40min from Split

Savour the gastronomic delights of **Šolta Island** (p186)
1hr from Split

Be dazzled by the glowing waters of ethereal caves of the **Vis Archipelago** (p190)
30min from Vis

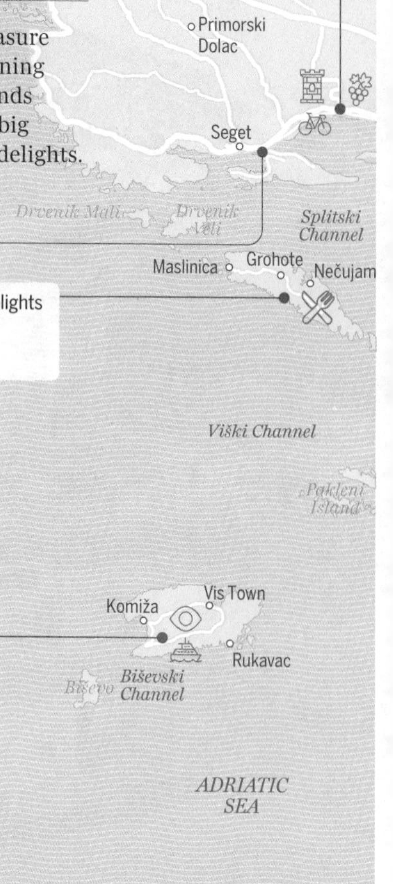

Discover the creations of **Ivan Meštrović**, Croatia's celebrated sculptor, in Split (p176)

15min from city centre

Take a stroll along the buzzing **seaside promenade** in Split (p174)

5min from the main bus station

Hike to a remote hillside hermitage locked in time on **Brač** island (p184)

30min from Dragavoda

Get to know the exquisite wines of **Hvar** island (p192)

2hr from Split

FROM LEFT: BKOLODZIEJ/SHUTTERSTOCK ©, MICHAEL WARWICK/SHUTTERSTOCK ©, TRABANTOS/SHUTTERSTOCK ©, PREVIOUS SPREAD: DALIU/GETTY IMAGES ©

Practicalities

MARKUS MAINKA/SHUTTERSTOCK ©

ARRIVING

Split Airport (pictured) has direct air connections to many European destinations. A shuttle bus takes passengers from Split Airport (located in Kaštela) to Split's city centre, 22km away.

Split Bus Station has intercity services that link all major towns and cities along the Dalmatian coastline, as well as the capital of Zagreb.

Split's port is adjacent to the bus station. Ferries sail to the islands of Central Dalmatia and beyond.

HOW MUCH FOR A

coffee
€2.50

glass of *plavac mali* wine
€2.50

bowl of brodet (fish and polenta)
€9

WHEN TO GO

JAN–MAR
Sunny winter days are perfect for hiking and cycling.

APR–JUN
The tourist season begins, but the islands can still be quiet.

JUL–SEP
Temperatures and crowds peak in July and August, but September is perfect.

OCT–DEC
Coastal towns slow down, while tourist spots close on the islands.

GETTING AROUND

Car Having your own transportation is the easiest way to get around, especially if you're travelling with family. Beware of high parking fees during the summer season. Fares for car ferries to the islands are expensive, so consider hiring a vehicle on arrival instead.

Bus Buses connect major towns and cities along the Dalmatian coast.

Ferry Regular car and passenger ferries connect Split to nearby islands. Travelling by boat is also an option between coastal destinations on the mainland, providing a quicker and more comfortable way to get around, albeit at a higher cost. Look for taxi boats or private boat transfers and tours.

EATING & DRINKING

Not surprisingly, fresh fish and seafood dominate menus in coastal Dalmatia. Fried octopus and squid (pictured right top) are firm favourites while *crni rižoto* (cuttlefish risotto) is a local delicacy. *Peka* is the name of a bell-like pan and the traditional method of cooking meals on an open fire that adds a distinct flavour to meat, fish and vegetables. No meal is complete without a generous dose of extra virgin olive oil and a glass of excellent Dalmatian wine, rounded off with a stiff shot of homemade *rakija* (pictured right bottom; grappa).

Must-try wine
Drnekuša, Hvar's rare red (p193)

Best olive oil
Olynthia (p187)

CONNECT & FIND YOUR WAY

Wi-fi Most cities and towns have public internet hot spots, especially those with high visitor numbers. All hotels and many cafes, bars and restaurants provide free wi-fi access. Connection speeds can be spotty in the summer tourist season when networks reach saturation.

SIM cards Many mobile providers offer special SIM cards and data packages catering to tourists at a reasonable cost.

WHERE TO STAY

Set yourself in the centre of the action or search for a quiet escape. Choose your destination according to the vibe you're looking for.

City	Pros/Cons
Split	Croatia's second city is the hub of the region and a launchpad to the islands. Overtourism is becoming an increasing concern.
Trogir	Charming Trogir is a good alternative to busy Split, thanks to excellent bus connections.
Makarska	A summer beach destination with a dramatic mountain backdrop that attracts hikers throughout the year.
Supetar	Brač Island's main town is well connected to Split and appeals to those who prefer to avoid city hubbub.
Stari Grad	A quiet alternative to the 24-hour party atmosphere of Hvar Town.

DISCOUNT BUS FARE

Use the Promet app to buy discounted bus tickets for travel in Split and its surroundings. Avoid overpriced local taxis and use Uber or Bolt instead.

MONEY

Debit and credit cards are accepted at almost all hotels and most restaurants. However, some cafes and bars may insist on cash only. Don't expect to be able to pay fares by card on buses.

33 A Seaside Stroll IN SPLIT

WALKS | OUTDOORS | SIGHTS

Split is made for walking. A sea-hugging pathway stretches from the main port westwards to Marjan Hill. Along the way, you'll come across ports, parks and plenty of spots to take in sweeping views of the sea and the city.

STOCKINASIA/GETTY IMAGES ©

The Big Picture

Just opposite the southern gate of Diocletian's Palace at the eastern end of the Riva, keep your eyes peeled for a bronze 3D architectural model of Split's old town. Compare it with the 3D model of Diocletian's Palace as it looked in the 4th century, just a few metres away.

Trip Notes

Getting here Start at Split's beloved seaside promenade, called the Riva by locals, an easy walk west from the port.

All dressed up On Saturday mornings, Splićani dress up in their Sunday best and head to the Riva for their weekly ritual of coffee and chitchat.

Mineral waters At the Riva's western end, you'll catch a whiff of sulphur coming from the therapeutic waters that spring up here.

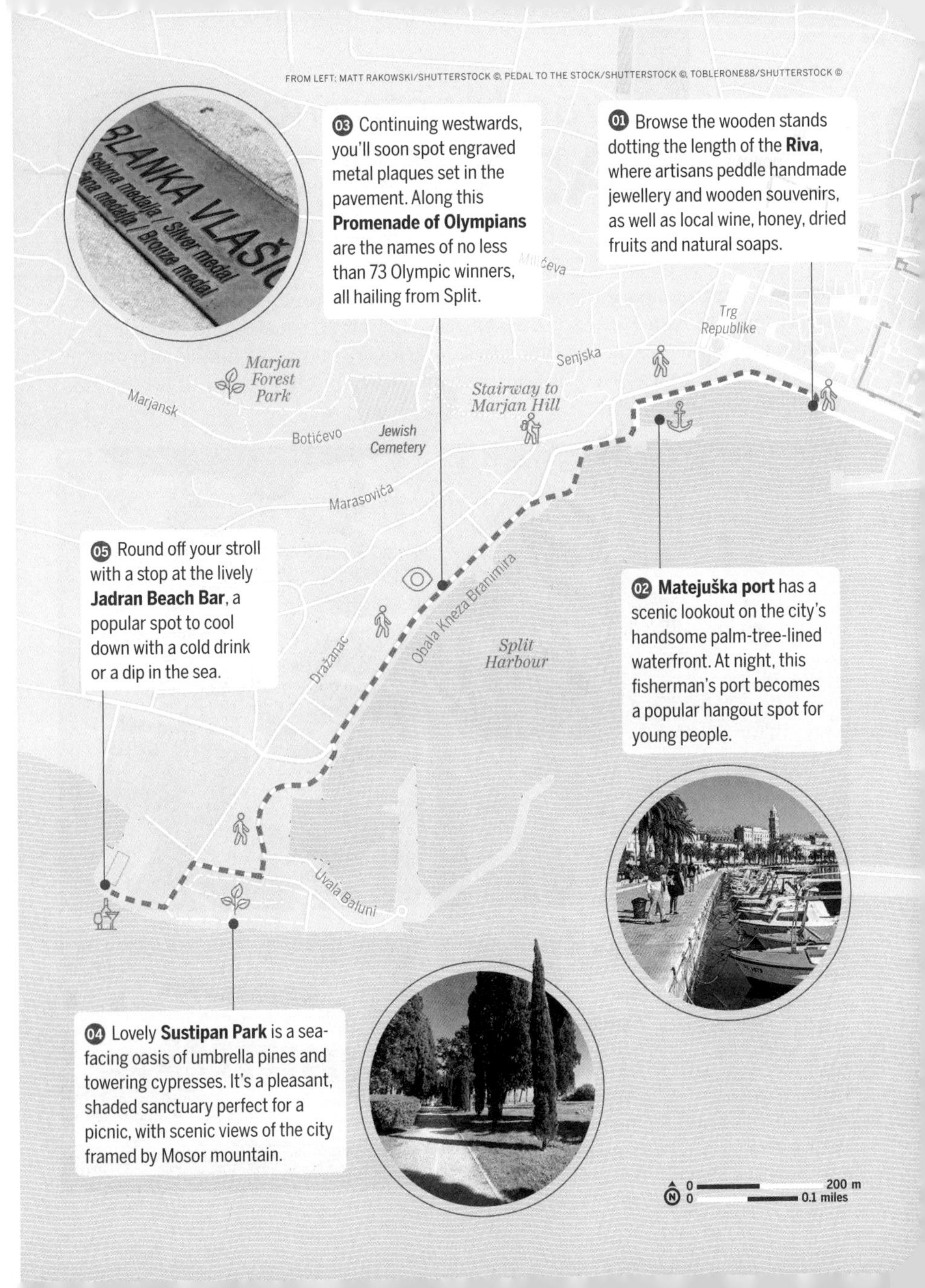

01 Browse the wooden stands dotting the length of the **Riva**, where artisans peddle handmade jewellery and wooden souvenirs, as well as local wine, honey, dried fruits and natural soaps.

02 **Matejuška port** has a scenic lookout on the city's handsome palm-tree-lined waterfront. At night, this fisherman's port becomes a popular hangout spot for young people.

03 Continuing westwards, you'll soon spot engraved metal plaques set in the pavement. Along this **Promenade of Olympians** are the names of no less than 73 Olympic winners, all hailing from Split.

04 Lovely **Sustipan Park** is a sea-facing oasis of umbrella pines and towering cypresses. It's a pleasant, shaded sanctuary perfect for a picnic, with scenic views of the city framed by Mosor mountain.

05 Round off your stroll with a stop at the lively **Jadran Beach Bar**, a popular spot to cool down with a cold drink or a dip in the sea.

34 Ivan Meštrović ART TRAIL

ART | SCULPTURE | MUSEUMS

It's hard to miss the creations of Croatia's most prominent sculptor. The masterpieces of Ivan Meštrović are showcased in urban squares and historical buildings in Split and many other cities. Meštrović's sea-facing family villa and studio are open to art lovers as a permanent gallery of his works, and his bronzes are on display in the gardens.

HANS GEORG ROTH/GETTY IMAGES ©

How To

Getting there The Meštrović Gallery is 2km from Split's main promenade, while Meštrović's Crikvine-Kaštilac is a further 400m down the same road named after the artist. The museums can be reached on Split Promet bus lines 7, 8, 12 and 21.

Opening times Both galleries are open to visitors from 9am to 7pm Tuesday to Sunday.

Tip The same entry ticket allows entry to both museums.

SOPHIE LZD/SHUTTERSTOCK ©

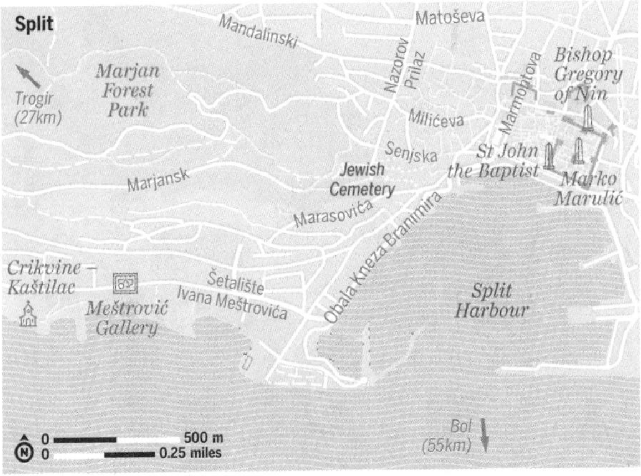

Split: A Meštrović treasure trove Start outside the northern gate of Diocletian's Palace to admire one of Meštrović's best-known works: the 8.5m-high 1929 bronze of **Bishop Gregory of Nin**. Note his shiny big toe that's been rubbed by passers-by for good luck. Next, duck through the gate towards the Baptistery (once a Roman temple to Jupiter) just off the pillared Peristyle. Inside, under its ancient barrel-vaulted ceiling, stands the sculptor's 1953 bronze of **St John the Baptist**. From here, it's a short walk to Braće Radić Sq, where you can marvel at Meštrović's statue of the renowned poet **Marko Marulić**.

The artist's seaside villa below Marjan Hill is now the handsome home of the **Meštrović Gallery**. Get up close to his bronzes in the sculpture garden before moving indoors to examine his other works of bronze, marble and wood, as well as a collection of charcoal drawings. Set in a nearby olive grove is Meštrović's **Crikvine-Kaštilac**, a sea-facing chapel whose walls are decorated with Meštrović's 1916 *Large Crucifix* and 28 wooden reliefs depicting the life of Christ.

Creations in Trogir and Bol Inside the **Venetian loggia** on Trogir's main square, catch sight of a stylised relief sculpture on its south wall of Trogir-born bishop Peter Berislavić, created by Meštrović in 1950. The **Branislav Dešković Art Gallery** in Bol is another showcase of this master sculptor's creations.

Left *Bishop Gregory of Nin*
Below left Meštrović Gallery

Must-See Works in the Meštrović Gallery

Vestal Virgin (1917)
This striking bronze of a seated female figure symbolises a woman as a protectress of the family and the continuity of human life.

Roman Pieta (1942–43)
Meštrović sculpted his own features in the face of Joseph, while Mary Magdalene's face is his daughter's, and Christ's features were modelled after his son. This is a plaster model of a bronze donated to the University of Notre Dame in the USA, where Meštrović was a professor of sculpture.

Job (1946)
Created during his expressionist period, this stylised bronze of a tormented biblical character evokes a traumatic period during WWII when the artist was imprisoned.

35 Living Monuments of ANCIENT STONE

WORLD HERITAGE SITES | HISTORY | ARCHITECTURE

Lovers of architecture should not miss these two star attractions of central Dalmatia, both protected as UNESCO World Heritage Sites. These exquisite open-air museums are living monuments where people still live and work among the ancient walls.

DAVE Z/SHUTTERSTOCK ©

How To

Getting there Split and Trogir are only 25km apart, linked by Promet bus 37, with up to three departures an hour. A quicker option is to hop on an intercity bus headed to Šibenik or Zadar.

When to go These star attractions see many visitors during the summer peak season. Visit early in the day to explore without the crowds.

Tip Pause for a cold drink and people-watching on the seaside promenade.

TMP - AN INSTANT OF TIME/SHUTTERSTOCK ©

Diocletian's Palace in Split

Emperor Diocletian built his massive sea-facing **palace** as his retirement home in the 4th century. Its fortifications cover 38,700 sq metre, enclosing a complex of about 200 age-old buildings: a veritable mini-city.

When nearby Salona fell in the 7th century, the palace welcomed a swarm of new residents, and structures started springing up beyond its walls, creating the foundations of the city of Split. The palace has been continuously inhabited for more than 2000 years, though only a few hundred residents still live within its ancient walls today.

Step through the **Golden Gate** in the northern wall to enter the section of the palace that served as a military garrison.

MATT RAKOWSKI/SHUTTERSTOCK ©

UNESCO Recognition

UNESCO has protected Diocletian's Palace since 1979 as one of the world's biggest and most complete Roman monuments, while the island city of Trogir was inscribed on the organisation's list in 1997 for its old town, which has exceptionally maintained its urban fabric while largely avoiding modern interventions.

Above left Diocletian's Palace
Left Cathedral of St Domnius (p180)
Above *Klapa* singers, Diocletian Palace

From here, follow the **Cardo** (Dioklecijanova), the north–south Roman thoroughfare, to the **Peristyle**, the palace's sublime main square framed by Roman columns, which marks the southern section of the palace that enclosed the emperor's living quarters.

Dominating the square is the octagonal dome built as Diocletian's mausoleum, which became the **Cathedral of St Domnius** in the 5th century. Brave the climb up the 12th-century bell tower for fabulous views over the entire palace complex.

The emperor addressed his subjects from the porch on the Peristyle's southern end, opening onto a domed rotunda and his living quarters beyond. Under the large dome, catch a free concert of *klapa*, a Dalmatian a cappella tradition recognised by UNESCO.

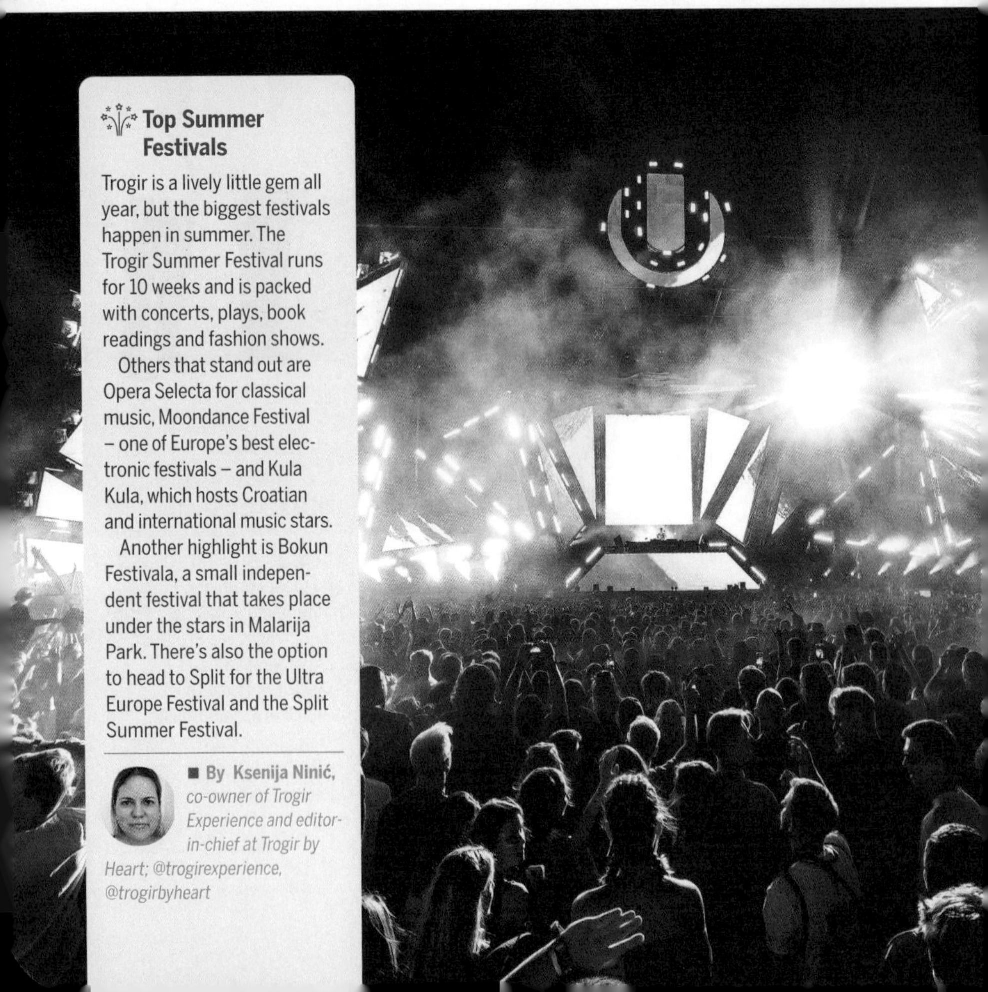

Top Summer Festivals

Trogir is a lively little gem all year, but the biggest festivals happen in summer. The Trogir Summer Festival runs for 10 weeks and is packed with concerts, plays, book readings and fashion shows.

Others that stand out are Opera Selecta for classical music, Moondance Festival – one of Europe's best electronic festivals – and Kula Kula, which hosts Croatian and international music stars.

Another highlight is Bokun Festivala, a small independent festival that takes place under the stars in Malarija Park. There's also the option to head to Split for the Ultra Europe Festival and the Split Summer Festival.

■ **By Ksenija Ninić,** *co-owner of Trogir Experience and editor-in-chief at Trogir by Heart; @trogirexperience, @trogirbyheart*

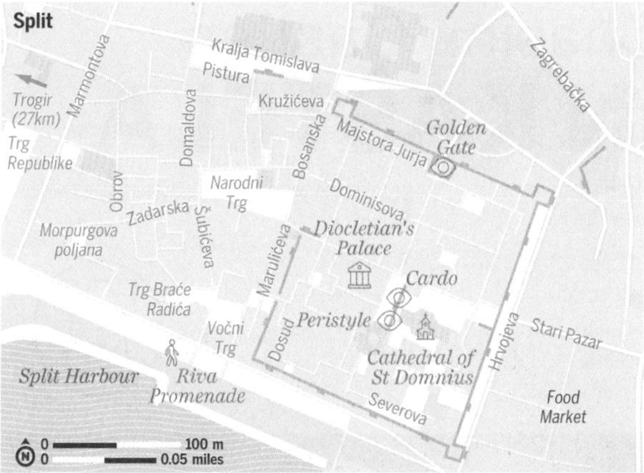

Left Ultra Europe Festival
Below Trogir main plaza

The Island City of Trogir

This historic island city is linked to the mainland and adjacent Čiovo Island via two short bridges. Trogir's old town covers an area of only 6.4 hectares, but it's chock-full of Renaissance and baroque buildings, Gothic *palazzos* and Romanesque churches.

Many of its highlights are concentrated on its lovely main plaza, John Paul II Sq. Start at **St Lawrence's Cathedral**, which has an exquisitely sculpted arched portal depicting scenes from the life of Christ and Adam and Eve balancing on the backs of lions. For a panoramic view over the main square, head up the winding stairwell of the 47m-high bell tower. From here, you have an excellent view of **St Sebastian's Church** and its moon-faced **Town Clock Tower**, one of Trogir's iconic symbols. To the right is the pillared Venetian-style **Town Loggia**, once a meeting place for townsfolk.

Wander Trogir's narrow maze-like lanes of cobblestone and you're bound to come across a church – the city has more than a dozen – or stumble upon a flower-filled courtyard or artist's studio. In any case, you can't get lost, and you'll eventually end up on the buzzing seaside promenade. On the island city's southwestern corner looms the imposing **Kamerlengo Castle**, a 15th-century Venetian fortress. For another viewpoint of Trogir, scale its tower for a panorama over the coral-coloured rooftops and Čiovo Island.

36 Chasing Castles IN KAŠTELA

ARCHITECTURE | HISTORY | WINE

Kaštela is a cluster of seven charming seaside towns connected via a sea-hugging promenade. Each grew up around castles constructed between the 15th and 17th centuries to protect against Ottoman invaders. This coastal stretch is also an important winemaking region.

XBRCHX/SHUTTERSTOCK ©

Trip Notes

Getting here Each of the seven settlements making up Kaštela – from east to west: Kaštel Sućurac, Kaštel Gomilica, Kaštel Kambelovac, Kaštel Lukšić, Kaštel Stari, Kaštel Novi and Kaštel Štafilić (pictured above) – is linked on Split's suburban Promet bus network.

Getting around The seven settlements stretch 8km along crescent-shaped Kaštela Bay, connected by a pleasant, car-free promenade.

Tip Look for NextBike bike-share stations (available everywhere except Kaštel Štafilić).

Zinfandel's Deep Roots

Growing in Kaštela's fertile soil is the native *crljenak Kaštelanski* grape varietal, better known as Zinfandel in California and Primitivo in Puglia, Italy. DNA testing has determined that the three have the same genetic profile and are one and the same, but the grape has its origins in Kaštela.

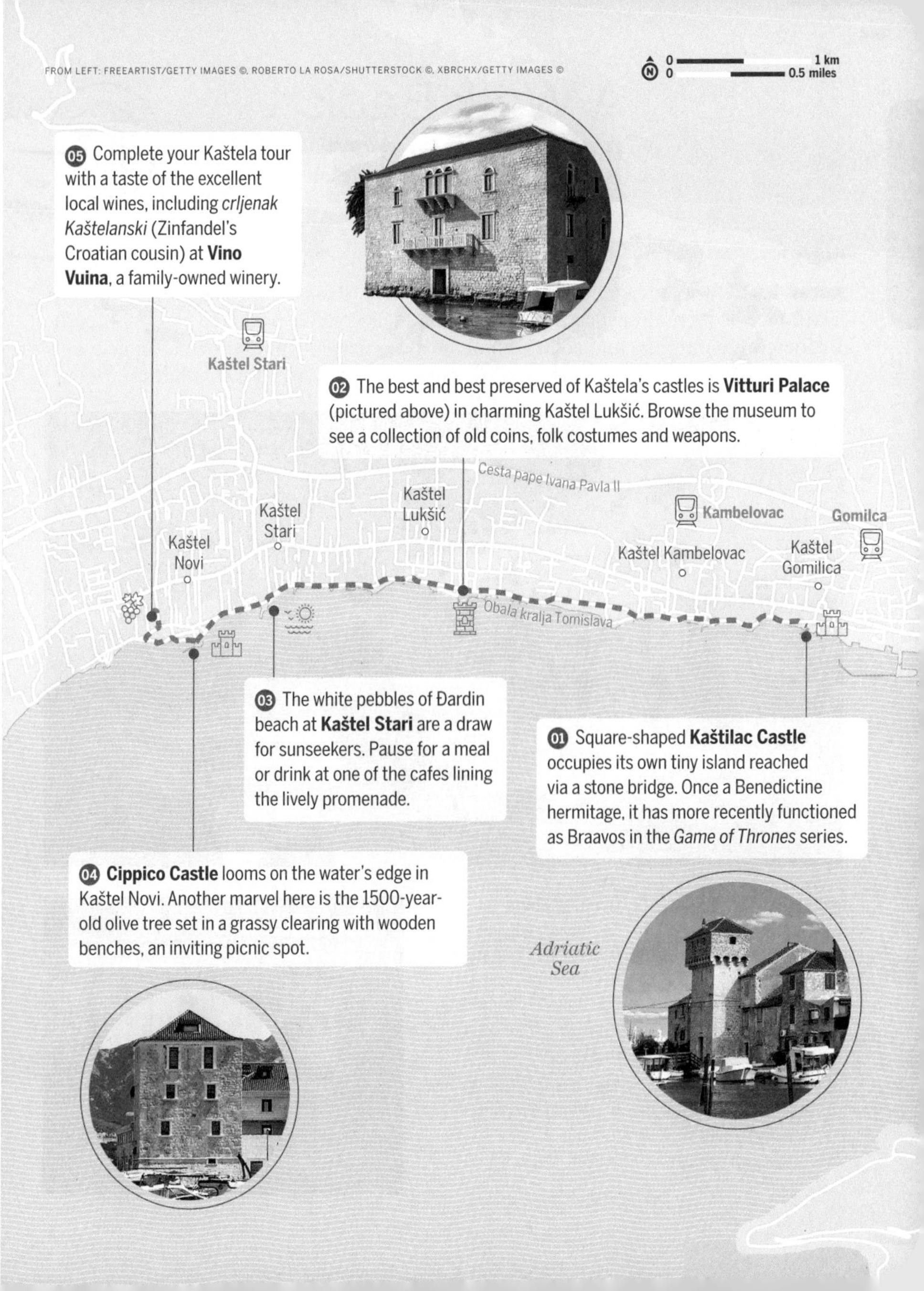

05 Complete your Kaštela tour with a taste of the excellent local wines, including *crljenak Kaštelanski* (Zinfandel's Croatian cousin) at **Vino Vuina**, a family-owned winery.

02 The best and best preserved of Kaštela's castles is **Vitturi Palace** (pictured above) in charming Kaštel Lukšić. Browse the museum to see a collection of old coins, folk costumes and weapons.

03 The white pebbles of Đardin beach at **Kaštel Stari** are a draw for sunseekers. Pause for a meal or drink at one of the cafes lining the lively promenade.

01 Square-shaped **Kaštilac Castle** occupies its own tiny island reached via a stone bridge. Once a Benedictine hermitage, it has more recently functioned as Braavos in the *Game of Thrones* series.

04 **Cippico Castle** looms on the water's edge in Kaštel Novi. Another marvel here is the 1500-year-old olive tree set in a grassy clearing with wooden benches, an inviting picnic spot.

37 A Walk Back IN TIME

HISTORY | HIKING | MUSEUMS

Part of the intrigue of Blaca Hermitage, a cluster of stone buildings built into a cliff face, is its remote location on Brač island, accessible only by a rocky footpath. Its incredible interiors and collection of antique curios seem untouched since the 19th century. Today, it is preserved as a museum, and a visit is a step back in time.

MRAK_HR/GETTY IMAGES ©

How To

Getting there Blaca Hermitage is accessible by two routes that can be negotiated only on foot. From Dragavoda, follow the 2.5km-long marked forest trail downwards or arrive by boat at Blaca Bay and follow the path uphill.

Opening hours The hermitage is open from 9am to 5pm, 15 June to 15 September, and until 3pm from 16 September to 14 June. It's closed on Mondays.

Tip The rocky trail is not demanding but requires sturdy walking shoes.

GORAN_SAFAREK/SHUTTERSTOCK ©

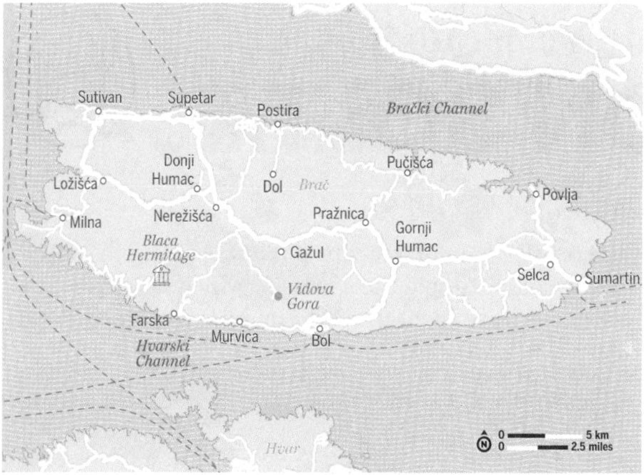

Left Blaca Hermitage
Below left Kitchen, Blaca Hermitage

A secluded sanctuary Monks first arrived in this remote spot in 1551 on the run from Ottoman persecution. Since then, **Blaca Hermitage** was continuously inhabited until 1963 when Fr Nikola Miličević, the last of the monastic order and a well-known mathematician, poet, teacher, musician and astronomer, died here.

More than a monastery In the primitive kitchen, you'll spot the cave where the hermitage had its beginnings before eventually morphing into a small complex of stone buildings, including a chapel. This religious refuge also functioned as a school, a library, a printing house, an astronomical observatory and a farm. The monks tended vineyards and 1000 olive trees growing on the surrounding rocky cliffs, producing wine, olive oil, honey and cheese.

Step through time Wander through the complex's interconnected rooms spread over several buildings and you'll see they contain an astonishing time capsule of period furniture and everyday objects, which have remained untouched for decades. A stark and cramped room of antique wooden desks served as the former schoolhouse. Head upstairs to the opulent music room embellished with decorated ceilings, velvet sofas and oil paintings to admire the grand piano transported here from Vienna, Austria.

Chock-full of treasures The museum also contains many other intriguing treasures: a collection of antique clocks, a library of more than 8000 books in five languages, a 3m-long telescope and the island's first printing press.

Goods Transport

Visitors to Blaca Hermitage can't help but ponder how the heavy furniture and grand piano were transported here, given the remote location and challenging terrain.

The massive pieces of furniture arrived on a boat from Vienna via Italy and were lugged uphill by donkey. As for the 400kg Viennese piano, 12 labourers hauled it up the cliff, a task that took eight hours and was compensated with 56L of wine. Weighing 1 tonne, the huge 3m-long telescope was also carried by donkey, and it was the hermitage's most expensive acquisition, paid for with a whole year's production of wine, oil, cheese and honey.

38 Slow Food ON ŠOLTA

LOCAL FLAVOURS | TASTINGS | WINE

Get a taste of island life on a slow-food adventure that takes you to the family farms and wineries of Šolta. Sample the exquisite wine and olive oil produced here and learn why bees are so vital to the island's ecosystem.

LUNGHAMMER/SHUTTERSTOCK ©

Trip Notes

Getting there Up to seven ferries a day connect Split with Rogač, Šolta's main port.

Getting around Bus services are limited. Scooters or e-bikes are good options to get around this small island.

When to go Tourist numbers peak in July and August. Come in autumn to catch the grape and olive harvests.

Top tip Many visitors come on a day trip from Split. Stay overnight to get a feel for island life.

Šolta's Home-Grown Varietals

Šolta has some grape and olive varieties that are native to the island and have grown here for centuries. The indigenous Šoltanka olive (pictured above) thrives in the island's rocky soil and resists heat well. *Dobričić* is our red grape varietal and one of the parents of *plavac mali*, the other being *crljenak Kaštelanski*, Zinfandel's Croatian ancestor.

By Frane Kaštelanac *founder of Olynthia Natura and Discover Šolta, @olynthia.natura, @discover_solta*

02 Stop at **Marinac Winery**, run by a family of passionate winemakers in Srednje Selo, for a tasting journey of Šolta's excellent bottles. Don't leave without a sip of the home-grown *dobričić* red.

03 Learn all about bees and why they are needed for much more than honey at **Tvrdić Honey**. Don't miss the rare opportunity to have a taste of pure Šolta honey.

05 Visit the age-old olive groves at **Olynthia Natura**, followed by a tour of its mill in Gornje Selo and a guided tasting of its exquisite monovarietal and infused olive oils.

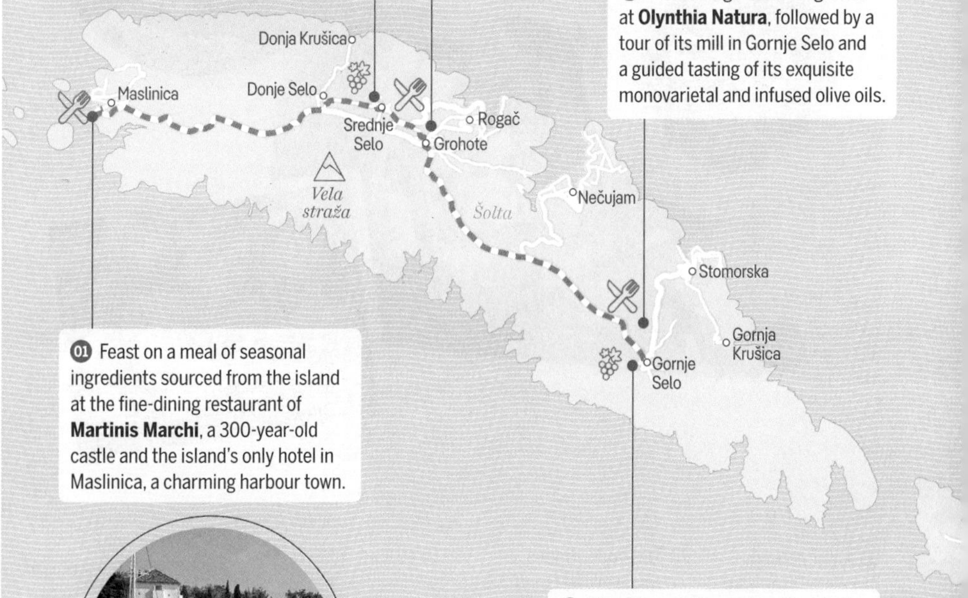

01 Feast on a meal of seasonal ingredients sourced from the island at the fine-dining restaurant of **Martinis Marchi**, a 300-year-old castle and the island's only hotel in Maslinica, a charming harbour town.

04 Walk through the vineyards and olive groves at **Agroturizam Kaštelanac** and then taste some island delights: olives, capers and anchovies washed down with local red and white wines.

Central Dalmatia's Gastronomic HIGHLIGHTS

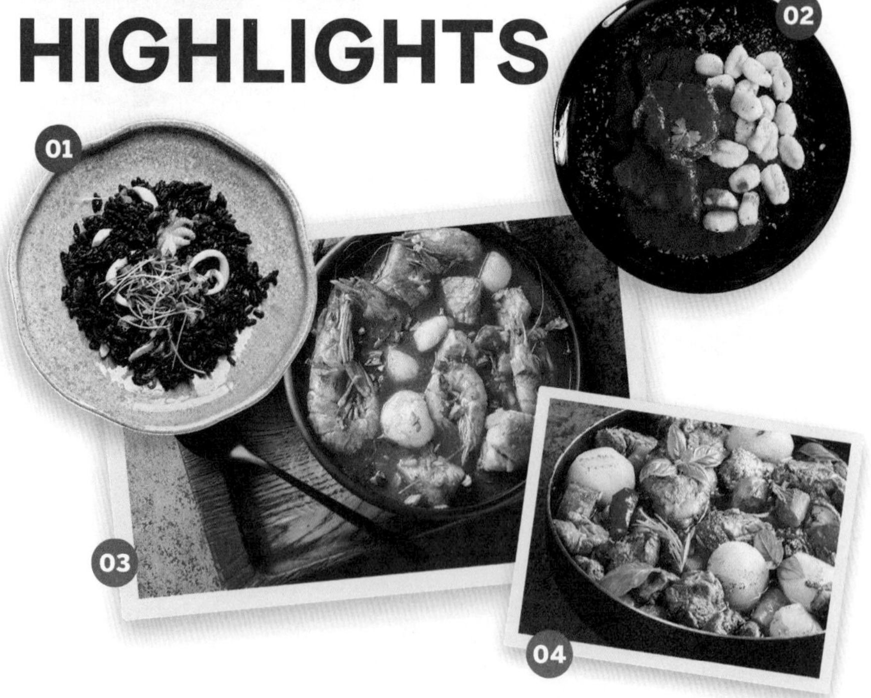

01 Crni rižoto
Black squid ink adds colour and flavour to this typical Dalmatian dish prepared with risotto rice and cuttlefish.

02 Pašticada
An elaborate dish of marinated beef slow-cooked with tomatoes, prunes, parsnips and sweet *prošek* wine and served with fresh pasta.

03 Brodet
This classic Dalmatian fish soup is cooked up with onions, garlic and tomatoes to create a thick and hearty broth.

04 Peka
This traditional cooking method uses a pan with a bell-shaped lid placed in an open fire to slow roast lamb, octopus, potatoes and vegetables.

05 Soparnik
A speciality of the Poljica region, this large, flatbread is filled with a mixture of Swiss chard and onions or garlic.

06 Gregada
A hearty dish from Hvar Island prepared with sea bream or monkfish stewed in white wine and parsley.

07 Viška pogača
Sandwiched between two layers of dough is a filling of anchovies and onions, creating this savoury flatbread from Vis Town.

08 Komiška pogača
Komiža, Vis Island's other big town, lays claim to its own version of *pogača* (pizza-like pie) with tomato added to the anchovy filling.

09 Rafioli
This half-moon-shaped sweet is filled with an almond mixture and is a specialty from the town of Trogir.

10 Plavac mali
Dalmatia's beloved red is a cross between two grape varieties: *crljenak Kaštelanski* and *dobričić*, creating a rich and flavourful wine.

39 Hidden Caves & BLUE WATERS

ISLANDS | DAY TRIP | OUTDOORS

Be dazzled by surreal caves whose waters glow in luminous shades of blue and emerald, a rare natural phenomenon. Tucked away on islets forming the archipelago just off the coast of Vis Island, these ethereal attractions are secluded but not so secret. Their increasing popularity means queues are to be expected, but it's well worth the wait.

STJEPAN TAFRA/SHUTTERSTOCK ©

How To

Getting there The easiest way to visit the blue and green caves is on a boat tour organised by the many travel agencies operating in Vis Town and Komiža.

Entry fees To enter each cave, you'll need to pay an entrance fee. The cost varies by season.

Tip Another option is to hire your own boat – no licence is required for boats with a 5HP engine.

SAM OAKES/ALAMY STOCK PHOTO ©

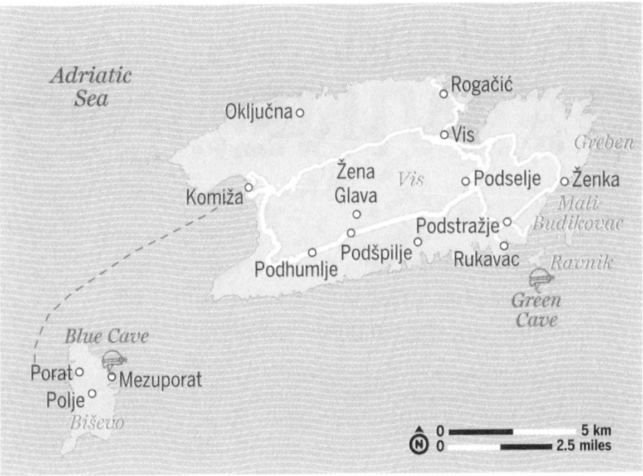

Left Blue Cave
Below left Green Cave

Biševo's Blue Cave About 5km off the southwest coast of Vis lies tiny Biševo Island, whose claim to fame is its astonishing **Blue Cave**, so-called because of the sublime blue light of its waters. On arrival at Biševo dock, you board a fishing boat for a short ride to the cave accompanied by a guide who tells passengers when to duck their heads to get through the low, narrow opening. When inside, darkness slowly gives way to the blue luminous glow of the waters in the cave's interior. This surprising natural phenomenon is created when sunlight enters an underwater shaft and reflects off the sandy bottom.

Swimming is not allowed in this protected natural monument, and boats linger inside for only a few minutes. This popular attraction sees high numbers of visitors in summer and is managed with a take-a-number queuing system. Expect long waits at peak times.

Green Cave on Ravnik Island The **Green Cave** is part of a rocky cavern on Ravnik, an islet off the southeast coast of Vis. Unlike the Blue Cave, you can swim inside (or enter on a small boat) and watch in wonder as you come across green shafts of light illuminating the water. The sunlight enters two holes in the cave's roof, creating glowing green spotlights in the murky waters.

Fascinating Facts about Vis

Vis is the furthest inhabited island from the Croatian mainland.

The island covers an area of 90.3 sq km and has a population of 5000.

Until 1992, Vis served as a secret military outpost and was off limits to non-islanders.

During President Tito's time, an underground network of more than 30 bunkers was built, as well as a bomb shelter and submarine tunnel.

Vis and its archipelago of nearby islands are geologically the oldest islands of the Adriatic Sea.

Vis is one of the few islands with its own water supply thanks to its unique geology of karst aquifers and springs.

40 The Island OF WINE

VINEYARDS | TASTINGS | FESTIVALS

Winemaking is a Hvar tradition that goes back to the 4th century, when the Greeks first planted vineyards here. Get to know the island of wine through your taste buds by sampling the varietals indigenous to its soil.

GORANSTIMAC/GETTY IMAGES ©

Trip Notes

Getting here Car ferries run between Split and Stari Grad, while foot-passenger services link Split, Bol and Milna on Brač Island to Hvar Town. A foot-passenger ferry also connects Bol and Jelsa.

Getting around A limited bus service links Hvar Town, Stari Grad port, Stari Grad and Jelsa. Hire a car or scooter for more flexibility.

ABV Hvar's wines are potent. White wines have 11% to 14.5% alcohol content, while reds pack in 12% to 18%.

Jelsa Wine Festival

Jelsa Wine Festival is Hvar's most important wine event and takes place every August. All the island's wineries gather here, with a jury awarding the best vintages. It's an opportunity to sample many different wines. Don't miss a taste of *bogdanuša* and *prč*: these are white wines native to Hvar and in danger of disappearing.

By Siniša Matković-Mikulčić *founder and CEO of Secret Hvar, @secrethvar*

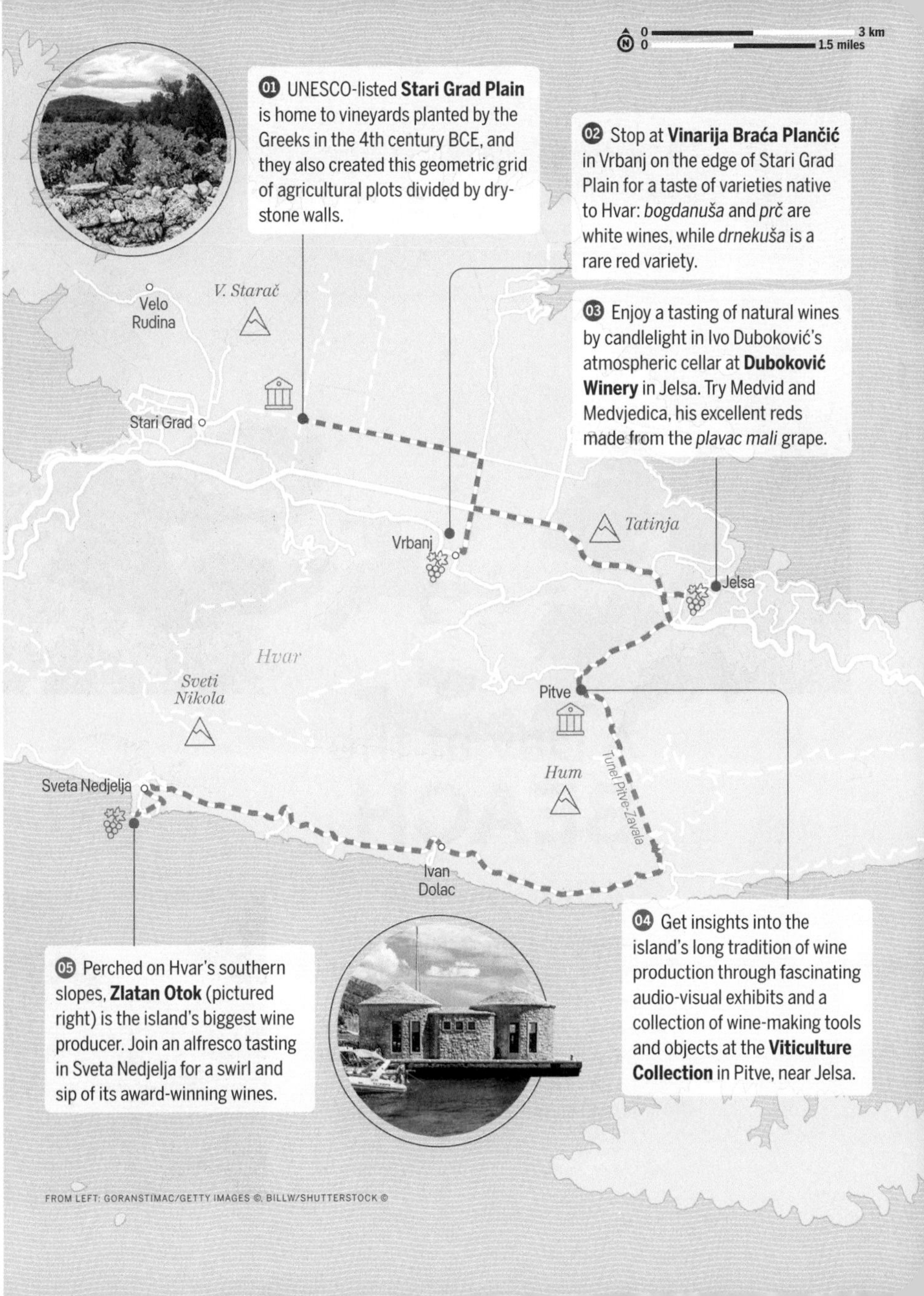

01 UNESCO-listed **Stari Grad Plain** is home to vineyards planted by the Greeks in the 4th century BCE, and they also created this geometric grid of agricultural plots divided by dry-stone walls.

02 Stop at **Vinarija Braća Plančić** in Vrbanj on the edge of Stari Grad Plain for a taste of varieties native to Hvar: *bogdanuša* and *prč* are white wines, while *drnekuša* is a rare red variety.

03 Enjoy a tasting of natural wines by candlelight in Ivo Duboković's atmospheric cellar at **Duboković Winery** in Jelsa. Try Medvid and Medvjedica, his excellent reds made from the *plavac mali* grape.

04 Get insights into the island's long tradition of wine production through fascinating audio-visual exhibits and a collection of wine-making tools and objects at the **Viticulture Collection** in Pitve, near Jelsa.

05 Perched on Hvar's southern slopes, **Zlatan Otok** (pictured right) is the island's biggest wine producer. Join an alfresco tasting in Sveta Nedjelja for a swirl and sip of its award-winning wines.

FROM LEFT: GORANSTIMAC/GETTY IMAGES ©, BILLW/SHUTTERSTOCK ©

41 A Day at the BEACH

SEA | ISLANDS | SWIMMING

Central Dalmatia is known for its gorgeous stretches of pristine pebble beaches (and even a few sandy ones) lapped by impossibly blue waters. Visitors have plenty to choose from along the long coastline and many islands.

FG TRADE/GETTY IMAGES ©

How To

Getting there Taxi boats in coastal towns are a convenient way to reach more remote beaches and nearby islands.

Tips All beaches in Croatia are public, which means you can lay down your towel where you please. Most beaches are equipped with simple changing facilities and showers.

Dangers Look out for jellyfish. On rocky seabeds, sea urchins are common.

Accessibility Download the Plaja Beach Finder app (plaja.hr) for a list of accessible beaches.

BORISB17/SHUTTERSTOCK ©

Bol's Beaches

Zlatni Rat (Golden Horn) is a fitting name for this quirky beach with a horn-like shape near Bol on Brač Island. Croatia's most photogenic beach also impresses with its soft white pebbles and see-to-the-bottom turquoise waters. A good breeze often kicks up on its eastern side, making it a great spot for windsurfing. The pine-scented stroll along the 2km-long promenade from Bol is a bit of a hike, but you can hop on a taxi boat or leave your car or scooter at the parking area nearby.

Closer to Bol and just east of its port are two other fabulous pebble beaches: **Kotlina Beach** stretches along a cove near the Dominican Monastery, while further east of this landmark lies

GORAN_SAFAREK/SHUTTERSTOCK ©

FKK OK

FKK (*freikörperkultur* in German) translates as 'free body culture'. These three letters are code for a nudist beach where swimwear is optional. Nudist beaches are common in Dalmatia, and they can usually be found in secluded sections on the edge of beach areas and often on rocky stretches of beach.

Above left Zlatni Rat
Left Kotlina Beach
Above Brela Stone, Punta Rata (p196)

Martinica Beach.

Makarska Riviera

The Makarska Riviera is a top destination for sunseekers, with more than 60km of pebble beaches ribboned by seaside walkways and soaring Mt Biokovo providing a dramatic backdrop.

Some of the most breathtaking beaches lie on the northern stretch in **Brela**, where postcard-perfect white pebble beaches are lapped by aquamarine waters. Stroll the 7km-long waterside promenade under the shaded canopy of Aleppo pines to stake out the perfect sunbathing spot. At **Punta Rata**, the shoreline bends at a sharp angle. Look for the Brela Stone, a giant rocky outcrop and well-known natural landmark.

Vis Beaches

From small secluded coves to expansive bays, Vis island has plenty of beaches to stretch out on. In Vis Town, head north from the ferry terminal to the Prirovo peninsula.

Beware of the Bura

The Adriatic's *bura* wind (*bora* in Italian) is a strong, cold wind blowing from the northeast that can wreak havoc on travel plans. It's regularly responsible for motorway closures and ferry cancellations and can upend a planned boat trip or day at the seaside.

When the *bura* is forecast, beware. It often strikes quickly and suddenly, taking those who are unaware of its power by surprise. The Croatian Mountain Rescue Service warns visitors in coastal areas to avoid going on the sea in any kind of vessel or engaging in any kind of watersport when the *bura* comes to town.

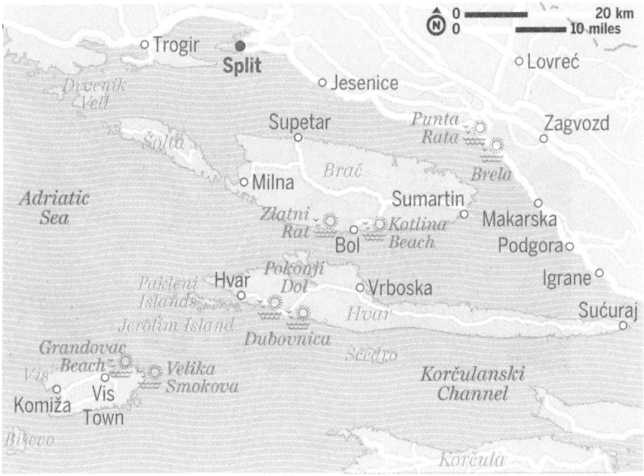

Left Dubovica Beach
Below Promenade, Makarska Riviera

On its eastern end behind St Jerome's Church, you'll come across a pretty stretch of pebbles. Tucked behind the British Cemetery at the other end of town lies the less-visited horseshoe-shaped **Grandovac Beach**.

If you're staying in **Komiža**, you can choose between Gusarica Beach at its northern end or Kamenica Beach, which sees a younger crowd drawn by the buzzing beach-bar scene.

Those who prefer the untamed vibe of wild beaches should head to serene **Srebrna Beach** on the island's south coast or hop on a boat to **Velika Smokova**, a rare sandy beach with crystal-clear waters.

Hvar's Beach Scene

Beach clubs line the waterfront in Hvar Town, but if you're looking for a beach experience without the loud music, head 2km east to **Pokonji Dol**, set on a pebbly bay within walking distance. Alternatively, catch a taxi boat to **Dubovica Beach** to find a lovely cove strewn with white pebbles.

The car-free **Pakleni Islands** also entice, with plenty of options for sunseekers. Choose Palmižana on Sveti Klement Island if you're up for a party scene. Mlini on Marinkovac Island is for those who prefer a quiet escape, while **Jerolim** island is known for its nude beach.

WIRESTOCK CREATORS/SHUTTERSTOCK ©

Jadranska Magistrala

CROATIA'S MOST BREATHTAKING DRIVE

When it was completed in the 1960s, the coastal highway along the Adriatic (Jadranska Magistrala in Croatian) linked Yugoslavia's seaside towns and cities. It also boosted local economies and transformed everyday life for people living along the coastline, sparking the beginnings of tourism in the region.

The Adriatic Highway twists and winds 818km along Croatia's indented Adriatic coastline, passing scenic coastal towns topped with fortified towers and castles, and picturesque bays and fishing ports. For most of its journey, the shore-hugging highway is sandwiched between the Adriatic Sea and the Velebit mountain range, opening onto panoramas of the sparkling sea and floating islands on one side. Meanwhile, on the other side, varied landscapes rush past, as the road snakes down the coast: pine forests, Mediterranean macchia, verdant vineyards and olive groves, and dramatic mountainscapes.

As the D8 state road, this single carriageway is Croatia's longest state road, stretching from the Croatian–Slovenian border south via Rijeka, Senj, Zadar, Šibenik, Split and Dubrovnik and continuing to Montenegro. Finished in 1965, the Jadranska Magistrala was Yugoslavia's biggest infrastructure project at the time, creating a road link between the Adriatic's coastal towns and cities from Italy to Albania for the first time.

In some sections, the route follows the paths of ancient Roman roads or arteries dating from the 18th and 19th centuries. In 1945, this coastal road ran from Rijeka as far as Novi Vinodolski, only 42km away, before being extended 181km to Zadar in 1959 and then a further 75km to Šibenik in 1963. Construction accelerated considerably after this, with close to 300km of road laid in two years.

The new highway became a lifeline between the coastal settlements it connected, providing an important

Views of the Jadranska Magistrala

TUPUNGATO/SHUTTERSTOCK ©

MOIAN ADRIAN/SHUTTERSTOCK ©

economic link that soon accelerated development. Everyday life was transformed thanks to increased connectivity and a boost in trade and employment opportunities. Also significant is the fact that by connecting the north and south Adriatic, the highway opened up the country to tourism. Its inauguration was followed by a boom in the construction of hotels up and down the Adriatic coast.

> The new highway became a lifeline between the coastal settlements it connected.

For a long time, the Jadranska Magistrala was the only road link to the coastal parts of Croatia until the expansion of the country's highway network in the 2000s. With the opening of the A1 Zagreb–Split highway in 2007 and its extension to Dubrovnik in 2008, traffic largely moved inland to this modern multilane highway and away from the Adriatic coast.

Today, it's much faster to travel by road from the northern or inland parts of Croatia south to Split or Dubrovnik on the modern highway network. As a result, the Jadranska Magistrala sees significantly less traffic, and the long summertime queues of cars snaking down the narrow coastal road are a thing of the past.

Though travelling along the now iconic Jadranska Magistrala is considerably slower than the new highway, the panoramic views it offers are unparalleled. Croatia's longest and most scenic coastal road offers the ultimate slow travel experience.

Building the Magistrala

More than 10,000 labourers engaged by over a dozen construction companies worked on the mammoth project of building the Jadranska Magistrala. Its construction presented numerous obstacles and technical challenges because of the sharply indented Adriatic coastline of rocky limestone. Workers had to cut and blast through the rock to create passageways and tunnels, excavating 6 million cu metres of stone in the process and using more than 2000 tonnes of explosives.

Numerous bridges were also constructed along the highway's route. The 482m-long Bistrina bridge passing over the river of the same name near Ston was built in just 10 months, breaking a world record at the time.

Listings

BEST OF THE REST

Cultural Festivals & Events

Sudamja

On 7 May, Split celebrates the day of Sv Duje (St Domnius), its patron saint, with a religious procession along the seaside promenade followed by much merrymaking, outdoor concerts and fireworks.

Hvar Summer Festival

From mid-June to mid-September, Hvar's public spaces host an eclectic programme of concerts, dance performances and theatre as part of an annual cultural festival staged since 1961.

Split Summer Festival

Split becomes an open-air stage from mid-July to mid-August, with concerts, classical dance performances, theatre and opera put on at cultural venues across the city.

Kaštela Cultural Summer

Kaštela's biggest cultural event of the year features concerts, art exhibitions, children's activities, dance, drama and comedy shows from the end of June to September.

Ultra Europe

For three days every July, Split is the host of one of the world's largest festivals of electronic music. Big-name DJs spin tunes on multiple stages before moving to Hvar and Vis islands to continue the dance party.

Brač Film Festival

Film lovers flock to Supetar on Brač Island for four days in August to watch films by emerging filmmakers on screens under the stars. During the day, renowned screenwriters and producers put on masterclasses.

Bol Summer Festival

Bol's cultural festival has been a summer highlight since 1989. The town's churches and public spaces become open-air venues for art exhibitions, plays for children, concerts and an international graffiti festival.

Concept & Design Shops

Trogir Experience

A concept store in the heart of Trogir's old town with a fabulous collection of handmade ceramics, jewellery, textiles and natural beauty products crafted by Croatian artisans and designers.

More Eco Souvenir Shop

This tiny shop in the heart of Split's Diocletian's Palace is the place to pick up fabulous handmade gifts. Everything is plastic free, ecofriendly and made in Croatia.

Isola Design Store Hvar

Small batch and high quality is the ethos behind this design shop in Hvar Town's historic centre. You'll find stoneware, ceramics, natural cosmetics and quirky bow ties, all handmade locally.

BOAZ ROTTEM/ALAMY STOCK PHOTO ©

Zrno Soli at ACI Marina

Atelier SU

Pop into this delightful shop in Supetar on Brač Island to find sustainable handmade creations, such as hats, bags, cushions, rag dolls and decorative objects made of driftwood.

Concept Vis

A design shop on Vis Town's main seaside promenade showcasing handmade souvenirs, vegan cosmetics and original artwork by Croatian artists, as well as a selection of local wines.

Cakes & Coffee Breaks

Oš Kolač

The place to go in Split for divine sweet treats. This pastry shop peddles artisan cakes and pastries that look almost too beautiful to eat.

D16 Coffee

Looking for a coffee fix in Split? Head to this specialty coffee shop and roastery in the heart of the palace. Try Dominus, its signature blend: a light roast with deliciously nutty notes.

Cukar

A pocket-sized cake shop in Komiža on Vis Island with delectable treats. Have a bite of savoury *komiška pogača*, Komiža's tomato- and anchovy-filled flatbread, followed by a slice of exquisite cake.

Đovani

Don't leave Trogir without a taste of *rafioli*, the city's beloved almond-filled sweet. Đovani is a local institution famed for its superb *rafioli*, as well as other yummy cakes and pastries.

Nonica

Step into this traditional pastry shop in Hvar Town for *medenjak*, a specialty infused with ginger, honey, spices and aromatic island herbs. Have it the traditional way: with a glass of prosecco.

Split Summer Festival

Elevated Dining

Konoba TRS €€

Tucked in a 13th-century stone building in the heart of Trogir's old town, this relaxed tavern is a firm favourite for its delightful open-air terrace and beautifully presented dishes of fresh fish and meat.

Il Ponte €€€

A skip and a jump from Trogir's historic old town, bright and airy Il Ponte entices with its stylish interiors and Mediterranean-inspired cuisine prepared with the season's freshest ingredients.

Dvor €€

Overlooking Split's Firule Beach, this sun-filled restaurant delights with a menu of imaginative fish dishes: ceviche, tuna cannelloni filled with foie gras, and seafood risotto. Snag a table in the shady garden with sea views.

Zrno Soli €€€

Be dazzled by the exquisitely plated dishes and panoramic views from the light-filled upper level of Split's ACI Marina. Choose the seafood tasting menu to savour the flavours of the season.

Konoba Kala €€
Situated near Supetar's port, this family-run restaurant tantalises with wood-fired dishes of lamb and fish, and alfresco seating at rustic tables on an enchanting courtyard terrace.

Otok €€
Modern decor and an atmospheric patio filled with olive trees provide a sublime setting at Hotel Osam's restaurant in Supetar. On the menu of island cuisine, you'll find tuna steak and fried octopus, as well as crowd-pleasing favourites like burgers and pizza.

Mediterraneo €€
Book your table in advance to eat at this family-run Hvar institution smack in the centre of the old town. An extensive wine list complements the large menu, and the consistently excellent service gets top marks.

Maslina €€€
Located in the resort of the same name, Maslina uses ingredients sourced fresh from the property's vegetable garden. In the evening, choose from the dinner menu of contemporary Mediterranean-inspired cuisine.

Drinks with a View

AURO Bol
Buzzing cocktail bar on the edge of gorgeous Zlatni Rat beach. Once you plonk yourself on one of the beachside beanbags, you won't want to get back up.

Frutarija
Popular sea-facing hangout with a youthful vibe just outside Vis Town on the seaside promenade to Kuta. Sip your morning coffee with a sea view or savour the sunset with a G&T.

Paradox Wine & Cheese Bar
Steps from Split's Riva promenade, this stylish wine and cheese bar entices with a fabulous rooftop terrace and a huge selection of Croatian wines and platters of local cheese.

Falko
This chill-out spot in Hvar is set among towering pines on the edge of the water. The menu includes expertly mixed craft cocktails and a selection of tempting bites for lunch and dinner.

Sol Lounge Bar
Get a front-row seat and watch the spectacle of the sun setting into the Adriatic Sea from this relaxed beachside lounge bar next to St Peter's lighthouse in Makarska Town.

Corte Bar
Right on Trogir's atmospheric square, Corte is a place you'll want to linger for a while. The drink list is extensive, and the cocktails are top notch.

Hugo's Bar
Stretch out on a deckchair with a cocktail or two at this cosy beachfront spot on the seaside promenade from Brela to Baška Voda.

Outdoor Adventures

Zipline Croatia
Soar 150m in the air on a zip line adventure across the Cetina River canyon near Omiš. Of the eight zip lines, the longest runs for 700m.

Rafting, Cetina River

Rafting Pirate
Get close to the flora and fauna of the Cetina River and canyon near Omiš on a guided rafting or canyoning trip. You'll take plenty of breaks for swimming under waterfalls, exploring cave pools and cliff jumping.

Vortex
Take off on an exhilarating off-road quad tour of Vis Island. The fascinating military tour takes you up mountains and into underground bunkers to once-secret sites that were strictly off limits.

Via Crucis Underwater Museum
Go under the surface for a snorkelling or diving adventure near Trogir. Spot a military plane resting on the seabed, an 8m-high statue of Jesus and 52 other life-size sculptures.

Hvar Adventure
Discover the caves and coves of the beautiful Pakleni Islands off the coast of Hvar by kayak. Pause along the way at quiet pebble beaches for a spot of swimming or snorkelling.

Zip Line Tučepi
Fly above the treetops of Gornji Tučepi canyon near Makarska while taking in the sweeping views of Mt Biokovo. Descend through the canyon on six different zip lines of varying lengths and speeds.

Biokovo Skywalk at Biokovo Nature Park
Take a step onto the glass-bottomed semi-circular Biokovo Skywalk protruding 11m from a cliff face at a height of 1228m. From here you'll have a birds-eye view of Biokovo Nature Park spreading below you and the coastline of the Makarska Riviera beyond.

Explore Brač
Get to know Brač Island with a guided jeep tour of its cultural sights, such as the quarry from where the island's famous white stone was excavated. Afterwards, make your way to the top of Vidova Gora, the highest point in the Adriatic islands.

IRINA WILHAUK/SHUTTERSTOCK ©

Biokovo Skywalk, Biokovo Nature Park

Veg-Friendly Restaurants

Up Cafe €€
Dig into tofu burritos, veggie burgers, falafel wraps and plant-based cakes at this casual vegetarian cafe located an easy 15-minute walk from Split's waterfront.

Fabrika €€
This colourful bistro on Komiža's harbourfront on Vis Island has plenty of options for plant-based diners. Vegan burgers, pesto pasta and smoothie bowls include some of the pickings.

BioMania €€
This bistro in Bol on Brač Island serves up vegan dishes with a sea view in town or at its street-food stand on Zlatni Rat beach.

Masha Vegeteria €€
When on Hvar Island, head to Jelsa to dine alfresco in this charming port town and savour its veggie delights. Menu standouts include the tofu fish and chips, lavender cottage cheese and spicy pumpkin soup.

Scan to find more things to do in Split & Central Dalmatia

DUBROVNIK & SOUTHERN DALMATIA

ORNATE | HISTORY | SPLENDOUR

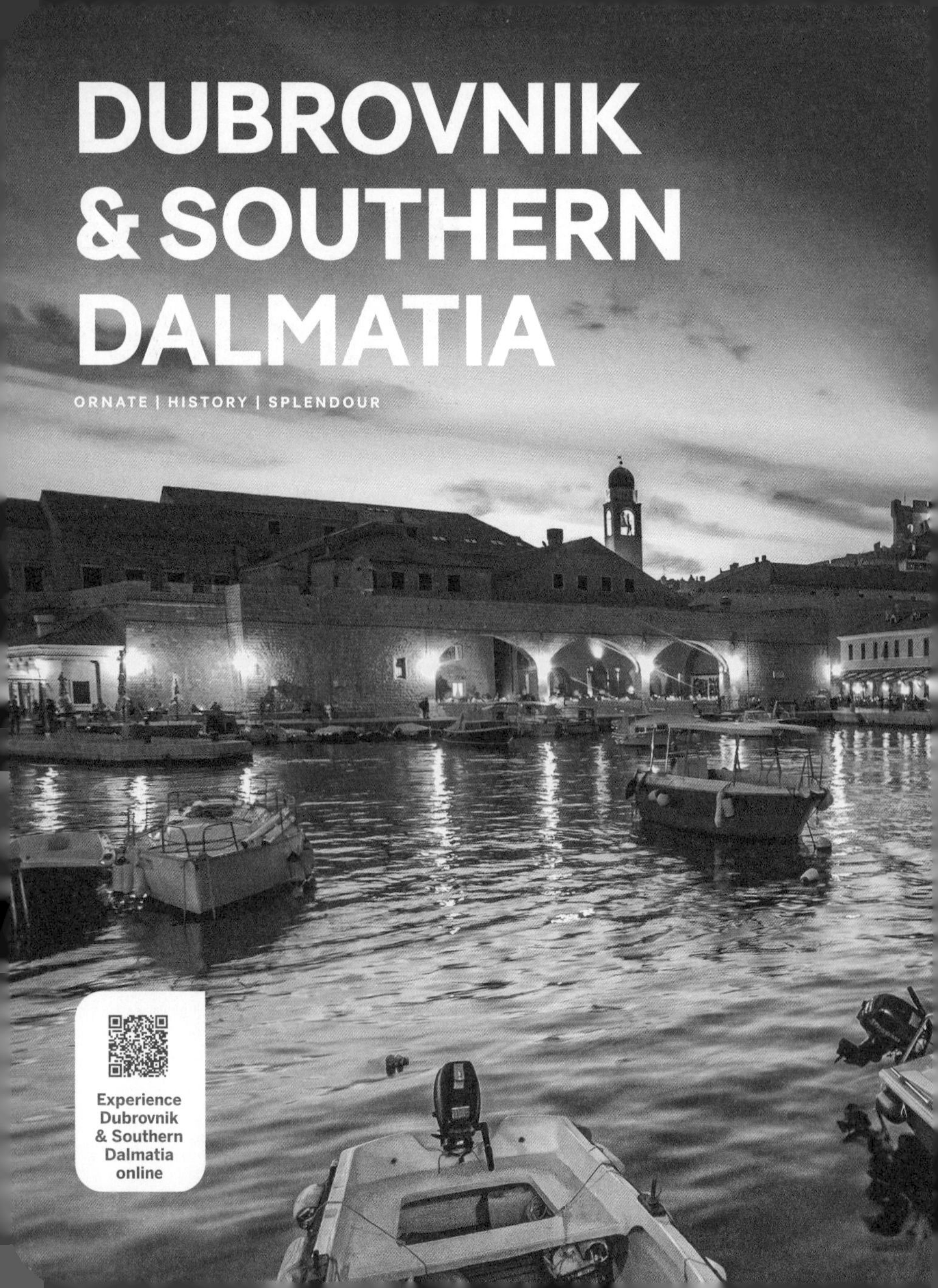

Experience Dubrovnik & Southern Dalmatia online

Sip local *grk* (white-wine varietal grown on Korčula) at vineyards in **Lumbarda** (p229)

2hr from Dubrovnik

Island hop to **Mljet** and its incredible lagoons (p223)

1½hr from Dubrovnik

DUBROVNIK & SOUTHERN DALMATIA

Trip Builder

All the hype is right: Dubrovnik is dazzling. Plus, alluring islands, a sprawling beach-lined coast, vineyards, olive groves and magnificent towns all neighbour the city known as the 'pearl of the Adriatic'.

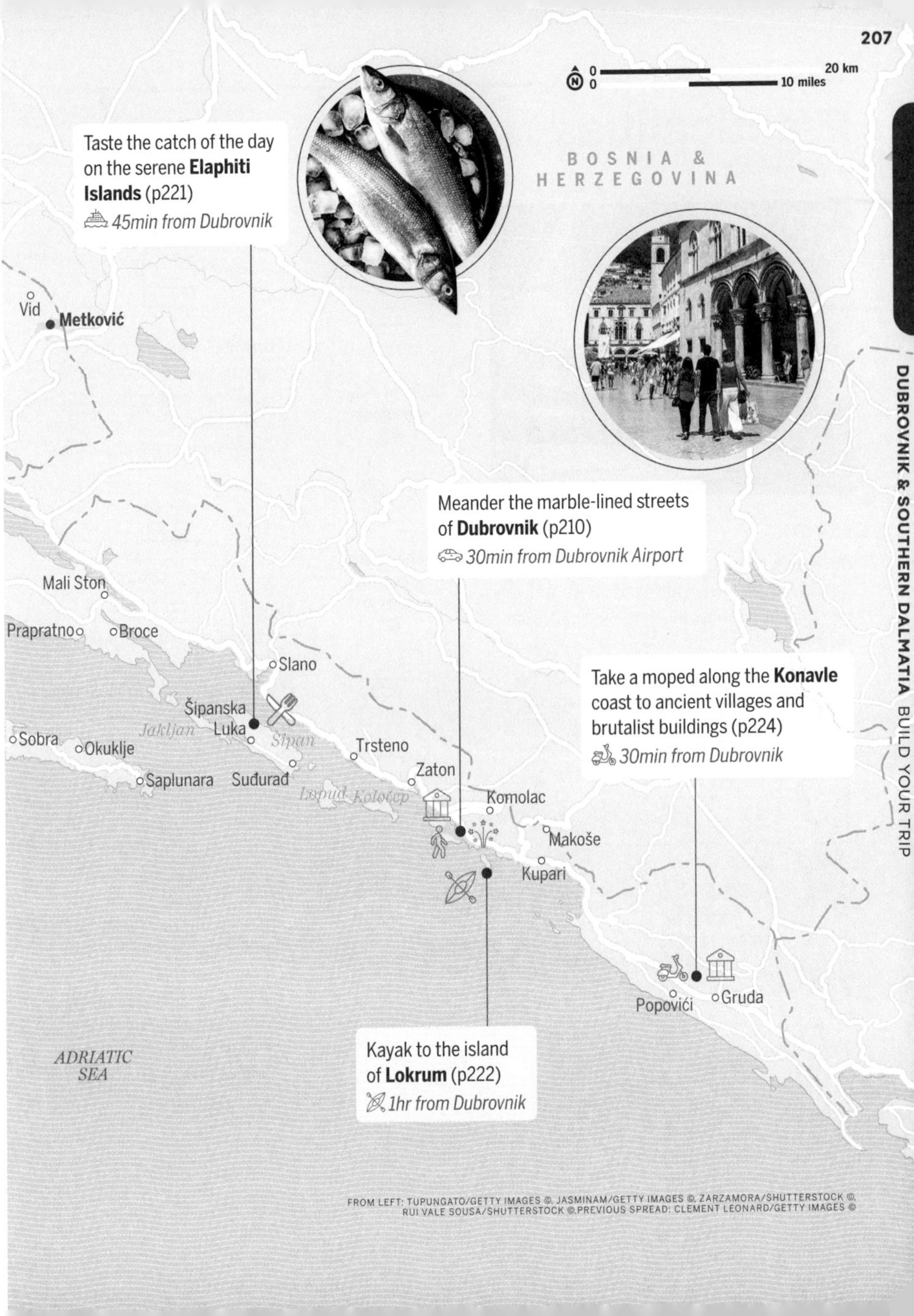

Taste the catch of the day on the serene **Elaphiti Islands** (p221)
45min from Dubrovnik

Meander the marble-lined streets of **Dubrovnik** (p210)
30min from Dubrovnik Airport

Take a moped along the **Konavle** coast to ancient villages and brutalist buildings (p224)
30min from Dubrovnik

Kayak to the island of **Lokrum** (p222)
1hr from Dubrovnik

Practicalities

© RVILLALON/SHUTTERSTOCK

ARRIVING

Dubrovnik Airport (pictured) is 30 minutes from the old city, with direct flights from New York City, London and European capitals landing from spring to late autumn. Arrivals wind down in winter, when you'll have to transfer through Zagreb.

Krilo and Jadrolinija ferries link Dubrovnik Gruž Port to the neighbouring islands of Mljet and Korčula before heading onwards to Hvar and Split. Services run twice a day from May to October.

HOW MUCH FOR A

glass of *rakija* (grappa) €5

cheese *burek* (cheese-filled pastry) €2

City-Walls ticket €35

WHEN TO GO

NOV–FEB
The off-season has blissfully quiet streets and reasonable accommodation prices.

MAR–MAY
Spring is the season for culture vultures who like to avoid the crowds.

JUN–AUG
Peak summer is packed, and prices and temperatures soar.

SEP–OCT
Shoulder season is best for beach lovers with warm days and seas.

GETTING AROUND

Bus Public buses run up and down the coast from Dubrovnik. It's an hour north to Ston or 30 minutes south to Cavtat, ideal if wine tasting is on the agenda.

Boat A handful of small boats run to Cavtat, with daily departures from Dubrovnik's pint-sized old harbour in the northeast corner of the old city. You can also catch group boat trips or chic speedboat services to the Elaphiti Islands from here.

Car Hiring a car is theoretically convenient, but parking is extremely tricky in Dubrovnik. You're better off hiring a moped or using a Mynt scooter, which is cheaper and lots of fun.

EATING & DRINKING

With a centuries-old sea-to-table dining scene and an olive-oil and viniculture tradition that dates back millennia, this ancient region knows how to eat right. Much of the cuisine has a deep-rooted Italian connection from the region's time as a Venetian outpost and as a long-time trading partner with Bari and Sicily. Expect excellent seafood pasta (pictured right bottom), risotto and grilled fish dishes. Sniff out the best restaurants by skipping those on the main drags that try to reel you in. Top quality doesn't hustle for patrons.

Best gelato
Peppino's (p232)

Must-try seafood
Octopus fritters at Trattoria Carmen (p212)

CONNECT & FIND YOUR WAY

Free wi-fi is available in public areas in Dubrovnik's old town. Elsewhere, you're at the mercy of local cafes, so buying a local SIM card is a cheap and effective way to stay online. T Mobile, A1 and Telemach are solid network options and charge about €15 for a sizeable amount of data to use within 30 days.

WHERE TO STAY

Bijou hotels, quaint B&Bs, holiday apartments and buzzy hostels are all readily available in Southern Dalmatia, Croatia's most-visited region.

City	Pros/Cons
Dubrovnik	Expect to pay top euro to stay in a hotel or hostel at the heart of the action.
Gruž	Dubrovnik's port is a vibrant neighbourhood with cheaper accommodation.
Cavtat	A quiet, seaside town that has large hotels and apartments aplenty as well as a chilled-out vibe.
Korčula	This beloved island has good-value stays outside of the old town.
Mljet	Come for the national park, stay for the idyllic small villages and affordable accommodation.
Elaphiti Islands	A peaceful archipelago offering serenity and good B&B stays, particularly on Šipan.

DUBROVNIK PASS

The Dubrovnik Pass includes entry to museums and the City Walls (which costs €35 alone) and free rides on public transport.

MONEY

Southern Dalmatia is one of the most expensive areas of Croatia, and Dubrovnik is notoriously spendy. If you're on a budget, avoid peak season and stay outside the old town, taking the bus into the centre.

42 Dubrovnik Old Town LIKE A LOCAL

COMMUNITY | HISTORY | CAFES

Scratch beneath the surface of one of the world's most popular tourist destinations to find the bars, cafes and restaurants where a dedicated community of locals quietly go about their business of keeping the old town well-maintained, warm and welcoming.

WOJTEK CHMIELEWSKI/SHUTTERSTOCK ©

How To

Getting around Choose buses or mopeds to avoid the turmoil of finding parking in packed Dubrovnik.

When to go Dubrovnik in summer is an extremely busy place. To avoid the dense crowds and enjoy a more relaxed pace in the old town, visit in spring or autumn.

Hit the beach This coastal city is awash with swimming spots, but none are as beautiful as Sveti Jakov Beach.

LIDERO/SHUTTERSTOCK ©

Life in the Old Town

Contrary to how some people treat it, Dubrovnik's old town is not a museum or theme park. About 1500 residents live here, and you won't meet locals more passionate about their hometown than Dubrovnikers. 'What's specific here is it's not just a place where you live; it's part of you,' says Miheala Skurić, director at the Institute for the Restoration of Dubrovnik, which maintains the old buildings. 'Every individual here is made of the city, and the city is made of us'.

It's easy to wander around the old town in awe without really taking it in. Stop and chat with locals in their favourite bars. Travel slowly and stay in the city as long as you can – this way, you'll get a richer and more in-depth understanding of Dubrovnik and get much more from your time there, as you

DARIOZG/SHUTTERSTOCK ©

Follow the Smoke

Most Croatians smoke like chimneys, and smoking is still allowed in cafes and bars across the country. If you're not sure whether a bar or cafe is a good local haunt, look for the clouds of cigarette smoke. No smoke clouds means probably no locals.

Above left Stradun
Left Ploče Gate
Above Street cafe, Stradun

begin to find the treasures hidden in plain sight.

Museums, Cafes, Bars & Beaches

Check out the **War Photography Museum** to gain important insights into what the city went through in the Homeland War of the 1990s. Grab a coffee at **Bikers Cafe**, a good place to find locals, and go for evening beers in Gruž. **Dubrovnik Beer Company** is a local favourite. Swim in the sea below **Hotel Belvedere** and check out the exhibitions and parties at the beautifully restored event space **Lazareti**. If you're a party animal, **Club Revelin** is where to join the ravers.

Support Local Crafts

At 6 Prijeko St, a hectic lane full of restaurants and bars, **Suveniri Bačan** is a must-visit spot. Proprietor Lena Bačan Janjalija and her

Old Town Favourites

Beach Bar Dodo
This sea-facing spot is open all day, so enjoy a few beers, the burger menu and the chilled vibes under the watchful eye of Fort Lovrijenac next door.

Glam Bar
A cosy nook with the most reasonably priced drinks in the old town, Glam is tucked away down a quiet side street and stocks a selection of international and local craft beers.

Trattoria Carmen
This fantastic, hole-in-the-wall spot near the old harbour has expanded ever so slightly, so you're more likely to get a table and enjoy the incredible seafood, steaks and pasta at good prices.

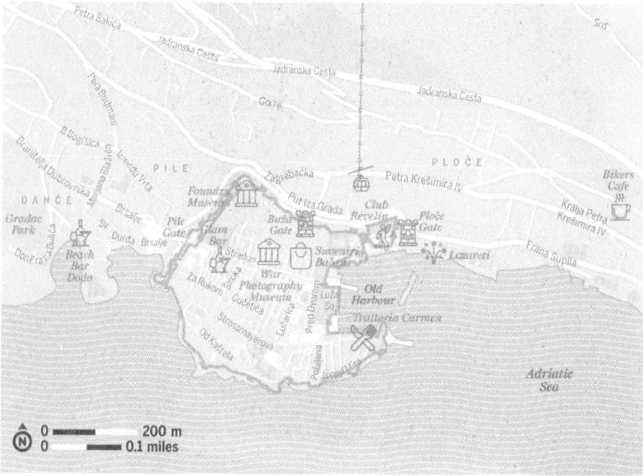

Left Lazareti
Below Prijeck St

family keep a local art tradition alive at their colourful family store, which sells blouses, bags, bookmarks and more embroidered with rare hand-sewn patterns unique to the region. The humble little shop marked its 50th anniversary in 2023. Lena's mother opened the store in 1953, moving from the Konavle region as the city modernised and opening the shop in the old town. It's now the last of its kind.

'Avoid entering by Pile Gate, as all the cruise ship tour groups come in this way. Instead, use the Buža and Ploče gates. Walk around the side streets, which have lots of steps, but it's worth it to see where locals still live. If someone is outside the restaurant with a menu and inviting you in, it's probably not going to be good, and if the menu has pictures, that's a big no. You can play basketball with the locals. There's a tiny door by the Foundry Museum leading to the magnificent court, and they play every evening from 6pm'.

■ **Recommended by Ivan Vuković**
photographer and tour guide
@Dubrovnik_tourist_guide

43 Party Like IT'S 1699

FAITH | TRADITION | FESTIVALS

Dalmatian saints' days are legit local celebrations that long predate tourism. Attending one of these huge, moving events is a guaranteed way to have an authentic local experience, as you witness age-old traditions that show off a deep faith and sense of community.

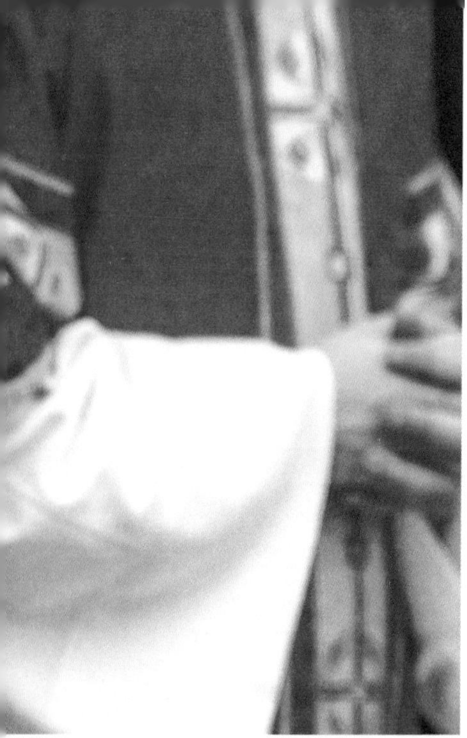

MARTIN SEPERIC/SHUTTERSTOCK ©

How to

Getting there Fly into Dubrovnik from Zagreb or take the ferries from Dubrovnik or Split, which serve Korčula all summer.

When to go February sees Dubrovnik alive with its age-old festivities, while Korčula parties all June and July.

Book in advance Traditional festivals across South Dalmatia are popular with locals, who visit their ancestral homes from Zagreb, Europe and beyond. Expect accommodation during festivals to be booked up quickly.

DAVE Z/SHUTTERSTOCK ©

A Blaise of Glory

The **Feast of St Blaise** (Sveti Vlaho or Sveti Blaž) is a unique Dubrovnik event. Every year on 3 February, the whole county puts on traditional costumes and floods into the old town to celebrate its patron saint. Women wear self-embroidered vestments resplendent in reds, yellows and occasionally greens sewn from homemade silks, while men don white shirts, black and red waistcoats and red felt pillbox caps. Dressed to the nines, locals line the streets as the saint's relics are paraded down the **Stradun** to the **Church of St Blaise**.

MICHAEL PASCHOS/SHUTTERSTOCK ©

Carnival Crew

Following the Feast of St Blaise, usually in mid-February depending on when Easter alls, Dubrovnik hosts a 10-day **Carnival**

Sword Play

If you can't visit during Korčula's saint's day but are still intrigued by the 400-year-old sword dancing traditions on the island, performances of *kumpanjija* (from Blato and Žrnovo) and *moreška* (from the old town) run from June to September in Korčula old town (moreska.hr).

Above left Procession, Feast of St Blaise
Left Carnival masks
Above Church of St Blaise

just before Lent. The city has put on these wonderfully ornate celebrations since the 14th century, even though at times some historical rulers banned masks in favour of traditional local costumes. Theatre has always played a huge part in Dubrovnik's Carnival, and that's still the case, as the celebration brings out dramatic productions, concerts and traditional dancing, and culminates in a masked ball. More Venice-like than Rijeka's Carnival, which has a more Eastern European vibe with animal costumes, Dubrovnik's is all masks and elegance – no beast heads here.

Swords of Steel

While *kumpanjija* traditional sword dancing still thrives in villages across central Korčula, it's rare to see it performed outside of a staged-for-tourists theatrical environment – unless you find yourself in the town of **Blato** on its annual saint's day, the **Feast of St Vincent** on 28 April. The whole of the town and villagers from around the region come out to celebrate.

The morning sees a brass band complete with majorettes parade through the square before an afternoon programme of *kumpanjija*

More Modern, Still Classy

Started in 1950, the Dubrovnik Summer Festival is a classy affair of classical music, poetry and theatre productions. Taking place throughout July and August, the events showcase local and international artists who play within the city's stunning churches and palaces. Performers over the decades have included Duke Ellington, Dizzy Gillespie, Ravi Shankar and Daniel Day-Lewis.

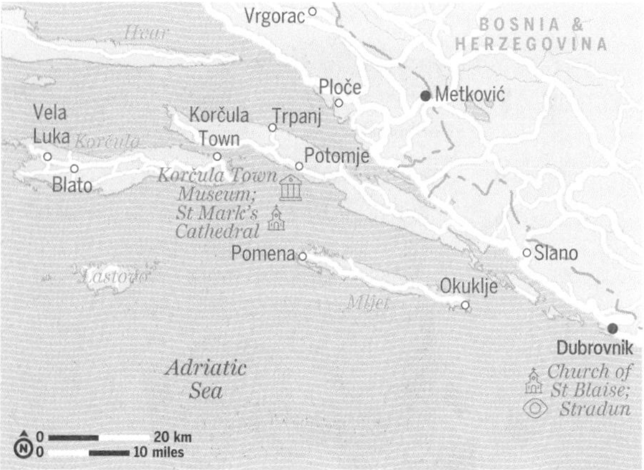

Left *Kumpanjija*
Below Korčula Town Museum

moves through the streets, often with young dancers proudly performing a part of their heritage for the first time. It's a truly special event to witness.

Two Saints are Better than One

Korčula's grandiose old town was built in the 15th century, densely packed with Gothic and Renaissance beauties that line the cleverly laid-out streets. The fishbone formation was designed to allow in the breezy summer maestral winds but keep out the punishingly forceful winter *bura* gales. Architectural must-sees include the soaring 15th-century **St Mark's Cathedral** and the **Korčula Town Museum** in the 16th-century Gabriellis Palace, which gives a neat overview of the history of the town through its arts, crafts and archaeology.

One of the most festive days for the folks of Korčula old town is 29 July, as everyone takes to the streets to celebrate St Theodore, the town's co-patron saint (along with St Mark, who was adored by the Venetians). The locals revere St Theodore, and his feast day is the biggest celebration of the year. Free events take place in Korčula's main square of Plokata, including the procession of the saint's statue, traditional *klapa* singers (similar to a church choir) and *moreška* sword dancing, a rare opportunity to see it performed in a non-staged, non-touristy way.

Mysterious Origins: Who Built Dubrovnik?

THE HISTORICAL DEBATE PLOUGHS ON

Dubrovnik and the neighbouring regions of Southern Dalmatia were formerly known as the Republic of Ragusa. It was a beating heart of justice and democracy and was the first country in the world to outlaw slavery. This centre of commerce became a key player in the Renaissance, but who founded the great city?

Left Ploče Gate
Centre Stradun
Right Onofrio Fountain (p232)

SAM TANNO/SHUTTERSTOCK ©

Breathtaking Dubrovnik-Neretva County is Croatia's southernmost region, out on a limb for centuries and sequestered by Bosnia and Herzegovina and Montenegro. The regional capital of Dubrovnik is the best-preserved walled city in Europe, and it deserves the hype it receives. Its wide, marble-paved streets lined with monumental baroque churches and Gothic palaces dazzle visitors. Beyond Dubrovnik, the sophistication of the Republic of Ragusa is still evident, from Ston and its great wall (the largest in Europe) to the gardens in Trsteno, the *palazzos* in the Dubrovačka estuary, creative Cavtat, and the villages and fortresses of the Konavle Valley. The scenery across the county is nothing short of sublime: rolling hillsides as you glance inland and crystal blue waters along the never-far-away coast.

But who founded the great Republic of Ragusa? Historians and archaeologists have debated conflicting claims through the ages as to who first formed Ragusa. They scour manuscripts written by kings, emperors and priests at different points in history and dig up evidence in excavations within the old-town walls, but it doesn't add up to one origin story.

The most accepted take is that Dubrovnik was built by refugees from Epidaurum (present-day Cavtat), a busy Greek city that fell for unknown reasons, causing

NIGHTMAN1965/SHUTTERSTOCK ©

ANAMARIA MEJIA/SHUTTERSTOCK ©

its inhabitants to relocate. This story suited Ragusans as they could claim to have links to Greece and elevate their status in the Renaissance period. An earthquake that hit the city in 1979 shed some light on the debate, as the broken foundations of the cathedral revealed fragments of Hellenistic glass and pottery, so maybe the Greeks were here after all.

Another theory says that Byzantines built a fortress here over a much older Illyrian hillfort to protect themselves from Ostrogoth invasions well before the demise of Epidaurum.

Whoever founded Dubrovnik, modern visitors can absorb more than 1000 years of culture.

The Slavic Bosnian kings had a great story too, suggesting that King Radoslav, a half-Bosnian, half-Roman ruler, built a castle that founded Dubrovnik in the 6th century CE on his journey home to Bosnia. While this story is generally known to be a myth, Slavs did populate the area, particularly around Mt Srđ, so it's not entirely implausible either.

Whoever founded Dubrovnik, modern visitors can absorb more than 1000 years of culture. Dubrovnik's walled old city is magnificent.

An Orlando Measure

An emblem of Dubrovnik, the statue known as Orlando's Column, has been standing outside the Church of St Blaise for 600 years. The monument means a lot to locals: he's their version of the ancient knight Roland, who was famed for his service to Charlemagne and worshipped for representing the independence of free cities.

This Roland was renamed Orlando by the Italians in Ragusa, which makes this statue the most southern Roland in Europe and more than just an emblem of freedom. The Dubrovnik textiles industry historically used Orlando's forearm, 51.25cm long, as their measure for buying and selling fabric.

44 Island Hopping in THE ADRIATIC

BOATING | SWIMMING | DAY TRIP

Dubrovnik is a former thalassocracy, so seafaring is in the city's blood. Locals are as at home on the waves as anywhere, so the jet-skiing, kayaking and speed-boat tours on offer are top quality, and various island-hopping options can get you to the Elaphiti.

LAZYLLAMA/SHUTTERSTOCK ©

How to

Getting around Ferry services wind down their links after September, so check the websites of Jadrolinija (jadrolinija.hr) and Krilo (krilo.hr) before making off-season island-hopping plans.

When to go Summer is the best season to enjoy the sea, and the waters glitter and provide inviting hues of blue and green.

Wear sunscreen It's easy to get caught out by the cool sea breeze and forget to reapply.

PUNTACRISTO/SHUTTERSTOCK ©

Kayak vs Jet Ski

Energetic, thrill-seeking travellers can find loads on offer on the shores of Dubrovnik. Sea-kayaking companies set off from Banje Beach, Sveti Jakov Beach and dinky Šulić Beach under Fort Lovrijenac, where guides take you out to paddle on a loop around the old town and even around Lokrum island.

If your need for speed is greater than a good old kayak, jet-ski tours also leave from Dubrovnik's shores. **Jet Ski Dubrovnik** (jetski-rent-dubrovnik.com/jet-ski-safari) runs themed tours, including a sunset tour, a *Game of Thrones* tour or the three-hour-long Total Experience, which covers Cavtat, the Elaphiti, Lokrum and Dubrovnik's City Walls.

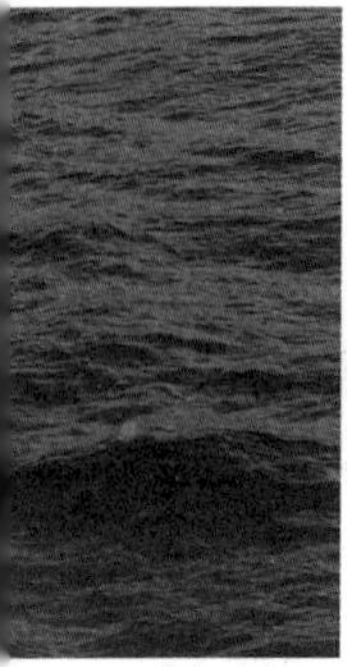

ANTONIO PRISTON/SHUTTERSTOCK ©

Sweet Treats

If you're heading to the Elaphiti Islands, have a meal in Lopud at Mandrac Seafood Restaurant, a quaint spot with a local vibe. Get a table outside by the pier and pick from the menu of fresh seafood, including delicious calamari. The incredible house-made desserts truly steal the show.

Above left Kayaking, Dubrovnik coast
Left Jet skiing
Above Šulić Beach

Ferried Away to Lokrum

A protected holy island with heaps of character, verdant Lokrum is a beautiful little island a 10-minute ferry ride from Dubrovnik's old harbour. It's the perfect place to escape the hubbub of the old town for an afternoon, with many swimming spots and interesting sights, such as the island's large Benedictine monastery, with lovely cloisters and gardens, or the island's 'Dead Sea', a saltwater lake that's blissful to float on. *Game of Thrones* fans will love the small museum dedicated to the island's time as a filming location. There's even an iron throne to sit on.

Speed Off to the Elaphiti Islands

A small archipelago in the Adriatic, the Elaphiti has three main islands: Šipan, Lopud and Koločep. **Šipan** is the largest, and is famous for its sprawling olive groves, lush vegetation, cute villages and the occasional goat.

Lopud is loved for its sandy beaches and medieval ruins, and you might even find a granny selling her recently spun lace – the island has had a weaving industry for centuries.

Elaphiti Dreaming

Why should anyone go to Elaphiti? Because of how clean the Adriatic Sea is: it's crystal clear. Go snorkelling in the caves of Koločep. Lopud has amazing sandy beaches, the only sandy beaches in this region. You must go to Šipan for the amazing local cheeses and olive oils. The islands are busier since I was a kid, but the roots are the same. There are still schools, and people live there. They're living, breathing community islands. Dubrovnik locals head over on the weekends too. Just 20 minutes by boat and you're feeling a totally different energy.

■ By Lukša Malohodžić
director of Rewind Dubrovnik
@rewinddubrovnikbyboat

Ferries run to all three islands from Dubrovnik's Gruž port, or myriad boat trips can take you to the captivating islands for a day trip from Dubrovnik's old-town harbour. Most of these boat trips operate large vessels and pack on as many folks as possible. If you can stump up for a private speedboat tour, it's worth it to have your own trip around the gorgeous archipelago. **Rewind Dubrovnik** (rewind dubrovnik.com) caters trips to your interests with expert local guides.

Book a table at **Bowa** on Šipan island. This upscale restaurant includes a boat pick-up service to the island from the mainland to enjoy mussels, charcuterie board and the classy atmosphere. Book a cabana table if you can.

Hop to Korčula & Mljet

If you have time to unwind after a Dubrovnik city break, tag on a stay in **Korčula** or **Mljet**, the nearest islands to the city and two of the most impressive in Croatia. Let the beaches, gastronomy and vini-culture on Korčula fill your days, or cycle, hike and swim your way around the lagoons within Mljet National Park. Jadrolina and Krilo catamaran ferries take 90 minutes from Dubrovnik to Mljet, and it's another 30 minutes to Korčula.

Left Beach Sunj, Lopud
Below Benedictine Monastery, Lokrum

45 Scoot Along THE COAST

ROAD TRIP | ARCHITECTURE | SCENERY

Do as the locals do and hop on a moped to cruise around the greater Dubrovnik region. Bypass the traffic and whizz along the sweeping coastal roads to visit impressive architectural and natural sights in Southern Dalmatia.

GORAN JAKUS PHOTOGRAPHY/GETTY IMAGES ©

How to

Getting around Companies in Dubrovnik hire out mopeds and motorbikes. Prices start from €50 a day for a 125cc bike, and you can negotiate weekly rates.

When to go May to September is the perfect time for driving the coast with balmy weather.

Take a tour Vespa Tour Dubrovnik (vespatourdubrovnik.com) runs guided drives in summer. Choose from the panoramic loop or the tour to the Ombla River, which lasts about two hours.

GORAN JAKUS PHOTOGRAPHY/GETTY IMAGES ©

Drive to the Bay of Hotels

A gorgeous sweeping coastal drive south of Dubrovnik into Konavle takes you to the majestic Bay of Hotels. Five structures adorn the shore of Župa Bay in Kupari, but they now all stand derelict in all their angular, concrete glory. **Hotel Pelegrin**, **Hotel Kupari**, **Hotel Goričina I** and **Hotel Goričina II** were built from the 1960s onwards and encircle the stylistically incongruous, 1920s-era **Hotel Grand**.

As with many masterpieces of Yugoslavian brutalist architecture, these hotels are dilapidated and have been abandoned since the Homeland War of the 1990s. The architecturally unimpressive but oldest of the bunch, Hotel Grand is a listed and protected building, but for some reason, the more significant work of revered Sarajevo-

PAWEL KLOBUKOWSKI/GETTY IMAGES ©

Mynt Mopeds

The easiest way to whip around Dubrovnik's suburbs and beaches is by hopping on a pay-as-you-go Mynt moped. It's simple to sign up on the app and top up your credit. Helmets are included in each of the electricity-powered 50cc bikes' trunks.

Above left Bay of Hotels
Left Hotel Grand
Above Hotel Goričina

born architect David Finci, who built the magnificent Hotel Pelegrin (the almost inverted pyramid, the northernmost in the bay) has not been listed or protected, despite his designs and contribution to the international canon of architecture being noted by a huge exhibition at the Museum of Modern Art in New York City.

Zip to Trsteno Arboretum

A smooth 30-minute drive along the gleaming coast from Dubrovnik gets you to the **Trsteno Arboretum**. Built in the 15th century by one of the wealthiest noble families in Dubrovnik, the Gucetic-Gozze, the sprawling arboretum is perched on a hilltop with glorious views over the Adriatic Sea and the Elaphiti Islands. Paths twist past rare trees, shrubs and plants, as the founders requested that merchants and explorers bring back seeds and saplings, which continue to flourish centuries later. The impressive water features include an aqueduct to keep the gardens irrigated and an imposing fountain and pond with a grotto and statue of Neptune watching over it all.

Where to Stop & Swim

Hotel Belvedere
This goliath of a building, an abandoned Yugoslavia-era hotel, is a favourite local swim spot and a *Game of Thrones* filming location a few minutes' drive from Dubrovnik's old town.

Trsteno Brsečine Beach
A divine little pebble beach a stone's throw from Trsteno in a nice cove protected from big waves. Ease yourself into the shallow, bright-blue waters.

Mali Ston Beach
A small swimming spot near the seafood restaurants and harbour, this pebble beach is well shaded. A dip is well deserved after conquering the length of the walls.

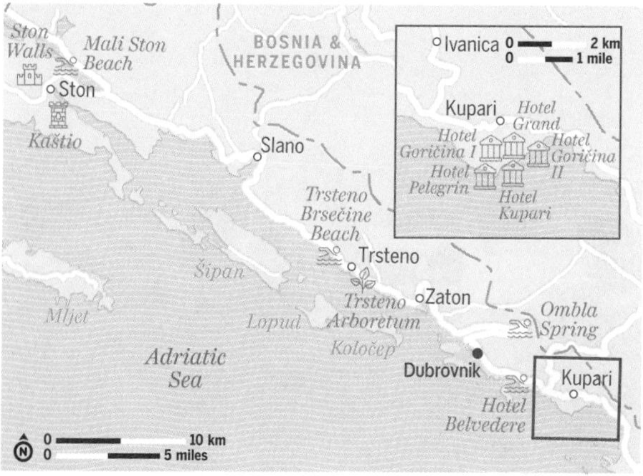

Left Hotel Belvedere
Below Trsteno Arboretum

Jump into Ombla River

Undoubtedly one of Dubrovnik's best-kept secrets, the unfathomably dinky **Ombla Spring** is one of the shortest in the world, and it's a summer hangout and hallowed swim spot for locals. At a mere 30m in length, the river springs straight from a karst cave within the looming mountain that frames it. You can jump in the cold waters from the small piers and abandoned water mill that surround it. It's a gorgeous spot, lined by lush greenery and old-world houses, protected by the Ombla Bridge before it flows off into the infinitely larger Dubrovačka River, which in turn leads to the sea.

Cruise the Scenic Route to Ston

It's a beautiful one-hour drive from Dubrovnik to the Walls of Ston, which stretch from **Little Ston** (Mali Ston) – a small village near excellent oyster farms – to **Ston** proper, an unspoiled small town, home to the **Kaštio** fortress and paved roads. It takes about 30 minutes to walk from one end of the walls to the other, but don't rush – take in the gorgeous views of the bays and towns below. While the steps that traverse the **Ston Walls** aren't too steep, we don't recommend taking them on in the midday heat of the summer months, lest you boil like the oysters in the pots beneath you.

46 Wine WARS

VINEYARDS | FOOD & DRINK | TASTINGS |

With a 2000-year-old viniculture, three major wine regions vie for the title of 'best in Southern Dalmatia': the idyllic island of Korčula, the hills of Konavle Valley and the plains of the Pelješac Peninsula. You can also try bottles in downtown Dubrovnik.

DONNEBRYANT/SHUTTERSTOCK ©

How to

Getting there Dubrovnik Airport is the easiest access point for Southern Dalmatia, but you can also reach Korčula by ferry from Split.

When to go Visit from May to August for guaranteed wine tasting. By autumn, stocks run low.

DIY visits Wine tours and tastings are popular to book from Dubrovnik, but if you're on Korčula or the Pelješac Peninsula, vineyards dot the landscape, and it's easy to visit the wineries yourself.

GORAN SAFAREK/GETTY IMAGES ©

Hints of Korčula

Sprawling rural Korčula is home to more than 20 wineries, all producing delectable grapes and bottles of wine that have given the island a reputation as a wine haven. Eight of those wineries can be found in **Lumbarda** (southeast of Korčula's old town), where families have been producing wine for centuries before opting to open to the public. The region has so many excellent *grk* (local white wine) tasting options that you'll be hard pressed to choose one, so schedule a few if you can.

When you visit is important. Because the wineries sell their house-made bottles, if you come too late in the season (after mid-September), some are likely to be sold out. Once the *grk* is gone, it's not available until next year.

PER KARLSSON-BKWINE.COM/ALAMY STOCK PHOTO ©

Sipping Wine in Šipan

Aside from being known for its immensely chilled-out atmosphere, beautiful old-world buildings in the small towns and the sparkling blue waters, Šipan in the Elaphiti archipelago is a haven for small family-run vineyards. One to visit is Goravica (goravica.com), where host Mato Goravica serves the white, red and rose made at his family farmhouse.

Above left Lumbarda
Left Matuško winery (p230
Below Pelješac grape varieties (p230)

Cork Pops on the Pelješac Peninsula

The long, thin 70km of land that stretches above Mljet and Korčula – with short and easy ferry links to both – the Peljesac Peninsula is famed for its vineyards. Many Dubrovnik wine-tasting day trips head this way. The region is known and loved for its hearty reds, particularly *plavac mali*, a variety of grape specific to Southern Dalmatia that's reared on the slopes of Dingač and Postup. This robust red has whiffs of cherry and spices.

Head to the hillside village Potomje to visit popular wineries **Matuško** or **Madirazza**, which have been open to the public for years, or the newer kid on the block, **Vina Antičević**. The enthusiasm of the staff will undoubtedly win you over. For a more unusual experience, swing by **Edivo Vino**, Croatia's only underwater winery. It's located in the village of Drače, near Mali Ston, where owners Edi and Ivo had the genius idea of ageing their wine in Roman amphoras in the

Unmissable Wineries in Korčula

Popić Winery
In the family for 300 years, Popić Winery in Lumbarda offers not only the most delicious *grk* wine tasting but also the most scenic, with sweeping views of the vineyards and the sea from the serene terrace.

Pošip 'PZ' Čara
This exceptional winery is an agricultural cooperative, and the whole village joins forces to produce the best *pošip* in Croatia.

Tasovac Winery
This charming spot in a renovated family house in Žrnovo is an intimate affair. Welcoming host Sanja serves award-winning *pošip* and 2022 *grk* in the tasting set.

Left Edivo Vino winery
Below Madirazza winery

cool depths of the lagoon. Bottles of Edivo Vino's *plavac mali* are stored in the bay for 700 days before being fished out, by staff – or visitors if they so wish – followed by a waterside wine tasting on dry land.

Low-Key Konavle

Petar Crvik's family has been making wine at their home in the Konavle Valley since the 1800s, and visitors can sample the bottles at **Crvik Winery**. The merlot is astounding, which Crvik attributes to the microclimate in the area and the soil that's not too acidic. You'll want to take home the award-winning Vilin Ples, a fine blend of cabernet sauvignon, merlot and the local grape *plavac*. Email crvik.vino@gmail.com to arrange a wine-tasting visit.

Taste it all in Dubrovnik

If you're staying in Dubrovnik, **D'Vino Wine Bar** in the old town offers an excellent range. You can stop by any time, but it's smart to reserve a table during peak summer season. For wine pairing with dinner, wine expert Domagoj Žeravica gives the best food and wine tour in the city. Email him at info@deliciousdubrovnik.com for availability. Tours run at 4pm and 7pm daily.

47 Walking the MARBLE

HISTORY | ARCHITECTURE | DESIGN

Catapulted to international popularity by HBO's hit show *Game of Thrones*, Dubrovnik is busier than ever. The city's dazzling, well-preserved Gothic, Renaissance and baroque architecture provided the backdrop for the show, standing in as King's Landing.

KIM WILLEMS/SHUTTERSTOCK ©

Pre-Walk Pit Stop

Before you start a tour around the old town, stop at Peppino's Gelato for a scoop of its mouth-watering flavours, such as Rookie Cookie or Lady's Lemon Cake. This legendary ice-cream vendor has two branches inside the old City Walls: one underneath the Dominican Monastery near Ploče Gate and the other on od Puča.

Trip Notes

Getting there Flights land at Dubrovnik Airport from spring through autumn. Otherwise, take a coach from Split or fly in from Zagreb.

When to go Summer in downtown Dubrovnik is gridlocked. Visit in spring or autumn for smaller crowds or in winter if you want the dazzling pavements to yourself.

Where to start Local guide Ivan Vukovic recommends beginning a walk of Dubrovnik's old town from Ploče Gate, the eastern entrance, which is less busy.

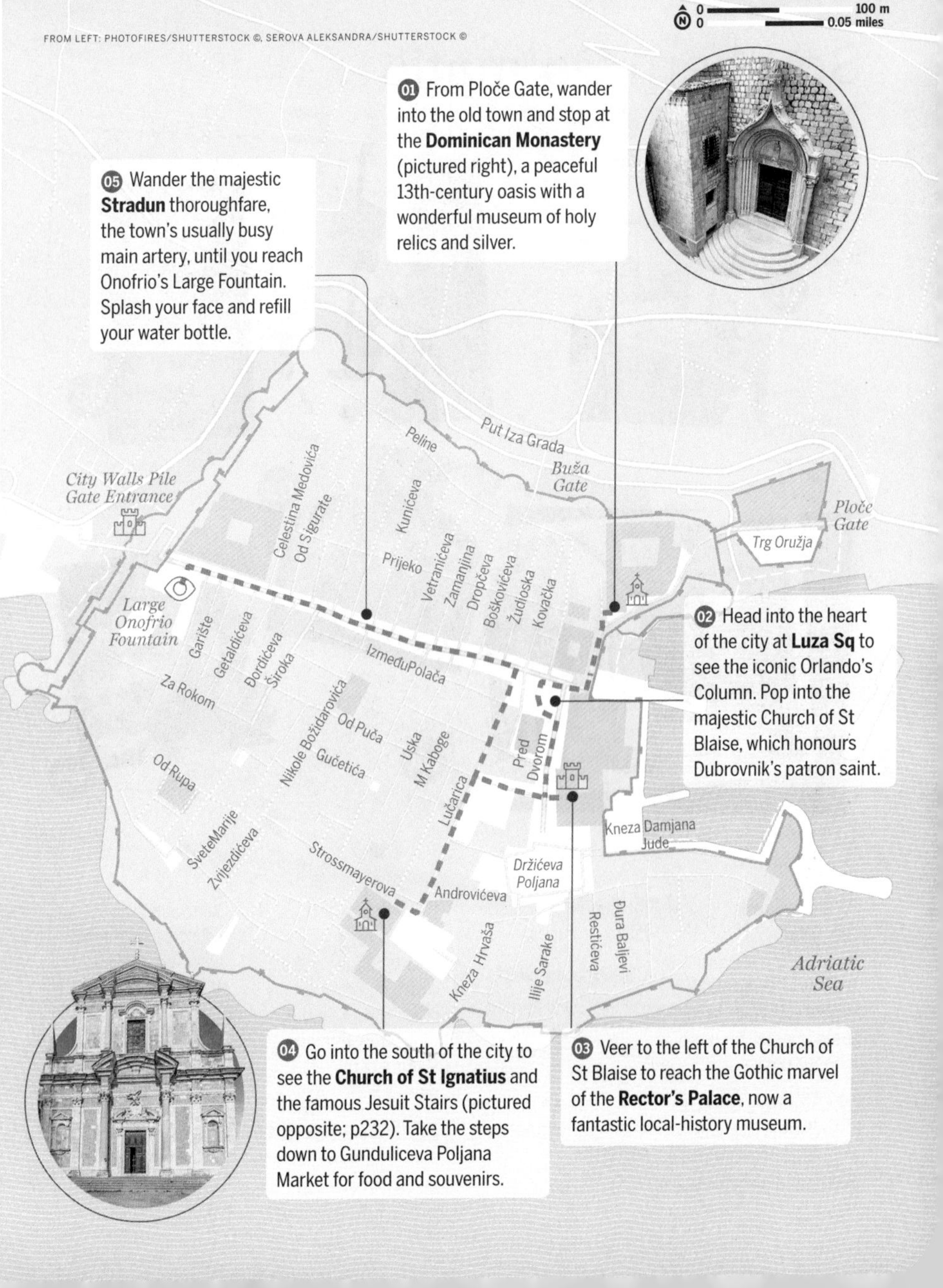

01 From Ploče Gate, wander into the old town and stop at the **Dominican Monastery** (pictured right), a peaceful 13th-century oasis with a wonderful museum of holy relics and silver.

02 Head into the heart of the city at **Luza Sq** to see the iconic Orlando's Column. Pop into the majestic Church of St Blaise, which honours Dubrovnik's patron saint.

03 Veer to the left of the Church of St Blaise to reach the Gothic marvel of the **Rector's Palace**, now a fantastic local-history museum.

04 Go into the south of the city to see the **Church of St Ignatius** and the famous Jesuit Stairs (pictured opposite; p232). Take the steps down to Gunduliceva Poljana Market for food and souvenirs.

05 Wander the majestic **Stradun** thoroughfare, the town's usually busy main artery, until you reach Onofrio's Large Fountain. Splash your face and refill your water bottle.

Southern Dalmatia
ICONS

01 Dubrovnik City Walls
Croatia's top tourist attraction, Dubrovnik's mighty City Walls have stood 25m tall for more than 500 years.

02 Orlando's Column
An emblem of Dubrovnik, the statue of Orlando has been standing outside the Church of St Blaise for six centuries.

03 Konavle vest
Worn by local women on feast days and special occasions. Green, red and gold silk threads adorn these ornately embroidered vests.

04 Dominican Monastery
A 13th-century oasis with a museum of holy relics and silver, this monastery reminds visitors of the city's devout faith.

05 Red pillbox hat
Pillbox hats are common across Croatia, but Dubrovnik's is a distinctive bright red and is worn at local celebrations.

06 Grk wine
Grk is a white-wine grape variety grown on Korčula, specifically in the sweeping vineyards around the village of Lumbarda.

07 Korčula Old Town Gate
A lion overlooks the steps that lead to the old town's gate, hinting at the island's historical association with Venice.

08 Ston cake
Pasta in a cake? Yes, coupled with chocolate, walnuts, almonds, cinnamon and a cheeky dash of rum. It's only found in Ston, and it's delicious.

09 Ston Walls
First built by Ragusans in 1358, these walls are the longest in Europe and once protected the town and its valuable salt pans.

10 Jadrolinija catamaran ferry
Connecting Dubrovnik, Korčula and Mljet with Hvar and Split, the national ferry line is a Croatia institution you're bound to board.

Listings

BEST OF THE REST

Dubrovnik Old Town Tipples

Soul Caffe & Rakhija Bar
Excellent wines, beers and *rakija* (grappa) are lovingly poured while you enjoy live jazz musicians in the alley most nights. The huge, beautifully presented charcuterie board is a nice treat.

Buža Bar
You're undoubtedly paying for the view and the experience here, but it's worth having a few beers in this nook in the City Walls, watching the divers launch themselves into the sea from the cliffs.

D'Vino Wine Bar
The best spot in the city for wine tasting, with friendly staff whose knowledge of Croatian wines is second to none. You'll be vowing to go back to this atmospheric tavern.

MILK
The old town's first gay bar serves a mean cocktail and guarantees a fun night out, with friendly staff and excellent pop tunes until the small hours.

Pizza the Action

Papillon Pizzeria €
Heaven-sent Neapolitan-style pizzas with cloud-like bases come at reasonable prices for Dubrovnik. Book a table on the terrace and treat yourself to a burrata on the side.

Pizzeria Pape €€
Friendly servers seat you at a table in Korčula old town's city walls. The delicious and extensive pizza menu sets you up for a busy day of sightseeing or swimming.

Desetka Pizzeria €
Cavtat's best pizzeria serves fluffy bases with layers of toppings. It also has a lengthy Italian menu to choose from at its waterside spot with sweeping views of the bay. €

Vegan Heaven

Nishta €€
Stalwarts of the plant-based food scene in Dubrovnik's old town, Nishta has a seasonal menu that includes Asian fusion and Mexican dishes, full of flavour and made with love by chef Gildas Remy.

Vege Dub €€
With a tip-top menu of fast-food favourites, Dubrovnik's Vege Dub is fast becoming known for its vegan pizza, hands down the best of its kind in Croatia.

Urban & Veggie €€
The largest vegan restaurant in Dubrovnik has charming staff, a huge garden and a menu of delicious plates (order the eggplant tartare), including a mouth-watering vegan breakfast.

Buža Bar

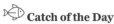

Catch of the Day

Lady Pi-Pi €€
This affordable favourite occupies a terrace that overlooks Dubrovnik's old city. The fresh seafood platter is popular for its size and rich flavours. Arrive early or reserve a table in advance at this popular spot.

Barba €€
The friendly staff at this joint by the Ston city gate serves delectable seafood with a modern twist, as well as the best Ston cake in town.

Kapetanova Kuća €€
A local institution for 50 years, this spot in Mali Ston is a classy affair – Croatians travel for miles to dine on the huge portions of fish.

Fine Dining

Restaurant 360 €€€
One of Croatia's finest Michelin experiences, Restaurant 360 sits within Dubrovnik's City Walls overlooking the old harbour. It has a tasting or a la carte menu, but don't skip the Ston oysters.

Bugenvila €€
The best menu, service and atmosphere of all the restaurants on Cavtat's main promenade. The menu and decor are elegant, and the staff have a down-to-earth approach.

LD Restaurant €€€
Korčula's premier Michelin restaurant is a treat. Dine on the city walls and enjoy the exceptionally well-presented tasting menu, including the famed gyoza or seasonal fish.

Go Local

Trattoria Carmen €€
This rustic hole-in-the-wall by Dubrovnik's old harbour serves incredible seafood, steaks and pasta at reasonable prices in a charming space.

Kapetanova Kuća

Atrij Žrnovo Simple Cuisine €
This bistro on Korčula does local dishes such as *žrnovski makaruni* (house-made macaroni) to perfection. Owner Petar runs an excellent grill where lamb and beef are mainstays.

Kameni Mlin €€
Just outside Čilipi, Kameni Mlin (which means 'stone mill') is a restaurant, museum and cooking school rolled into one. Feast on fish or meat from the *peka* (a bell-shaped lid that sits on top of a tray in the hearth) or learn to use one yourself.

Don't Skip Dessert

Peppino's Gelato €€
In Dubrovnik, Peppino's has 20 creatively named flavours. Highlights include Carob and Fig Nostalgia, Wolfgang Almondeus Mozart packed full of almonds and pistachios, and the unforgettable Golden Ticket Chocolate.

Restoran Pepper & Choco €€
This classy restaurant has awesome desserts and the best ice-cream window in Korčula's old town. Don't miss the traditional fig or almond desserts or the chocolate and apple tart.

Scan to find more things to do in Dubrovnik & Southern Dalmatia

Practicalities

Right Rovinj (p104)

Est 1967
Est 1967

EASY STEPS FROM THE AIRPORT TO THE CITY CENTRE

Franjo Tuđman Airport in Zagreb is the main entry point for many international travellers to Croatia, and it has the highest passenger numbers. The airports in Split and Dubrovnik are the gateways to Dalmatia and see high traffic in summer, with many seasonal connections operated by low-cost airlines. Each of these airports has a shuttle-bus service to the city centre.

AT THE AIRPORT

SIM CARDS
SIM cards are available at Tisak Media shops in the arrivals area of airports. Local mobile network providers A1, Telemach and T-Mobile all offer prepaid SIM cards for tourists that include 10- or 30-day plans, which cost between €8 and €12.

CURRENCY EXCHANGE
Currency exchange offices are available in the arrivals halls at all airports, but rates are not as favourable as those offered by national banks. Exchange a minimum amount of foreign currency at the airport only if you have no other option.

Zagreb airport

WI-FI Free wif-fi is available in all areas of the airports in Zagreb, Split and Dubrovnik.

ATMS ATMs are stationed in the arrivals area of all airports. Beware of Euronet ATMs, which have high fees and unfavourable exchange rates.

CHARGING STATIONS Power outlets and charging stations with USB ports are available at all airports.

CUSTOMS REGULATIONS

According to EU rules, arriving passengers can carry a maximum of 200 cigarettes, 1L of spirits, 4L of wine or 16L of beer. If you're carrying more than €10,000 in cash, you must declare it to the customs officer.

GETTING TO THE CITY CENTRE

Zagreb A shuttle bus connects Zagreb's airport to the main bus station every 30 minutes. The journey time is 25 to 45 minutes depending on traffic. Bus 290 runs twice an hour between the airport and Kvaternik Sq.

Split A dedicated shuttle bus departs every half hour, linking Split Airport to the city's main bus station, a 40-minute ride. A cheaper and only slightly slower option is to take bus 2 or 38 to the Sukoisan bus terminal in the city centre.

Dubrovnik Dubrovnik Airport is connected to the city centre via a shuttle bus leaving every 40 minutes, with stops at Ploče gate and the main bus station in Gruž.

HOW MUCH FOR

an airport taxi €25–30

an airport bus €8–10

car hire from €25 per day

Hire a car

Car-hire agencies have offices at the arrivals terminal of airports. Book in advance during peak tourist seasons, especially if you require an automatic vehicle.

Taxis

Find a taxi stand outside the airport arrivals terminals. Inquire at the taxi information desk for the official rate to the city centre.

Ride-share BlaBlaCar, a ride-share app that connects drivers with passengers, is popular in Croatia. It offers a convenient and affordable way to travel between cities by sharing the cost of transportation among passengers and the driver. Search for a ride and make a booking on the BlaBlaCar website (blablacar.hr) or the mobile app.

OTHER POINTS OF ENTRY

Trains connect the cities of Zagreb, Rijeka, Split and Vinkovci with destinations in Austria, Czechia, Germany, Hungary, Slovakia, Slovenia and Switzerland. Some of these routes operate during the summer season only. EuroNight Croatia is a night train between Zagreb and Zürich via Munich, Stuttgart and Feldkirch. From May to October, a night train travels from Split to Bratislava via Maribor, Graz and Vienna, with the possibility to also transport your car or motorbike.

Buses link Croatia with its neighbours (Slovenia, Hungary, Serbia, Bosnia and Herzegovina, and Montenegro) as well as several other countries in Europe, including Italy, Austria, Germany, Belgium and the Netherlands. Many of these bus lines run year-round.

Seasonal car ferries operated by Jadrolinija travel between the coastlines of Italy and Croatia, linking Ancona to Zadar (summer only) and Split (year-round), and Bari to Split and Dubrovnik from May to October. During the summer months, Venezia Lines operates daily passenger ferry services between Venice and Poreč, Rovinj and Pula.

TRANSPORT TIPS TO HELP YOU GET AROUND

If your visit to Croatia is limited to one or two cities, you can get from point A to B on the efficient intercity bus system. However, if you plan to travel extensively or explore rural areas or the islands, the most convenient way to get around is with your own transport.

BUSES

Croatia has an extensive intercity bus network, which almost always runs on schedule. Buses are comfortable and equipped with air-conditioning, sometimes USB ports and free wi-fi. Baggage is charged a small extra fee to be stored in the hold.

FERRIES

Foot-passenger and car ferries potter up and down the Adriatic coast, linking the Croatian mainland with its many islands. Foot-passenger ferries tend to be faster and are called *katamaran*, while car ferries are referred to as *trajekt* or simply 'ferry'.

RENTAL PER DAY

Car hire €25–75

Petrol from €1.40 per litre

Bike hire from €20

A road toll system is in place on all of Croatia's motorways, as well as the bridge to Krk Island, the Učka tunnel that connects Kvarner to Istria, and the road between Rijeka and Delnice. At the entrance to motorways, you receive a toll card, and you pay when exiting at your destination. Tolls for tunnels, bridges and shorter roads are paid upfront.

CAR HIRE Hiring a car requires a credit card and a safety deposit. A young driver's surcharge is imposed on renters under the age of 21. Reserve in advance in the peak season, especially if you need an automatic car, which costs extra.

DOMESTIC FLIGHTS Regular flights operated by Croatian Airlines link the capital of Zagreb to Zadar, Split, Dubrovnik, Osijek and Pula. During the summer months, a seasonal flight is added to Brač Island, though flying such short distances comes with a big environmental impact.

DRIVING ESSENTIALS

Drive on the right – the steering wheel is on the left.

.05 The blood-alcohol limit is 0.05%. It's 0% for drivers under 24.

50 The maximum speed limit is 50km/h in urban areas, 90 km/h on secondary roads and 130km/h on motorways.

On narrow roads or single-lane bridges, give way if the red arrow is pointing in your direction of travel.

Headlights must be switched on at all times between 1 November and 31 March.

NGCHIYUI/SHUTTERSTOCK ©

TRAINS Croatian Railways' network is limited and convenient for travel only within Istria and between Zagreb and destinations such as Rijeka, Osijek and Varaždin. Travelling by train is generally slower than bus travel but significantly cheaper.

CYCLING Riding a bike is a popular way to travel around Croatia. Look for an app-based public bike-share system called Nextbike, which rents out bicycles and e-bikes in 30 towns and cities across the country.

TAXI APPS In Zagreb and other major cities, look into using ride-hailing services such as Uber, Eko Taxi, Taxi Cammeo and Radio Taxi. At taxi stands in central Dubrovnik, signboards list official rates according to destination. Taxis are sometimes the only mode of transportation available on islands or in rural areas. Always determine the fare before starting the trip.

KNOW YOUR CARBON FOOTPRINT
A domestic flight between Zagreb and Split emits about 110kg of carbon dioxide per passenger. A train emits about 50kg. A bus emits 20kg for the same distance, per passenger. Native's carbon calculator tool (native.eco/for-individuals/calculators/#Travel) can be used to calculate and purchase carbon offsets to contribute to clean energy and carbon-reducing projects.

ROAD DISTANCE CHART (KMS)

	Dubrovnik	Osijek	Pula	Rijeka	Šibenik	Split	Varaždin	Zadar	Zagorje
Osijek	515								
Pula	710	540							
Rijeka	610	440	110						
Šibenik	685	620	400	300					
Split	232	430	515	415	85				
Varaždin	685	340	350	250	425	490			
Zadar	350	560	345	290	90	160	370		
Zagorje	500	350	240	145	250	320	165	190	
Zagreb	605	290	270	165	345	410	85	285	85

SAFE TRAVEL

Croatia is generally a safe country with a low crime rate. Incidents of violent crime are rare, and the threat of terrorist attacks is low. Safety incidents involving tourists are mostly due to road, boating or swimming accidents.

WILDFIRES Summer temperatures can be intense across the country, often causing a risk of drought conditions and potential wildfires as a result. During the summer months, it's forbidden to light outdoor fires or to use barbecues outside of authorised areas. If you see a fire, call the fire brigade immediately on 193.

JELLYFISH & SEA URCHINS Jellyfish and sea urchins are part of the Adriatic Sea's ecosystem and are more of a nuisance than a real danger. If you spot jellyfish in the water, it's best not to venture in and risk a painful sting. Prickly sea urchins are commonly found on rocky seabeds.

SNAKES Croatia is home to more than a dozen snake species, including poisonous vipers, and sightings are common. Avoid walking barefoot in long grass and exercise caution when picking mushrooms or wild asparagus. If hiking in forested areas, wear closed shoes and long trousers. Call emergency services on 112 if you're bitten by a snake.

MINE-AFFECTED AREAS Unexploded mines may be present in former war-affected areas of Eastern Slavonia, Brod-Posavina County, Karlovac County, areas around Zadar County and the more remote sections of Plitvice Lakes National Park.

HIKE SAFELY

The Croatian Mountain Rescue Service cautions against hiking in inappropriate footwear and straying from marked hiking trails. Take sufficient food and water, make sure your phone is fully charged, and be prepared for sudden weather changes.

TRAVEL INSURANCE

Travellers who need a visa to enter Croatia must also carry travel insurance. EU citizens are encouraged to travel with their European Health Insurance Card (EHIC), which grants them free emergency healthcare.

EMERGENCY NUMBERS

Emergency services can be reached 24/7 by dialling 112 or 192 for the police, 193 in case of fire, 194 for emergency medical assistance, and 195 for search and rescue at sea.

QUICK TIPS TO HELP YOU MANAGE YOUR MONEY

CREDIT CARDS Cash is still king in Croatia, but credit cards are sometimes accepted. You're not likely to have a problem paying by card at hotels and most restaurants, but many bakeries, cafes and bars may insist on cash only. Market vendors expect to be paid in cash, and bus fares are also cash only unless there's an option to book online.

VAT

The standard value-added tax rate is 25%. A reduced rate of 13% applies to accommodation and 5% to staple foods.

VAT REFUNDS

Look for shops displaying a 'Tax Free' sign. Non-EU residents can qualify for a VAT refund if more than €100 is spent on goods in one shop. Request a tax-free form.

CURRENCY

euro (€)

HOW MUCH FOR A

coffee
€2

glass of wine
€2

burek (pastry stuffed with meat or cheese)
€1.50

ATMS Cash machines, known in Croatian as *bankomat*, are found in all urban and tourist centres. Only use cash machines operated by national banks to avoid the excessive fees charged by Euronet ATMs. If you find yourself in an area with no ATMs, you can request a cash advance at any post office for a fee.

PAYING THE BILL In restaurants, servers will not present you with the bill until you request it. By law, a receipt must always be issued.

TIPPING

Tips are not obligatory in Croatia, which doesn't have a tipping culture. That said, gratuities are always welcome. Round up the bill in cafes and bars and leave 5% to 10% at restaurants.

BUDGET HACKS

To stretch your euros, keep an eye out for restaurants offering three-course lunch specials on weekdays called *marenda* or *gablec* for under €10. Served between 11am and 3pm, these hot meals cater to workers on their lunch breaks.

Students and senior citizens receive discounted fares on intercity buses and trains. Photo ID is required.

Avoid Croatia's expensive motorway tolls by opting for scenic secondary roads and a slow travel experience.

MONEYCHANGERS

The best place to exchange foreign currency is at branches of Fina (the Croatian Financial Agency, a provider of financial and electronic services) or banks. Private currency-exchange offices tend to charge higher fees.

RESPONSIBLE TRAVEL

Tips to leave a lighter footprint, support local and have a positive impact on local communities.

ON THE ROAD

Embrace slow travel by basing yourself in one region and taking time to explore the local history, culture and cuisine.

Look into the green credentials of accommodation options by inquiring about recycling practices, renewable energy sources, energy-efficient appliances, and heating and cooling systems.

Hire a hybrid or electric car for road trips. Charging stations are available at hotels and along motorways.

Go on a cycling tour and explore on two wheels. Riding a bike is a good way to slow down and get closer to nature as well as local culture.

Reconsider cruise ships. Cruise liners pollute the Adriatic Sea and harm its fragile marine ecology. According to Friends of the Earth, a cruise holiday is responsible for eight times more carbon-dioxide emissions per day than a stay on land.

BORIS EDELMANN/SHUTTERSTOCK ©

GIVE BACK

Volunteer at the Bear Refuge Project (kuterevo.org/bears) in the village of Kuterevo in the Velebit mountains to help protect and rehabilitate orphaned bears (pictured above).

Join a responsible dolphin-watching trip and get insights into marine conservation on Lošinj Island with the Lošinj Marine Education Centre (blue-world.org). At the Dubrava Falconry Centre (sokolarskicentar.com) near Šibenik, learn about falcons and other protected birds of prey. Get insights into bees and why they're an essential part of the ecosystem at Tvrdić Honey (tvrdichoney.com) on Šolta Island.

Donate to the Blue World Institute and help protect the fragile coastal and sea habitats of dolphins, turtles and other marine animals in the Adriatic Sea (blue-world.org/get-involved/donate).

DOS & DON'TS

Local authorities in popular tourist spots such as Split, Hvar Town and Dubrovnik are cracking down on behaviour seen as inappropriate, such as walking in the street in swimwear, which can earn you an on-the-spot fine. Other infractions include climbing on monuments, sleeping outdoors and drinking, spitting, urinating or vomiting in public places.

LEAVE A SMALL FOOTPRINT

BYOB (Bring Your Own Bottle). Tap water in Croatia is clean and safe to drink. Fill up a reusable water bottle instead of buying water in a single-use plastic bottle.

Hire an e-bike. Do the planet a favour (and get an extra push on uphill climbs) by hiring an e-bike instead of a gas-powered scooter or quad bike.

Stick to the trail. Respect Croatia's flora and fauna and protect natural landscapes by not straying off hiking and cycling trails.

BARBARA MILAVEC/SHUTTERSTOCK ©

SUPPORT LOCAL

Support local producers while reducing the carbon footprint of the food industry by visiting markets. Look for the *gradska tržnica* (city market) in every Croatian town and city, where you can buy fresh produce directly from farmers.

Croatian products such as wine, olive oil and honey (pictured left) are eco-friendly gifts and souvenirs that also support the local economy.

CLIMATE CHANGE & TRAVEL

It's impossible to ignore the impact we have when travelling, and the importance of making changes where we can. Lonely Planet urges all travellers to engage with their travel carbon footprint. There are many carbon calculators online that allow travellers to estimate the carbon emissions generated by their journey; try resurgence.org/resources/carbon-calculator.html. Many airlines and booking sites offer travellers the option of offsetting the impact of greenhouse gas emissions by contributing to climate-friendly initiatives around the world. We continue to offset the carbon footprint of all Lonely Planet staff travel, while recognising this is a mitigation more than a solution.

RESOURCES

Sustainable Tourism
(mints.gov.hr/odrziviturizam/en/sustainable-tourism/23096)

Friends of the Earth Croatia
(zelena-akcija.hr/en)

Ecofriendly accommodation in Dalmatia
(dalmatia-green.com)

Vegan restaurants in Croatia
(prijatelji-zivotinja.hr/index.en.php?id=405)

UNIQUE & LOCAL WAYS TO STAY

Where to bed down in Croatia depends on your destination. Cities have plenty of hotel options, ranging from budget to boutique. Rural areas offer opportunities for camping and glamping, as well as quirky options like lighthouse stays. Long-distance hikers can overnight at a network of mountain huts, while countryside villas appeal to families.

HOW MUCH FOR A

campground spot from **€20/night**

glamping **€150/night**

villa with pool from **€200/night**

HOLIDAY VILLAS

The largest share of tourist accommodation on offer in Croatia consists of privately owned properties, from self-catering apartments in cities and seaside spots to spacious villas in more rural areas. Many tourist villas entice with little extras like open-air Jacuzzis or outdoor swimming pools, which are coveted by families travelling with children.

LIGHTHOUSE STAYS

For something completely different, consider spending the night in a lighthouse. Many lighthouses across Croatia have been converted into holiday accommodation, offering a unique experience as well as panoramic sea views. Most are situated on secluded corners of the coastline and sometimes even on their own islands.

GLAMPING

Glamping is a growing trend in Europe, and it has caught on in a big way in Croatia. This upscale camping option appeals to those who like to be close to nature but also appreciate a touch of luxe. Luxury air-conditioned tents, yurts and rustic wooden cabins with private decks or terraces to relax on outdoors are set in scenic natural surroundings, often in seaside locations. On-site perks usually include swimming pools, luxury spas, yoga studios and lounge bars.

Above: Glamping, Lanterna, Istria; **Above left**: Holiday villa, Pula (p109); **Above right**: Lighthouse Sućuraj, Hvar (p197)

Josip Schlosser Klekovski mountain lodge, Risnjak National Park (p82)

MOUNTAIN HUTS

Croatia has a vast network of more than 150 mountain huts located in remote and often inaccessible areas. These huts have been built along mountain and hiking trails as overnight shelters for long-distance walkers and mountaineers. A complete list is available on the Croatian Mountaineering Association website (hps.hr/info/planinarske-kuce).

Mountain huts come in three different categories, each with its particularities. *Planinarski domovi* (mountain lodges) provide food in addition to shelter, often in a dormitory-style setup, and many (but not all) are open throughout the year. *Planinarske kuće* (mountain houses) are open only on weekends and holidays. These two categories must be booked in advance by contacting the manager by phone. *Planinarska skloništa* (mountaineering shelters) are more basic and are left unlocked. Hikers can take shelter free of cost and without prior notice but need to have their own sleeping bags.

A few mountain huts are especially notable for their location or design. The Ratkovo mountaineering shelter is a log cabin perched at 1174m in a cave-like niche on a cliff face in Gorski Kotar. Zavižan is the highest mountain lodge, located at an altitude of 1594m in the Velebit mountains and doubles as a meteorological station. The architect-designed mountain shelter of Ždrilo stands out for its contemporary style.

BOOKING

Accommodation in Croatia can be reserved online using booking platforms or by reaching out directly to the property, which sometimes allows for some negotiation on rates. Room rates peak in July and August, as well as during the Easter and Christmas holidays – book as far ahead as possible for these periods. Prices are slightly reduced during the shoulder seasons of spring and autumn, while winter is the best time to get a good deal. The daily tourist tax is usually included in the nightly room rate. In some cases, villa bookings start on a weekend and often require a minimum stay of one week. Many hotels and other tourist accommodation close during the winter months in rural and coastal areas.

Glamping.com (glamping.com/destinations/europe/croatia) Unique glamping destinations across Croatia.

Book a Lighthouse (bookalighthouse.com/rentals/croatia) Lighthouse holiday rentals in Croatia.

Mountain Huts (mountain-huts.net) An interactive map of mountain huts in Croatia and neighbouring countries.

CAMP OUT

Wild camping is forbidden in Croatia, but campsites are ubiquitous all over the country. Campsites welcome tents, caravans and campervans, and on-site amenities range from basic to upscale.

ESSENTIAL NUTS & BOLTS

EUROPEAN UNION

In 2013, Croatia joined the EU, and it adopted the euro currency in 2023.

VISAS

Citizens of 90 countries do not need a visa to enter Croatia and can stay for up to 90 days within a six-month period.

SCHENGEN AREA

Since 2023, Croatia is one of 27 countries in the EU's border-control-free Schengen Area, which has no internal border controls or passport checks.

FAST FACTS

Time Zone
GMT+1 hr

Country Code
385

Electricity
XXV/XXHz

GOOD TO KNOW

The legal minimum age to buy alcohol is 18.

Smoking is prohibited in enclosed public spaces, including public transport, shops, and most restaurants and bars (though some may have smoking areas).

According to the 2021 census, nearly 80% of Croatians are Catholic.

Order tea at a cafe and you'll get fruit tea. Ask for black tea.

Swimming pools at seaside hotels are often filled with sea water.

ACCESSIBLE TRAVEL

Hotels & buildings New constructions are required to be fully accessible and feature lifts and ramps. While many hotels in historic buildings do not have lifts, newer hotels have been designed with accessibility in mind and may have a few accessible rooms on offer.

Accessible beaches The Plaja Beach Finder app (plaja.hr) features a 'Disabled Accessible Beach' category, which includes a list of accessible beaches across Croatia.

Public transport Public-transit systems in many cities, including Zagreb, Split and Dubrovnik, have accessibility features such as kneeling buses and low-floor trams designed for wheelchair users and others with mobility requirements.

Train travel The newer trains operated by Croatian Railways have low steps, but these carriages are not available on all routes. Contact Croatian Railways (hzpp.hr/en) to inquire about the accessibility of the train you plan to travel on before booking a seat.

Ferry travel Travellers with mobility needs have the right to free assistance on all ferries. Some car ferries have lifts, while passenger ferries are fully accessible and feature ramps to ease embarcation.

PAPERLESS TICKETS
Digital tickets for buses, trains and ferries are available when you book online.

PUBLIC TOILETS
All large supermarkets and shopping centres have free public toilets available for customers.

INTERNET
Free wi-fi hot spots are available in many cities, as well as airports, public transit and many businesses.

FAMILY TRAVEL

Hotels All hotels supply cots for babies, but be sure to reserve one in advance. Hotel chains often have plenty of kid-friendly amenities, such as kiddie pools, play areas and children's clubs.

Restaurants Many eateries provide high chairs, but kids' menus are not common. Staff are happy to whip up a kid-friendly dish such as pasta or pizza if it isn't already on the menu.

Public transport Fares are reduced by up to 50% for children under 12.

DIGITAL NOMADS

Croatia introduced a temporary-stay permit for digital nomads in 2021. Any non-EU/EEA national who works remotely as an employee or is self-employed can apply for the permit, which is valid for up to a year as long as services are not provided to Croatian companies.

SUNDAY SHOPPING

According to a 2023 law, shops can open for business on only 16 Sundays a year. This law exempts shops at airports, bus and train stations, ports, petrol stations, hospitals, hotels, museums and a few other locations.

GIOVANNI VALE/SHUTTERSTOCK ©

LGBTIQ+ TRAVELLERS

Attitudes towards the LGBTIQ+ community are slow to change in Croatia, a conservative country influenced by traditional values. Members of the LGBTIQ+ community prefer to keep a low profile.

The 2014 Life Partnership Act grants the right to same-sex couples to enter into a civil partnership on an equal basis as married couples.

Zagreb Pride (pictured left; zagreb-pride.net) is the LGBTIQ+ community's biggest event, which takes place on the second Saturday in June.

Split Pride (facebook.com/lgbt.pride.split) is an annual Pride march in June.

LANGUAGE

In Croatian, every letter is pronounced and its sound does not vary from word to word. Let's get started.

To enhance your trip with a phrasebook, visit **shop.lonelyplanet.com**.

BASICS

Hello.	Dobar dan	*do·bar dan*
Goodbye.	Zbogom	*zbo·gom*
Yes.	Da	*da*
No.	Ne	*ne*
Please.	Molim	*mo·lim*
Thank you.	Hvala vam/ti (pol/inf)	*hva·la vam/ti*
Excuse me.	Oprostite	*o·pro·sti·te*
Sorry.	Žao mi je.	*zha·o mi ye*

What's your name?
Kako se zovete/zoveš? (pol/inf)
ka·ko se zo·ve·te/zo·vesh

My name is ...
Zovem se ...
zo·vem se

Do you speak English?
Govorite/Govoriš li engleski? (pol/inf)
go·vo·ri·te/go·vo·rish li en·gle·ski

I don't understand.
a ne razumijem.
ya ne ra·zu·mi·yem

NUMBERS

1	**jedan**	*ye·dan*	6	**šest**	*shest*
2	**dva**	*dva*	7	**sedam**	*se·dam*
3	**tri**	*tri*	8	**osam**	*o·sam*
4	**četiri**	*che·ti· ri*	9	**devet**	*de·vet*
5	**pet**	*pet*	10	**deset**	*de·set*

DIRECTIONS & SIGNS

Where's (the station)?
Gdje je (stanica)? *gdye ye (sta·ni·tsa)*

What's the address?
Koja je adresa? *koy·a ye a·dre·sa*

Could you please write it down?
Možete li to napisati?/Možeš li to napisati? (pol/inf)
mo·zhe·te li to na·pi·sa·ti/mo·zhesh li to na·pi·sa·ti

Can you show me (on the map)?
Možete li mi to pokazati (na karti)?
mo·zhe·te li mi to po·ka·za·ti (na kar·ti)

Ulaz/Izlaz	Entrance/Exit
Otvoreno/Zatvoreno	Open/Closed
Slobodna Mjesta	Rooms Available
Bez Slobodnih Mjesta	No Vacancies
Informacije	Information
Policijska Stanica	Police Station
Zabranjeno	Prohibited
WC	Toilets
Muški/Ženski	Men/Women

EMERGENCIES

Help!	Upomoć!	*u·po·moch*
Go away!	Maknite se!	*mak·ni·te se*

Call the police!
Zovite policiju! *zo·vi·te po·li·tsi·yu*

Call a doctor!
Zovite liječnika! *zo·vi·te li·yech·ni·ka*

Index

000 Map pages

T

V

W

Z

'As a committed motorbike rider I thought looping the islands of Kvarner Bay in April on the back of a bike was a good idea and soon learned about the *bura* wind!

LUCIE GRACE

'I just love driving along the zigzag roads through the undulating hills of Zagorje as the sun drops over its vineyards, cottages and hilltop castles.'

ANJA MUTIĆ

'I love taking the train in Istria for the dreamy views and turn-of-the-century stations dating back to Austro-Hungarian times.'

ISABEL PUTINJA

THIS BOOK

Destination editor
Dan Bolger

Co-ordinating editor
Lauren Keith

Assisting editors
Victoria Smith, Fionnuala Twomey

Production editor
Claire Rourke

Cartographer
Mark Griffiths

Book designer
Fabrice Robin

Cover researcher
Lauren Egan

Thanks
Imogen Bannister, Alison Killilea

FROM LEFT: MATEJ_Z/SHUTTERSTOCK ©, KARL ALLEN LUGMAYER/SHUTTERSTOCK ©